In the Meantime

In the Meantime *Temporality and Cultural Politics*

SARAH SHARMA

Duke University Press Durham and London 2014

Printed in the United States of America on acid-free paper ∞
Designed by Courtney Leigh Baker. Typeset in Whitman by
Tseng Information Systems, Inc.

Library of Congress Cataloging-in-Publication Data
Sharma, Sarah, 1977–
In the meantime : temporality and cultural politics /
Sarah Sharma.
p. cm
Includes bibliographical references and index.
ISBN 978-0-8223-5465-9 (cloth : alk. paper)
ISBN 978-0-8223-5477-2 (pbk. : alk. paper)
1. Time—Sociological aspects. 2. Popular culture—
Effect of technological innovations on.
3. Culture and globalization. I. Title.
HM656.S53 2014
306–dc23
2013025573

For Jeremy Packer and our two metronomes,
ZYLA SHANTHI *and* DAHLIA RAI

Contents

Acknowledgments

I have a running joke (mostly with myself) that *In the Meantime* is the first book in the slow book movement series. It took a long time to write. In the doldrums of writing my mind would often wander to the moment I could write the acknowledgments. Finally getting to write these pages has left me feeling as if I am accepting an Academy Award. I'm going to go with that feeling.

Tucked between the pages of this book is an invisible itinerary made up of a series of places and journeying times. The people encountered along the way, and there are a lot of them, are the reason the book is what it is today. The idea for this book began when I was a PhD student in the Joint Program in Communication and Culture at York University and Ryerson University in Toronto. Jody Berland was an absolutely incredible advisor. There's nothing like working with someone whose work inspires you. She taught me where to look, how to look, and, most important, how to talk to people along the way. I want to thank a host of mentors, professors, and peers at York University: Stephen Bailey, Shannon Bell, Roberta Buiani, Barbara Crow, Lauren Cruikshank, Kevin Dowler, Fred Fletcher, Bob Hanke, Andrew Herman, Nathan Holmes, Guy Letts, Ravindra Mohabeer, Evren Oszelcuk, Scott Preston, Beth Seaton, Ed Slopek, Matthew Tegelberg. I want to especially thank Ganaele Langlois, Tanner Mirrlees, and Scott Uzelman for their intellectual camaraderie and friendship. And thank you to the following cast of genius characters connected to ComCult, purveyors of side splitting laughter, who will always be my Toronto family and who especially grounded me during these years by teaching me that there is more to life than "discourse or dat course": Mike Bickerton, Sara Chan,

Stephen Gilbert, Erin MacKeen, Sara Martel, Rebecca Morier, Nick Taylor, and Mark Kenneth Woods.

But this book truly came into being after I moved to the University of North Carolina, Chapel Hill, in 2006. The Department of Communication Studies, my academic home, has been the most intellectually supportive place I could do my thinking and teaching. I have immense gratitude for my colleagues who have fostered an environment of creative and rigorous inquiry. Lawrence Grossberg has been an incredible mentor and friend. His engagement in my research and my well-being in general is unparalleled for a colleague. Ken Hillis has been a sympathetic Canadian co-conspirator, cherished co-instructor of technology studies, and esteemed mentor. I also want to especially thank Dennis Mumby for being a fabulous department chair for the entire period leading up to tenure and the publication of this book. A special thank you to Carole Blair and Della Pollock for their constant and unwavering guidance for all things both big and small. Thank you to my at one time junior cohort: Renee Alexander Craft, Rich Cante, Sarah Dempsey, Michael Palm, Tony Perucci, Ed Rankus, and Kumi Silva. I must single out Christian Lundberg who started at UNC in Bingham Hall at the same time as me. I have valued our exchange tremendously, even when the conversation shifts to psychoanalysis. Thank you to Francesca Talenti and Gregory Flaxman for their friendship and warmth as soon as I arrived in North Carolina. At UNC at large I thank: Banu Gokariksel, Jordynn Jack, Mark Katz, Dick Langston, Cary Levine, John McGowan, Mai Nguyen, John Pickles, Inga Pollmann, Alvaro Reyes.

I have received financial support from UNC by way of the Spray-Randleigh fellowship and the Junior Faculty Development fund. This book was also supported by a semester-long fellowship from the UNC Institute for the Arts and Humanities. I want to especially thank the Hyde Family for the fellowship but also Julia Wood who ran the lively weekly meetings and Tim Marr (from American Studies) for his incredibly insightful feedback.

My graduate students helped shape some of the most important ideas in this book. I mean it when I say that they are the best part of my academic life—one that cannot be traded for anything. A tremendous thank you to Grant Bollmer, my very first PhD advisee, who provided RA work for this book and sustained a five-year conversation with me over its contents. What a treat to work and think alongside him for all of this time. Thank you to Nathan Taylor for his care with all of the images in this book and for managing to keep a straight face during my Luddite bouts. My other PhD advisees during the time of writing this book have all pushed my thinking and challenged me in innumerable ways. I leave every conversation with each of these individuals with more than I came with: Adam Rottinghaus, Armond Towns, and Grover Wehman. A number of unforgettable students enrolled in the three different iterations of my "Politics of Time and Space" grad seminar over the past six years as I was writing. A special thank you to (in order of appearance): Josh Smicker, David Terry, Sindhu Zagoren, Brett Lyszack, Dan Sutko, Kin Tsu Chung, Carey Hardin, Bryanne Young, Jade Davis, Bryan Behrenshausen, Calum Matheson, and Kurt Zemlicka. They are all doing such amazing political and intellectual work. Watch out for them!

I thank a disparate set of others whom I have run into, some regularly, on this long road of writing, whose questions, comments, answers, late night conversations, and emails and texts with links and photos have left their mark on this book. I thank Miranda Brady, Jack Bratich, Cathy N. Davidson, Radhika Gajjala, Ron Greene, Mark Hayward, Matt Jordan, Julia Kaisla, Chad Lavin, Marina Levina, Sara Martel, Matt May, Matt McAllister, Elizabeth Mazzolini, Rob Mitchell, Erika Polson, Craig Robertson, Michelle Rodino-Colocino, Gil Rodman, Chris Russill, Jennifer Darryl Slack, Jonathan Sterne, Patty Sotirin, Rebecca Walsh, Steve Wiley. I thank Ron Chan for opening up the entire world of business traveling for me which inspired an entire chapter. A special thank you to Kate Maddalena for helping me with my final draft. And then there are the distant mentors who you only realize much later completely altered your course. For this, I thank Paul Mier for his very early mentorship and his political theory courses at Capilano College in North Vancouver. By insisting that I should leave the continent to pursue a master's degree in London, he instigated the beginning of a life spent waiting in airports, bus stations, train stations, and visa- and immigration-processing centers—the very places that gave rise to many of the ideas explored in these pages. Finally, I want to thank James Hay whose serendipitous putting together of two panels at Crossroads in Cultural Studies in 2004 on mobility and space gave me a new perspective on my work. His very early support and excitement over this project made a huge difference. I believe it was him who forced me to talk to Ken Wissoker years before I wanted to.

And, ultimately there would be no *In the Meantime* had Ken Wissoker of Duke University Press not believed in this project when it was barely a book. He was always excited and always encouraging even when I felt it was impossible. I thank him for giving me this chance and for finding such capable anonymous reviewers who provided invaluable insight and advice through various stages of this project. Thank you also to Elizabeth Ault and Sara Leone for their good humor and care they have taken with my manuscript.

There are also the people who may or may not be part of my academic life but have provided the sustenance and forms of care that makes possible writing here: Grover, Claudia, Anna and Thomas, Steve and Myriam, Kumi and David, Nick and Danielle, Jina and Alan. Thank you to my family: my mother, Asha, for inspiring an entire chapter (and probably my next book as well) and providing (with Harry) so much childcare during summer writing sessions in Vancouver; my father, Bill, for teaching me the importance of the 7 Ps; my sister, Serena, for being my number one interlocutor; and Ineke, Sue and Scott, for all their support along the way.

And finally, this book is for Jeremy Packer. Where do I begin? He knows this book better than anyone else. I thank him for all the mornings he whisked Zyla away on mini-adventures so I could write. He is father extraordinaire. But most of all, I thank him for the conversations that never end, his passionate and smart heart, and being the one I travel with.

Introduction

TEMPO TANTRUMS

Speed and the Cultural Politics of Time

At the scramble crossing outside Shibuya Station in Tokyo, motorized traffic stops in all directions to allow the throngs of pedestrians to pass (see figures I.1 and I.2). Thousands of people move through the intersection at any one time. The subway lines below street level service two and a half million people daily. Underground there is another entirely separate shopping and business district, at least a mile in scope, called Shibuchinko. Shibuya is to transportation as Shibuchinko is to trade—its halls filled with high-end boutiques and trendy goods. The crossing at Shibuya pulses with an intensity incomparable to any other city street in the world.

To say that Shibuya is hypermediated is an understatement. Surveillance cameras hover above the crossing in every corner. The blinding flash of neon displays, with their constantly changing content, draw the eye up into an urban panorama of vertical space, where television screens hail the crowds in every direction. Visual spectacles are mounted and projected to cover the facades of the high-rises.

FIGURE I.1. (top) A skyline view of Shibuya scramble crossing.
FIGURE I.2. (bottom) Shibuya scramble crossing in the rain. Photos by Jeremy Packer.

Professional videographers and journalists are on site all day, every day, seeking the latest trends, interviewing passersby, editing on the spot, and then airing their products instantaneously on the media displays above. Everything is instantly, incessantly updated. The crowds on the street are sourced, inscribed on a screen, and displayed back to themselves in a matter of minutes. Fashions can go out of style before they reach the other side of the street. Shibuya pulsates with information turnover; goods, people, money, trivia, and ads circulate in a seemingly endless stream. Everyone is either looking up at the screens or staring down at their hands as they skillfully text while they wait to cross. Others have phones glued to their ears. Shibuya is said to have a higher density of cell phones than anywhere else on earth.[1]

For card-carrying members of the new information economy, such as gamers and game developers, technophiles, fashionistas, pop culture junkies, advertisers, and software engineers, the speed of life in Shibuya may well be pure magic, full of endless possibilities. In fact, the cyber utopian Howard Rheingold references Shibuya as proof of the coming technological revolution ushered in by cell phones and texting.[2] Shibuya signifies a future that is densely inhabited by creative, energetic, tech-savvy, and forward-thinking types. People and capital seem unencumbered and almost immaterial, flowing without inhibitions. Shibuya represents the evolution of technology and commerce in a networked and creative humanity. At Shibuya, the market effortlessly and instantly fulfills endless consumer needs.

For critical theorists of globalization and technology, Shibuya is emblematic of something much bleaker: what Paul Virilio terms the "overexposed city," where physical architecture is displaced by the nonplace spectacles of billboards, neon lights, and surveillance cameras.[3] The crossing is saturated with instant transmissions and real-time communications; even the buildings are screens. And the content of those communications are commodity; Shibuya's massive consumer spectacle mocks the political potential of public space. As Virilio argues, when space yields to time, democracy fails: "Today we have achieved three attributes of the divine: ubiquity, instantaneity, immediacy; omnivoyance and omnipotence. This is no longer a question of democracy; this is tyranny."[4] From Virilio's perspective, the crowds at Shibuya are full of cyborg-consumer-citizens: plugged in and plugging away, all consumed and consuming as they watch and are themselves watched. Shibuya feeds off of people and then feeds them back into the system. Surveillance is normalized and made pleasurable in fun, panoptic fashion shows. You have to look good because at any given minute you may be exhibited. The crowds may be informed and informative, but they are also information. For those alarmed by the new phase of hypercapitalism, Shibuya starkly demonstrates the new gods of sped-up, mobile information capitalism—Nokia and Sony—and their ability to turn people into weightless data.

Standing at a more figurative scramble crossing, a crossroads of schools of thought, one can veer right for utopia, with Rheingold and the fashionistas, or left for dystopia, with theorists like Virilio. But there is another way to cross this intersection that allows for more complex insight into the politics of time and space ushered in by global capitalism, and that way involves awareness of power relations as they play out in time—a concept I will call *temporality*. There are multiple interdependent and relational temporalities tangled together at Shibuya. People play and shop in Shibuya, but people are also at work. The crowds at Shibuya change and shift at different hours and on different days. At different moments luxury consumers, bargain hunters, salarymen, Harajuku Girls, drunks, high school students, the unemployed, retailers, construction workers, cleaning staff, tourists, taxi drivers, traffic-directing cops, delivery vans, private chauffeurs, garbage collectors, and commuters dominate the space. Around five in the morning, overworked salarymen, who have been up all night drinking (and who have grabbed a couple hours of sleep in one of the tiny capsule hotels nearby), make their way across the scramble, their gaits slow and unsteady. Just two hours later, a new set of salarymen in fresh suits appear with quick, determined steps—the two groups clearly demarcating yesterday and today. Cleaning staff members carrying brooms and mops come hours later. The streets temporarily empty after the morning rush; the shops open, and students with their book bags and mothers with children make their appearance. Transient figures emerge later in the afternoon and into the late night: tourists, drunks, *otaku*, and the homeless. In a hotel, situated above the rooftops in Shibuya, an even more complex sense of the multiplicity of time emerges. The tops of the buildings are full of workers taking time for cigarettes, food, and exercise. One building has a tennis court and another a makeshift track where uniformed workers can be seen doing slow laps.

I stayed in Shibuya for two weeks to see if I could tease out some individual threads in its temporal, material, technological, and cultural tangle. After a few days of observation, I began to recognize the same figures appearing at the same times throughout the day. I saw that Shibuya is hardly about speed or spectacle or a coming technological revolution. The people that move through Shibuya might all be speeding across the scramble, but as they move, they remain distinct; they represent discrepant forms of labor constituted in time in a variety of inequitable ways. The figures at the scramble crossing best exemplify not so much the speed of life in Shibuya but the different temporal itineraries that constitute social space there. The crossing is shared by masses of people whose convergence is not random but temporally ordered. They come to inhabit and experience time and the crossing differently, depending on where they fit within a larger grid of time(s).

At the beginning of the twenty-first century, a set of questions that focused on the impact of technologies built for acceleration and faster-moving capital on the democratic fate of a sped-up globe emerged across the disciplines. I call this line of critical inquiry *speed theory*. Virilio was one of the first to write of speed in this vein, in France during the 1970s, and he remains its most prominent figure.[5] As wild and aphoristic as Virilio's work is, it has given rise to research and writing within fields as diverse as media studies, cultural geography, political theory, sociology, critical theory, and cultural studies. The culture of speed, as it appears in such various conversations, goes by many terms: *24/7 capitalism* (Jonathan Crary), *the chronoscopic society* (Robert Hassan), *fast capital* (Ben Agger), *the new temporalities of biopolitical production* (Michael Hardt and Antonio Negri), *the culture of acceleration* (John Tomlinson), *chronodystopia* (John Armitage and Joanne Roberts), *hypermodern times* (Gilles Lipovetsky), and *liquid times* (Zygmunt Bauman).[6] Of course, the advent of the new millennium isn't the first time that speed has been the object of critical inquiry. Such work fits within an important trajectory of thought that includes histories of capital as it became coterminous with different technologies and their temporal and spatial effects. These critical histories describe clocks, trains, telegraphs, and other global metronomes with their attendant temporal dictates of ticks, tocks, nanoseconds, and light-years.[7] Speeding up gives rise to new cultural imaginaries as well as artistic movements.[8] Much of the focus in media theory has so far explored how changes in technological pace translate into entirely new social realities. In the 1970s, Marshall McLuhan famously prophesized that the speed of electronic communication would culminate in the harmonization and connection of all of humanity into a "global village."[9] That we are living in a 24/7, always-on, and on-the-go world continues to be the assumed starting point for much critical analysis of globalization, media, and democracy.

While critical theorists of speed examine different elements of speed culture, there is a shared sentiment: new technologies and faster moving capital herald grave political and social consequences. Unlike McLuhan and other cyber utopians, speed theorists are not so much interested in the liberating potential of sped-up technologies to connect Others. Instead, the contemporary theorist of speed is concerned about how a culture of speed is antithetical to democracy. They share a similar cautionary tale: Speed is the commanding byproduct of a mutually reinforcing complex that includes global capital, real-time communication technologies, military technologies, and scientific research on human bodies. Democratic deliberation gives over to instant communication. Political interaction is replaced by monetary transaction. Space, the apparent *real* ground of politics, is subsumed by speed and what Virilio calls the "tyranny of real-time."[10] Speed theorists argue that geopolitics (a politics based in space) is supplanted by chronopolitics (a politics based in time). The yielding of space to time not only dissolves the grounding of politics but also gives rise to a way of being in time that is adverse to a political public sphere. Moreover, rather than facilitating an egalitarian global village, the yielding of space to time divides the citizenry into a temporal binary. There are two temporal poles of chronopolitical life: fast classes and slow classes (Virilio), tourists and vagabonds (Bauman), inhabitants of chronotopia and chronodystopia (Armitage and Roberts), and the time rich and the time poor (Jeremy Rifkin).[11] These two temporal classes are imagined to be much like distant ships that never pass, unknown to the other.

This book argues that speed theorists have offered too simple an account of the acceleration of everyday life and temporal difference. Speed theorists have been the subject of substantial criticism for mimicking the tone of marketers and multinational corporations who want us all to believe the same thing: that we are again on the verge of utopia, living in new times.[12] But as wild and aphoristic as this theory is, it is worth paying significant attention to. It is not just a theoretical assumption that these are fast times. This notion has become rather common sense, if not a cultural fixation. In all this attention to time, however, the complexity of lived time is absent. It has not been addressed in speed theory, nor is it taken up in any substantial way by those who have critiqued speed theory for providing the digital age its "sacred canopy."[13] Recognition of differential lived time is also ignored in everyday discussions about life getting faster. But that is hardly surprising. Running out of time is largely felt and imagined to be an individual problem, even when the critique is aimed at society.

Speed theory is without a doubt indebted to Marx's formulation of the clock's quantification of work and the production of value and socially necessary time.[14] Speed theory is also largely sympathetic to E. P. Thompson's thesis in *Time, Work, and Industrial Capitalism*, which is concerned with how the new chronometers imposed by governmental, military, and capitalist interests have replaced earlier, collective perceptions of time that he believed flowed from the collective wisdom of human societies.[15] Marx has been fundamental to thinking about the annihilation of space by time, a change ushered in by chronometers and capitalist time frames. Marx and Thompson are both necessary to thinking about how capital robs the worker of time, whether by diminishing personal time, controlling the bounds of a working day, stalling clocks, or establishing the age limits of child labor. Yet the protagonist, in the contemporary work on speedup and time-space compression, is no longer the worker or any specific subjugated population. Instead, the protagonist is a generalized individual—an everyday subject—who is suddenly out of time. While pointing out the indentured conditions of contemporary labor and living brought on by ubiquitous technologies is an important analysis of contemporary life, it does not deal with the uneven cultural politics of time. In fact, ignoring differential time exacerbates inequitable temporal relations. Without attention to multiple temporalities, the subject of value in the critique of speed ends up being the same subject who will confirm speedup most readily as *the* reality—the consumer of new technological gadgets (tomorrow's garbage), the jet-setter who can't remember which airport he's in, the disoriented postmodern theorist, or the tired and overworked academic whose blackberry is keeping him or her "on" 24/7.

While the imposing world of clocks, trains, and temporal grids of empires and civilizations is central to the history of capital and social control, *In the Meantime* offers an approach to time that is about the micropolitics of temporal coordination and social control between multiple temporalities. In speed theory, synchronization accounts for the relationship between technology and the social body, political body, and biological body.[16] *In the Meantime* focuses instead on how synchronicity is at the heart of everyday material relations. Thus, the image of an observatory keeping the time of the ships as they move at different speeds, at different distances, scattered across the ocean, gives way to a more commonplace scenario within the urban fabric: a business traveler calling a taxi with a mobile device, and the taxi driver texting his wife to say that he won't be home until the morning.

This book traces these multiple threads of lived time: Frequent business travelers hail cabs to the airport, late for their flights. Taxicabs speed up and slow down at the will of their backseat passengers. Maids at high-end hotels clean suites designed to cater to the jet-lagged; some of them have been trained to deal specifically with jet-lagged travelers. Nine-to-fivers take express hour-long lunchtime yoga classes at work in order to get through the day. Mobile yoga instructors arrive at corporate offices, making pitches to managers about the benefits of yoga for employee productivity. Slow-food connoisseurs are seated in slow-food establishments across Europe and North America. They are enjoying their slow-cooked meals, but an exploited service staff hurriedly cleans their dishes. Fiber affects fiber across the social fabric. The fibers are not randomly scattered; they are entangled with one another in time. They are much like the ships and the "slave" clocks of Big Ben and the Royal Observatory, Greenwich, that are referred to in the histories of capital and world standard time.[17] These fibers, these temporalities, compose the chapters of *In the Meantime*.

Temporalities are not times; like continually broken clocks, they must be reset again and again. They are expected to recalibrate and fit into a larger temporal order. Temporalities do not experience a uniform time but rather a time particular to the labor that produces them. Their experience of time depends on where they are positioned within a larger economy of temporal worth. The temporal subject's living day, as part of its livelihood, includes technologies of the self contrived for synchronizing to the time of others or having others synchronize to them. The meaning of these subjects' own times and experiences of time is in large part structured and controlled by both the institutional arrangements they inhabit and the time of others—other temporalities.

By following and describing several examples of multiple, entangled temporalities—frequent business travelers, taxi drivers, yoga instructors, slow lifers, and desk workers—*In the Meantime* critiques a tacit acceptance that the world is getting faster by examining instead how the discourse of speedup is part of the problematic cultural context in which people understand and experience time. Such an approach means contending with the fact that the critique of speed is also a discourse—one that privileges certain populations and disavows others while it upholds normalizing conceptions of time. In the chapters that follow, I discover not a polarity between fast and slow classes, or a political choice between going fast or slow, but an uneven multiplicity of temporalities that is complicated by the labor arrangements, cultural practices, technological environments, and social spaces that respond to this so-called globalized, speedy world.

Temporalities, as this book describes them, exist in a grid of temporal power relations. The term *temporal*, here, does not imply a transcendent sense of time or the time of history. I mean for the temporal to denote *lived* time. The temporal is not a general sense of time particular to an epoch of history but a specific experience of time that is structured in specific political and economic contexts. The temporal operates as a form of social power and a type of social difference. Focusing on the issue of fast or slow pace without a nuanced and complex conception of the temporal does an injustice to the multitude of time-based experiences specific to different populations that live, labor, and sleep under the auspices of global capital. The social fabric is composed of a chronography of power, where individuals' and social groups' senses of time and possibility are shaped by a differential economy, limited or expanded by the ways and means that they find themselves in and out of time.[18]

Power-Chronography

This book sits at the crossroads of work on speed, biopower, media, and globalization and outlines a new approach to time I term *power-chronography*. I offer power-chronography as an extension of Doreen Massey's theory of power-geometry, a key intervention in geography in the early 1990s.[19] Massey's theory of power-geometry destabilized powerful masculinist discourses of "time-space compression" as they related to the politics of space. The prevailing notion within the theories of time-space compression that she was writing against at the time, specifically Fredric Jameson and David Harvey, was of a rising sense of a placelessness attributed to postmodernity. Social differences such as gender, class, race, and sexuality were either unacknowledged or lost from the view of the disoriented postmodern gaze into social spaces affected by the acceleration of capital and time-space compression.

Massey's power-geometry stresses differentiated subjectivity as opposed to the so-called universal and inevitable time-space compression: "Different social groups have distinct relationships to this anyway differentiated mobility."[20] For Massey, space is multiple and relational; it is a process rather than a container for social relations. She maintains, "We need to ask, in other words, whether our relative mobility and power over mobility and communication entrenches the spatial imprisonment of other groups."[21] As with the feminist response to the postmodern theorists who announced the end of the body, Massey questions Jameson and Harvey's invoking of placelessness: "Those who today worry about a sense of disorientation and a loss of control must once have felt they knew exactly where they were, and that they *had* control. For who is it in these times who feels dislocated/placeless/invaded?"[22] Theorists who once described place in the way Massey finds inadequate were unable to recognize their own privilege, or previous privilege.[23] I argue that the dominant descriptions of time today are similarly failing to recognize those same forms of privilege.[24]

The intellectual intervention known as the *spatial turn*, of which Massey's work is a canonical part, showed how space is a co-producer of social relations rather than just a backdrop for life.[25] Since the spatial turn, cultural theory has paid close attention to how space is imbricated in games of power—whether by extension, expansion, colonization, imprisonment, banishment, confinement, inclusion, or exclusion. In all these forms of spatialized power, a temporal counterpart is implied. But temporal power, it would seem, is more subtly and quietly asserted and as such has gone unremarked. Ultimately, the spatial turn did not acknowledge time as a form of power, a site of material struggle and social difference.[26] As the spatial turn continues to spin, the politics of time does not yet share a documented systemic record akin to that of the politics of space.[27] I suspect this is the case because space continues to be the valorized site of political life at the expense of time. *In the Meantime* seeks to balance the spatial imaginary with a temporal imaginary.

In the 1970s, Nigel Thrift argued that geography had neglected the time horizon of its own concepts.[28] The time geographers, most notably Torsten Hägerstrand, Allan Pred, and Thrift, introduced an approach to geography that involved both the spatial and temporal coordinates of human activity. In his body of work Hägerstrand argued that time was of utmost importance in how people and things fit together in order for different socio-economic systems to function.[29] Thrift's later work in the 1980s was seminal in pointing out the production of capitalism's varied time consciousness, what he called "owners' time and own time."[30] Likewise, Mike

Crang has made rhythm and the choreography of bodies, as they are tied to different complexes of technology, in time and space central to cultural analysis.[31] Routes, paths, modes of transport, forms of labor, and leisure practices have since been enlivened with a newly intertwined spatiotemporal significance. *In the Meantime* is indebted to time geography but seeks to move beyond the spatiality of paths, itineraries, and routes, and how bodies are orchestrated in space in order to delve further into distinctive temporal forms of power.

Making Space for Time

SPATIAL AND TEMPORAL BIASES

A significant source of inspiration for this project comes from the work of the Canadian political economist and media historian Harold Adams Innis. Contemporary theorists of speed share Innis's concern for the increasing pace of life and the downfall of democratic culture.[32] But unacknowledged in their writings is one of Innis's most important conceits: the temporal is political regardless of speed and is present no matter what the dominant technologies of the day are. For Innis, the temporal is a power dynamic—not a new condition resulting from speedup but an enduring political and economic reality with important cultural effects.

The critical questions about changes in space and time ushered in by technologies concern specific sorts of relations of power, what Innis calls monopolies of knowledge and power.[33] Rather than assume a uniform technological effect brought on by a particular media we must ask instead what kinds of social struggles, what kinds of power dynamics, are more likely to occur in particular technological environments as opposed to others.[34] The spatial and temporal politics will differ depending on the technology in question but also the populations in question. Underlying all of Innis's eclectic work was one enduring premise: a balanced space-time approach was necessary not only for a culture to thrive but in order to both understand and change the political and social world. For Innis, balanced conceptions of space and time within culture, awareness of spatial and temporal dynamics, could have the power to keep state and market power in check.

The major crux of Innis's media theory is his theory of space-time bias.[35] Depending on whether or not space or time is emphasized by a particular medium or complex of media, certain monopolies of knowledge and power arise in that civilization. Space-binding media, from papyrus to the radio, are light, and can be easily disseminated, thereby fostering the centralization of power. Civilizations that emphasize space over time tend to be imperial powers, involved in the conquering of space at the expense of the maintenance of culture over time. Time-binding media, such as stone, are heavy, resistant to decay, cannot be easily transported, and foster decentralization. They do not produce centers of power scattered across the globe. According to Innis, civilizations that emphasize time tend to be practical, oral cultures where time is treated in terms of continuity. In time-biased societies, space becomes a bounded sphere to be protected rather than a means to extend power outward. Civilizations biased in terms of space will spatialize time. Time becomes a resource, commodity, and sequence of events that can be managed and controlled. A technology that saves time, then, is in fact a spatially biased technology. A space-biased culture, remarks Innis, when left completely unchecked by technologies that foster time, can become overly invested in the present.[36]

Following from Innis, it becomes necessary to take a step back and question if the fixation on speedup, even as a form of critique, is symptomatic of a present mindedness fostered by a spatial understanding of time. The concern with speedup today reflects not a culture invested in the temporal but a culture that operates with a spatial sense of time. Spatial understandings of time lack recognition of the cultural politics of time. Instead, spatial treatments of time are individualistic, concerned with control and management.

Innis's work allows us to see that by all such determinations, global capital depends on a spatial treatment of time, on a spatially biased culture. It is not just that our dominating technologies are spatially biased; our ways of knowing, systems of power, and even notions of resistance tend to be spatial. For example, the very fact that shared space, social space, or the public sphere is the privileged ground of political life is symptomatic of the negation of the temporal. All of these are spatial concepts. And with this spatial sense of political life, time is treated as a mode, a way of being communicative or present. Certain temporal modes are valorized as appropriate to political space. For example, the slow intersubjective time of a contemplative and deliberative public sphere is the assumed form of a properly civic and politicized public. The uneven temporalities that are the condition of the possibility for political space are completely unacknowledged. But they are there and quite visible if one becomes temporally attuned.

In terms of theorizing publics, at every level from the local to the global, oppositional to the bourgeois public sphere, temporality is an invisible and unremarked relation of power.[37] For example, the *agora*, the venerated space of antiquity that continues to animate contemporary theorizing of the public sphere, was not merely a space. If the temporal is acknowledged, then the public sphere is also a time. It was a space of free time for political thinking for the minority of free citizens. It was an experience of time and social space produced by the time of women and slaves who worked in the *oikos* (household or intimate sphere). Contemporary laments over the revered public sphere are also unwittingly making claims on time. The temporal requirement of the public (i.e., that the public have time to devote to matters of governance) underlies the contested Habermasian model of the public sphere. Even theorists who refute his bourgeois ideal on the grounds that it is exclusionary and historically inaccurate valorize a contemplative and deliberative mode of being in time.[38] Theories of liberal democracy assume a way of being in time, but the assumption itself is not a time politics; it is one single, and albeit very powerful, discursive mobilization of time.[39] What continues to animate public-sphere theorizing is an expectation that political civic life is only political insofar as it takes place in a space and time separate from state and market. The right practice of time, a democratic one, must be free of institutional restraints, whether economic or cultural.[40] It is a time that must be unfettered in order to be contemplative. Such a provocation denies the reality that individuals and the productive arrangements they inhabit are not and cannot be beyond state and market.

Public-sphere theorizing is conditioned upon a particular politics of time that is about the *pace* of one's time rather than how its citizens or denizens are *constituted in* time. The democratic expectation, to be free and have time, is a liberal bourgeois demand, an ideal that rests on a particular conceptualization of time and relationship to capital and state power.[41] Likewise, the focus in critical works on globalization directed toward dismantling uncritical assumptions of the new "global now" privileges space as the locus of change. It is often pointed out that there are a myriad of flows, scales, and scapes—global corporate capital, labor, tourists, information, monies, people, and ideas.[42] Strangely, in contesting the global now, these are all spatially oriented terms. They account for movements across space, albeit at different speeds, where new borders, old borders, or the absence of borders becomes the central problematic.[43] *In the Meantime* seeks the temporal counterparts of these spatial dynamics and experiences.

Power-chronography is a corrective, a balanced space-time approach to understanding differential temporalities under global capitalism. I want to make this very clear: power-chronography is not an argument that points out the multiple, different, many, or plural times within some epochal condition, phase, or stage, of modernity.[44] The perspectival accounts of taxi drivers, business travelers, slow lifers, desk workers, and yoga instructors that I introduce through this book recognize these forms of labor as various positions within the multiple temporalized flows and time-spaces of globalization. They are not different layers of the modern. Instead, my purpose is to highlight how time is worked on and differentially experienced at the intersections of inequity. In terms of a political economy of time, this book provides insight into the processes where bodies are differently valued temporally and made productive for capital. By inhabiting the world with a critical eye toward the differential ways in which time is structured and experienced, power-chronography provides a politicization of time that dispels individualistic accounts of time and allows the social and relational contours of power in its temporal forms to emerge.

The Power-Chronography of It All

In Massey's groundbreaking essay "Global Sense of Place," she instructs the reader to step outside of the world in order to see the power-geometry of it all: "Imagine for a moment that you are on a satellite, further out and beyond all actual satellites; you can see 'planet earth' from a distance and, unusually for someone with only peaceful intentions, you are equipped with the kind of technology which allows you to see the colors of people's eyes and the numbers on their number plates. You can see all the movement and tune in to all the communication that is going on."[45] There is, as Massey argues, "a highly complex social differentiation. There are differences in the degree of movement and communication, but also in the degree of control and initiation."[46] For example, following Massey, there are people sending faxes out of New York City and women collecting water on foot in the sub-Sahara. The power-geometry of it all is concerned with how people are distinctly and unevenly placed.

When *In the Meantime* seeks to examine the power-chronography of it all, it does not stand outside the globe—such a vantage calls attention to space. Instead, this book's approach requires immersion in the rhythm, thus calling attention to time. The theorist must be able to stand in Shibuya and a slow city and see that there are power-chronographies. How are chronographies of power located? And what does power-chronography have to do with lived temporalities?

First, chronographies of power have to do with how different time sensibilities are produced. Power-chronography is based on a conception of time as lived experience, always political, produced at the intersection of a range of social differences and institutions, and of which the clock is only one chronometer. Power-chronography works to detangle the ways that time is differently worked on. In order to examine the power-chronography of it all, *In the Meantime* employs a mixed methodological approach that includes political economic analysis, attention to technological environments, thick descriptions, discourse analysis, and ethnographic interviews. I examine how discourses about time maintain lines of temporal normalization that elevate certain practices and relationships to time while devaluing others. The discourse of speed continues to offer a completely inadequate and limited view of the temporal. My turn to discourses about time reveals the inherently unstable nature of hegemonic discourses. But, an examination of popular discourses can only lead us so far.

Because speedup dominates the horizon of thought and action, describing how time is given meaning and experienced by historical subjects living in this particular discursive formation and cultural context is absolutely central to a cultural-critical consideration of time. In order to understand the chronography of power, I turn to subjugated knowledge, recognizing that most critical treatments of speed so far have only relied on theorists' observations of their own experience of the assumed fast world. I situate my analysis through interviews with people whose labor is explicitly oriented toward negotiating time and the time of others. While it could be argued that all labor requires laborers to manage their time, the forms of labor I focus on here provide insight into the differential and inequitable ways in which time both is made to matter and is experienced. These pages include interviews with frequent business travelers, city taxi drivers, and yoga instructors who teach in corporate settings. All of the interviewees have been given pseudonyms. These subjects destabilize and contest a uniform pace of life, revealing instead how the explanatory power of speed works to produce differential time and exacerbate structural inequalities experienced at the level of time. While using their own names was an option for each of my interlocutors, the most precarious of laborers, namely all of the taxi drivers and some of the corporate yoga instructors, asked not to be named. Being able to freely talk about one's conditions of labor and experience of time at work is also differentially experienced. As far as further discourse analysis in the book, I limit the array of surrounding discourses that I analyze to those that specifically relate to these interviewees' particular contexts or forms of labor.

Much of this book is based on immersing myself as an observer in the rhythm of the places where these people labor, live, and rest: airports, slow-living communities, express yoga classes, and slow-food events. I participated and observed corporate yoga classes, rode in taxis in Toronto, visited international business lounges, visited slow-living lifestyle communities in Tokyo, attended slow-food events across the United States, and went to conferences about speed culture. One of the most powerful conceptual commitments in popular discourses today is that the world is getting faster. How is it that individuals have radically inequitable relations to time yet uphold similar ideological attachments to time? And how does this attachment to the explanatory power of speedup provide more fodder, rather than resistance, to global capital's hold upon the time of life? Speed is not the reason for differential relationships to time. Instead, biopolitics provides a more compelling framework to see the power-chronography of it all. Biopolitics allows for an embodied as well as political economic understanding of lived time.

The Biopolitical Economy of Time

Speedup is not restricted to the confines of theoretical inquiry. It is manifest throughout popular culture, in workplaces, and in spaces of leisure. That the world is getting faster is an incantation uttered so often by media pundits, promised in ads for new technologies, and exclaimed in boldface from magazine covers and newspaper headlines that the conceit is rarely second-guessed. But in a world ostensibly short on time, there appears to be plenty of time to be had. Whether it is a GPS unit, mobile phone, or energy drink, a range of commodities are sold that promise efficiency in navigating this apparently fast world. The counters of supermarkets are filled with small bottles for quick doses of five-hour energy. And if life is moving too fast, you can "slow your roll" and drink Drank, the first extreme relaxation drink on the market. Cosmetic interventions such as Botox shots promise to hide the passing of time on weathered faces. The market is also full of experiences that can be purchased to better navigate the temporal demands of global capital.

Express yoga classes are now offered in many studios during lunch hours. "Employee-centered," "progressive" corporations in the industrialized parts of the globe incorporate meditation and other forms of spiritual healing as part of the workday. The Empire State Building and Vancouver International Airport are fitted with napping pods from MetroNaps, a company that offers pay-as-you-go naps in public spaces. The drug Modafinil, which was once reserved for soldiers on extra-long military missions, as it promises forty-eight hours of wakefulness, is now being sold as a productivity enhancer for corporate rat racers and others who are under tight deadlines.[47]

Other solutions for time scarcity include employing the labor of others. The international remote assistant in India is one such solution, celebrated by new business gurus such as Timothy Ferris, the author of the bestselling *The 4-Hour Workweek*.[48] The remote assistant will take care of those tasks that Americans are too busy to deal with, such as the apparently soul-draining monotony of data entry, responding to e-mail, ordering Christmas gifts, and sending family members birthday cards.

While these examples speak to the cultural currency of speedup to garner market responses and reactions, they also speak to the inextricable link between contemporary biopower, capitalism, and the control of time. I want to provide a cautionary tale, as well. Namely, that the fixation over the control of time today tends to leave individuals more vulnerable to biopolitical control. Foucault uses the term *biopower* to describe how the various institutions and disciplines arising in the eighteenth century monitored, intervened, and controlled the productive capacities of individuals and populations at large. Through different techniques and practices, these institutions of the state, as well as other institutions of modern power such as the army, family, police, schools, and medical professions, would administer life through the optimization and intensification of the life force. As Foucault argues, "Biopower was without question an indispensable element in the development of capitalism; the latter would not have been possible without the controlled insertion of bodies within the machinery of production to economic processes."[49] No matter what the specific contours of capital are, whether we call it fast capital, neoliberalism, late capitalism, or empire, capital develops at the expense of bodies. Processes of investment and disinvestment are not experienced as catastrophes and crises within the labor forces of capital, but are much more slow and arduous; they are also subtle, insidious, and practically invisible.

This book draws attention to the temporal aspects of managing the force of life. For example, I consider how the giving of meaning to time is a form of biopolitical time management.[50] That is, external control over time occurs increasingly in the realm of quality time; the meaning of one's lived time is central to one's workplace practices. While this is elaborated more fully throughout the book, it is important to acknowledge at the outset that within the biopolitical economy of time, interventions are made into the life force of certain populations in a way that elevates their time practices while normalizing them. With these interventions, however, there are also claims about time that lead to the disinvestment of the time of other populations. Through both disinvestments and investments, a normalizing and differential temporal order is maintained.

It is not speed per se but the explanatory power of speed that I argue has the undue effect of preparing more and more sites for the institutions of modern power to intervene in bodies in increasingly invasive and inequitable ways. The discourse of speed casts all individuals as extremely vulnerable, open to intervention. Shared across the temporal differential is not so much the general speed of life but rather the expectation that one must recalibrate. To recalibrate is to learn how to deal with time, be on top of one's time, to learn when to be fast and when to be slow.[51] Recalibration, as I suggest throughout this book, accounts for the multiple ways in which individuals and social groups synchronize their body clocks, their senses of the future or the present, to an exterior relation—be it another person, pace, technology, chronometer, institution, or ideology. When Foucault argues that biopower is the power to "make live or let die," the temporal is explicit.[52] Life is not taken. It is "let to live" through investment or "let to die" through disinvestment, slowly. This book illuminates the invitations and expectations to recalibrate time as those expectations permeate the social fabric differently for distinctive populations. Such recalibration occurs differentially and unequally.

In the Meantime reveals how the problem of time is a site of biopolitical intervention for traditional institutions of modern power such as the state, the market, the military, pharmaceutical companies, airliners, wellness enterprises, and the hospitality and tourism industry. Such institutions derive and exert power through their investment and control of people's time.

More significantly, institutions establish this control through the production and enhancement of people's qualitative experience of time. Together they compose a temporal order that normalizes people's experiences of time, including maintaining established lines of temporally experienced privilege and difference.

Whether it is theories of speed or cultural responses to speed, articulating the contemporary moment as one of all-consuming speed adds an element of novelty and urgent necessity to the demand and desire to exert more time control over one's quickly passing life "in these sped-up times." Too often the belief that we are living in a dangerously sped-up culture makes the demand for the labor of others justifiable as a systemic need "in these fast-paced times" rather than the structurally excessive privilege that it is. We're all so tired and overworked that the mundane tasks of daily living and getting by are relegated as meaningless pursuits and increasingly outsourced to others.[53] Claiming that speed is a universalized condition means that everyone is now precarious. The conceit masks the fact that many have long been temporally precarious. The imported domestic servants and housecleaners with no rights to education, health care, or other forms of social welfare and the unpaid labor of women at home are just two of the many examples of populations who have long been disinvested in by institutions of modern power.

It is time to cast aside the individualistic and privileged weight of busyness, sacred space, and generalized precarity found in the laments over speed. If we want to grasp the complex intersections of social differences under global capital, we need to take the temporal seriously on its own terms. The disjunctive horizons of political possibility under capital make necessary a consideration of power-chronography. We must pay attention to how the cultural fixation on time produces differential time.

Chapter Overviews

Chapter 1 examines the temporal experiences of the frequent business traveler and the rise of temporal architectures. The chapter is based on interviews with frequent business travelers, participant observation in airports and hotels, and analysis of business literature geared to the frequent business traveler. The bodies of the jet-lagged business travelers are particularly vulnerable to break down as they trample over time zones. The business traveler inhabits the architecture of global capital with speed and agility, making quick transfers within this temporal architecture between different conference centers, airports, and hotels. This population most readily insists that the world is speeding up. But it is also the frequent business traveler whose time unfolds within an elaborate infrastructure dedicated to his or her time maintenance. Temporal architectures are composed of built environments, commodities and services, and technologies directed to the management and enhancement of a certain kind of subject's time—a privileged temporality. For the business traveler, these temporal architectures of time maintenance are largely invisible. Instead, the business travelers encounter a solitary road and a culture of disorienting speed, one they feel that they are independently navigating as singular entrepreneurs of their own fates. Their very real need to keep up to speed unintentionally legitimizes the inequitable reorchestration of the time and labor of others. Their temporal architectures are supported by systems of temporal labor.

One of these forms of the temporal laborer is the taxi driver, the subject of chapter 2. The taxi driver in most major metropolitan cities in North America is almost always recently immigrated, seeking asylum, or waiting for accreditation papers. The taxi driver straddles multiple temporalities, such as the tempos of the travelers they must transport, the slow traffic, the changing cityscape between night and day, the ticking of the clock, and the running meter. The taxicab is both a technology of transport and a transit space—a mobile nodal point for the circulation of people, information, goods, and capital. The interior space of the cab is a site of business, transfer, and political exchange between driver and fare, as well as a place to conduct business for the passenger. The taxi driver is constituted in time in a way that is structurally related to the exceptional time of the business traveler. This chapter develops a theory of temporal interdependence. Relationships of synchronization infuse the entire social fabric. There is an expectation that certain bodies recalibrate to the time of others as a significant condition of their labor. As a result, specific temporal regimes and strategic dispositions are cultivated in order to simply survive within the normalizing temporal ordering of everyday life.

Chapter 3 examines the incorporation of yoga into the rhythm of the workday as an example of the significance of recalibration and the acquiring of a temporal disposition as a form of social control. This chapter is based on interviews with yoga instructors who teach in corporate settings and trade materials of these instructors, as well as my own participation in express yoga classes geared toward office workers. Yoga classes offered at the office is a practice indicative of a new set of rationalizations and technologies to control and discipline labor in the realm of the temporal. Yoga at work cultivates a sense of time wherein the demands of the sedentary life are both a place of comfort and fulfillment. In using a discourse for "living in the moment," the desk worker's station at the workstation is reconfirmed. "You may be stuck here [space]," the discourse chants, seductively, "but at least you are living in the now [time]." Mobile yoga instructors and spiritual healers are drawn to the sedentary labor force of contemporary capitalism, as they see an opportunity and a need to recalibrate bodies that are on the verge of giving out. They reinvigorate the time sensibilities of workers who feel that their lives are passing them by. Yoga espouses a nonlinear conception of time, seemingly resistant to the normalizing workaday world. But viewed through the lens of power-chronography, yoga, when practiced in the office, actually bends and bonds individuals to better fit within the various temporal requirements of late capitalism.

Chapter 4 examines the cultural currency of slowness as it has become a new, alternative pace that all kinds of people are supposed to choose. Slowness and speedup are two dominating mobilizations of time that appear to be competing stances within the contemporary social fabric. This chapter offers a deep description and examination of a series of slow spaces I observed and participated in: an organic grocery store in Bowen Island, British Columbia; the Caretta Shiodome, a slow-living condo in Tokyo; the ideal home for the great American staycation; and Slow Food Nation in San Francisco. Slowness, on the surface, actively resists blind acceptance of speedup. But the power-chronography of speed culture and slow culture reveal that they share a similar negation of the temporal. Slowness is beginning to occupy its own spaces, taking up room across the social fabric. But its spatial bias is deeper than its concrete infrastructures. It is space, and not time, that dominates the slow initiatives that I trace globally. As Harold Innis argued in the *Bias of Communication*, culture is sustained by spaces that are temporally biased, attuned to temporal continuity, tradition, and sustained over time.[54] These would include such spaces as meditation centers, churches, temple gardens, parks, and even universities. I ultimately argue that slow spaces are not in fact temporally biased. Slow spaces are spaces where anxieties about the pace of life are deliberately pacified in order to produce a different experience of time. As alternative temporal spaces they instead depend on the inequitable social relations of the fast and divisive world they rail against. And, more importantly, they are spatial solutions to cultural anxieties over time, revealing again the limits of our spatial imaginary to understand the political complexity of the social experience of time.

In the Meantime concludes with a chapter concerned with the fundamental political condition that these previous chapters bring to light: the sharing of space does not guarantee the sharing of time. The dream of shared space is a powerful political and cultural ideal. It is a dream of shared space that motivates the Left's critique of speed culture in the first place. The power-chronography that emerges within the pages of *In the Meantime* makes necessary the need to reckon with the largely unacknowledged yet enduring political condition of social life; there is no common or shared temporality to which the spatial ideals of democracy can correspond. I end with an outline for a way of theorizing and of inhabiting a public in time, what I call a *temporal public*.

Temporal Beginnings

The idea for this book began in Toronto many years ago during a series of otherwise mundane daily walks from my apartment to the subway station. The scenes are ongoing, so I want to describe them in the present tense. At the crack of dawn, I walk south on Christie Street. I pass by a rickety old multistoried building, an asylum hostel run by an international Christian organization. Every day I see lone men occupy their balconies in their bathrobes cupping coffees and smoking cigarettes. I can hear the clanking of their worry beads well before I reach the building. The men are waiting—for immigration papers, for a next step in this long process. They are also waiting for their wives to hand them breakfast, lunch, and dinner. The steam from hot pots on stoves fogs windows and escapes the basement floor of the hostel. If you peer in, you can make out a handful of women cooking together, waiting on the men above.

I enter the subway station and travel east. The subway car is full of tired people. In the back corner an elderly South Asian man who has finished his night shift and is on his way home is fast asleep. He is wearing a uniform with the insignia of a private security company. Middle-aged women from Trinidad sit across from me. They are eating out of plastic bags, conversing with one another while holding tight to their mops and buckets. They are rubbing their sleepy eyes. I get to Spadina Station and change lines in order to travel north. The station is mostly full of office workers, early morning yogis with their yoga mats, corporate types, retail employees, and students beginning their day. Some mornings I continue traveling east and, for a brief moment, am in the throngs of rat racers on their way to Bay Street, the financial district. As the subway pulls into Bloor-Yonge, the morning rush reverberates with the sound of determined feet in high heels as they click on the pavement.

The sounds of the rush are long gone on a late weekday night. Some nights I traverse this district on my home way after a later night out. On the surface, this walk in Toronto is not much different from a late-night stroll through Chicago's, Vancouver's, or New York's business districts. As I walk through the financial district of a major city late at night, I see that the foyers of skyscrapers are well lit. In almost every building there will be a lone security officer in the middle of their "working day." There is quite often evidence of the night cleaning crew. Lights go on and off as the cleaners make their way through the floors, their shadows and the outlines of their bodies visible as they push vacuums and empty wastebaskets.

On most mornings I bypass the whole financial district and just travel north of the city to Downsview Station. It is a remarkably somnolent station in contrast to the corporate rush at Bloor and Yonge. The atrium above the platforms has a quiet shuffling sound. For many, the station is a liminal space between work and sleep. Sleeping on the subway is necessary within a range of temporalities. There are the obvious morning commuters, students, and businesspeople, but there are also pilots, vacationers, and international business travelers headed to the airport. Among them are a larger number of night-shift workers who have been waiting a long time for buses to start morning routes. I learn, in crossing paths with them daily, that some of them are taxi drivers without their own cars. They have driven through the night and are traveling back home to sleep. There are also employees of the twenty-four-hour fast-food joints, mostly middle-aged Asian women and black youths. These establishments built for automobiles and suburban sprawl litter the strip malls of Toronto's suburbs and most outskirts of major North American cities. Some of these workers have waited more than an hour for transit.

It is morning in a subway station in a big city. There are rat racers, yogis, taxi drivers, business travelers, wage laborers, professors, students, and late-night revelers. The demographic compositions of these morning congregations and transversals will be different depending on where you are. But, regardless, the subway hours, the loud sounds of the morning rush, the "good mornings," and the weather reports that flash on the subway screens and are exclaimed by the radio jockeys, along with the smell of brewing coffee, interpolates only a few. For the night shifters this is evidence of a temporal ordering of the day completely inconsistent with their time. But it is a temporal order completely dependent on their labor.

I no longer live in Toronto, nor do I walk up and down Christie Street every day. My move from Toronto to Durham, North Carolina, was accompanied by a significant change in rhythm, from big city to small city. But mine was not simply a move from the fast life to the slow life. Rather, I had entered a new landscape of temporal power relations. There are variations to the gendered, classed, raced, and immigrant histories woven into the temporal politics of Toronto and Durham. Durham's city limits are composed of a vast forest, a recently revitalized downtown, farmers' markets, barrios and ghettos, the university high streets, and the old tobacco factories that have become lofts, restaurants, cafés, and artist studios. There are some reminders of the once thriving black Wall Street.

On my bus rides between Duke University and the University of North Carolina, I encounter different ways in which people share space but not time. It is a short commute on the express bus between Durham and Chapel Hill. The bus is full of students, professors, and service staff. In this part of America, the university service staff is not South Asian men or women from Trinidad. It is mostly African American men and women. They work shifts on campus, a place that is often thought to be outside of the workaday world. But on the bus you can see that the University of North Carolina and Duke are also places of low-waged work. If you walk through the upper-middle-class neighborhoods surrounding these campuses, you'll see driveways with rusty cars or a minivan or truck that pulls up only on Fridays, indicating that someone is cleaning someone else's house. Fridays are an important part of the temporal normalization. A clean house for the weekend is a temporal ritual. In this part of America, it is most likely Latina women, sometimes their entire families, who clean. There are cleaning people in Toronto's neighborhoods as well, but geopolitics changes the chronopolitical landscape of social relations. There you are more likely to encounter Filipina and Eastern European women cleaning. In Durham the composition is also differently gendered and raced, with Latino men and women often cleaning together.

The figures on the bus, in the asylum hostel, and on the subway, like the power-chronographies of the places and populations found throughout this book, are all interpolated by speedup in one way or another. While advertisers and capitalists are quick to portray a world speeding up, the work of the critical Left is not to confirm this world and simply flip it on its head, merely exposing it as corporate, capitalistic, dehumanizing, and antidemocratic. Instead, the goal of critical thought is to rescue the politics of time from domination by structures of power. In order to do this, we must learn to inhabit the world in time. First, such an intervention must recognize that more important than a perceived fast world full of busy people needing more time is the structural reality that not everyone is equally out of time. Second, the intervention must recognize how keeping people in and out of time is a form of social control, one of the conditions of possibility for contemporary global capital. Finally, the intervention must recognize how our time is entangled with the time of others. *In the Meantime* does not free time, but it provokes the question of what a politics of bounded time might look like. In order to do this we must begin by recognizing the power-chronography of it all.

Chapter One

JET-LAG LUXURY

The Architecture of Time Maintenance

During my layover in Atlanta between Raleigh-Durham, North Carolina, and Vancouver, a young man reading Plato's *Republic* strikes up a conversation. After a few minutes of small talk at gate B9, I find myself in a pretty heated discussion. My fellow traveler is a software developer for video games, with a particular interest in cell phone consoles. He is a Canadian citizen who moved to Buenos Aires when his company decided to "go global." He is perplexed that my area of research involves taking a *critical* approach to media and technology. Since I am a professor of media and cultural studies in a communication studies department, he first assumes that I will be a good networking opportunity. He hands me his business card almost as soon as I mention what I do. We start talking about what I teach. He soon realizes that what I profess is not akin to his unconditional blanket love for technology. I may even come off a little technologically unsavvy, in fact, probably quite a bit so, by comparison.

It comes as a surprise to me, though, when he asks if I am "like Zygmunt Bauman"—that is, someone who is angry and threatened by the inevitable future of technological progress. He goes on to tell me that multi-player video games on cell phones are a part of the future—a future that is fast approaching. In fact, "in many parts of the world this future has already arrived." This future is intrinsically "good because it is diverse" and is "diverse because it is fast moving." He then proceeds to paraphrase Bauman's *Liquid Life* at length. For Bauman, "liquid" men and women are the fragmented subjects of liquid modernity. In liquid modernity, social forms do not have enough time to solidify. Long-term thinking becomes impossible and liquid moderns must find new ways to exist in the new temporality of liquid life. People such as me (and Bauman) are bogged down by our heavy thoughts. According to my fellow traveler, Bauman and I have made careers out of critiquing technology because we are too conservative and fear change. This leads to a denial of the social diversity that global capital and new technology promise.

At one point he boldly states, "I *am* Liquid Man." Liquid Man then confesses that Bauman's writing was therapeutic for him because it describes who he is. Although, he warns, Bauman's take was much more negative than the way Liquid Man actually experiences liquid life. He exclaims, "I enjoy being Liquid Man." By this he means he relishes all the accouterments of a mobile and fast-paced lifestyle: the plane hopping, social networking, contract employment, and technological gadgets that keep him plugged in. Being without bonds in this liquid world means he can "keep going with the flow." Liquid Man tells me he feels free, not limited by the weight of the world.

While Liquid Man and I continue to have a conversation about how technological visions of the world are too often divided between dystopia and utopia, he gives me something else to ponder. Liquid Man says, "I love the airport." "Look around," he says, "look at all these people thrown here together. I just love airports, everything and everyone I need is probably right here, right now." He is excited by the new possibilities inherent in airport sociality. Strangers sharing space and the constant emptying out and filling up of the airport present a business opportunity for him. He can network, conduct market research, tap into the crowd, and even promote his new software. For Liquid Man, fast times are for the free and unfettered spirits. The obvious gathering place for these fast and free spirits is the modern airport. Liquid Man and I part ways at the first boarding call:

"I would like to invite all Gold Status Star Alliance members to board at this time." Liquid Man stands up, smiles, and shakes my hand. "That's me," he says, with all of the self-assurance of a card-holding member of the Gold Status Star Alliance.

Liquid Man's appreciation of airport sociality is echoed in *Aerotropolis: The Way We'll Live Next*, a book written for business leaders, urban planners, and other "global visionaries." It makes the argument that the potential of the airport lies less in its spatial location than in how it is a site of connectivity, keeping everyone from "workers" to professionals connected to the global market.[1] If new leaders of the twenty-first century pay more attention to the airport, the book argues, they can remap the world. Airports are places where the dueling goals of capitalism—global homogenization and local diversification—can be realized together. While this excites capitalists, it horrifies the critical theorist of speed.

In speed theory, the airport is a (lamentable) structural transformation of the public sphere and material evidence of the fall of the public man. Spaces such as airports, speed theorists argue, signal the demise of political space and the rise of an apolitical time. In this literature, spaces of transit are denigrated for their homogeneous architecture, purified and pacified interiors, and lack of local referents to situate the individual traveler.[2] At the airport, the retreat of individuals into their own personal technospheres mimics a larger withdrawal of citizens from activating public space. In *Crepuscular Dawn*, Paul Virilio maintains that the new architecture of globalization is based on modular standardization and synchronization.[3] In *Pure War* he argues that airports are the new capital city, no longer a spatial capital but a temporal capital where departing and arriving are more important than dwelling.[4] He argues: "When we know that every day there are over one hundred thousand people in the air, we can consider it a foreshadowing of future society: no longer a society of sedentarization but one of passage; no longer a nomad society, in the sense of the great nomadic drifts but one concentrated in the vector of transportation." He goes on to say: "People are no longer citizens, they are passengers in transit."[5] Similarly in Bauman's case it is Liquid Man who replaces the political category of the citizen; the contemplative and deliberative subject gives way to one who is open, malleable, fragmented, unattached, and—of course—fast moving.

As it turns out, Liquid Man, Virilio, and I have something in common. The airport transfixes us all. The meeting between an international business traveler so affirming of speed and me, both well versed in cultural theories of speedup, indicates that perhaps speedup is a narrow and uncomplicated worldview characteristic of a privileged relationship to time. Far from the airport bar, distinct temporalities—in the air-traffic-control tower, at the baggage claim, and on the tarmac, for example—unselfconsciously carry out their machinations to make our conversation possible. As the concretized infrastructure for the maintenance of global capital's accelerated flows of goods, money, people, and information, the political and economic importance of the airport cannot be understated. But the importance of the airport has less to do with how it fails as a public space or how it is speed space and more to do with the way it operates as a routing mechanism for different temporalities within the larger biopolitical economy of time.

In airports people wait, serve, sleep, rush, and work within a highly uneven relationship to time. At any given moment there are new visitors, residents, citizens, laborers, and denizens who are spilling out of various flights and enduring different plights. Many travelers breeze through security. Immigrants and visa holders move through passport control at speeds determined by some combination of socioeconomic status and geopolitical context. The range of service workers in the airport includes baggage handlers, taxi drivers, janitors, shoe shiners, retail clerks, servers, bus drivers, parking attendants, and beauticians. In this list we must now include nutritionists schooled in the science of jet-lag dietary requirements and acupuncturists who prick and poke bodies to help them overcome sleep deprivation.

In a time-obsessed culture, the airport is a particularly vital node for the reproduction and maintenance global capital's most valuable subject: the frequent business traveler.[6] Upon arrival at the modern international airport, the frequent business traveler is met by a multimediated infrastructure—one that consists of technologies, commodities, programs, and laborers, all oriented toward the enhancement and protection of their time. "Keeping up to speed" is a discourse that reverberates in the corporate speak of the companies the travelers work for, the ads for their mobile technological devices, and the business literature they read. Speedup is a perception of time constantly confirmed by the elaborate system of temporal support that greets travelers in airport lounges, hotels, their offices, and the air. This ideological belief in speed operates as a scaffold: one that holds up while it hides the temporal infrastructure that keeps travelers on pace and along the paths that are commensurate with the aims of global capital.

The temporal value of the frequent business traveler is largely unparalleled by any other tired population that labors under the auspices of global capitalism. Frequent business travelers experience the world as accelerated and fast paced. They describe their lives and their labor as largely lived outside normal time. My careful consideration of three representative case studies draws attention to the relationship between frequent business travelers' position within the biopolitical economy of time and their subsequent perceptions of speedup. Frequent business travelers' unwavering belief in the speed of life indicates less about the new realities of a sped-up world than it does about their position within the biopolitical economy of time. It is no wonder that the fellow traveler I met in Atlanta loves being Liquid Man; he enjoys the maintenance of his privilege now found in liquid form at the modern airport. In his uncritical affirmation of a world of speed, what Liquid Man doesn't see is that he is being quickly carried along and ushered through, liquefied by a temporal architecture designed especially for him.

Three Itineraries: The Frequent Flyers

CLAIRE

Claire is an independent consultant in her mid-fifties with adult-aged children. I meet Claire at her home office in Toronto, which is where she spends her workdays when she is not on the road. She typically travels for work once a month, this after a decade of traveling every week. On the day we meet, she is taking an afternoon break from writing an article for one of the city's major newspapers. Her article is on the subject of "time management and balancing acts in the time-crunched workplace."

Claire has a degree in psychology. She is a consultant who specializes in business psychology, specifically "helping people to maintain balance, including diet, health, and domestic issues related to work—spousal issues, life planning, and time management." She describes her profession as an "on-site psychologist who teaches certain echelons of a host-company 'emotional intelligence.'" Claire "helps people to feel comfortable in their own skin in order to eradicate the dysfunctional behavior that takes up too much time." She works with people's emotions in order to keep up the increasing demands that come with "tighter cycles of production." Given speedup, "there is less time nowadays for posturing and positioning." According to Claire, "emotional intelligence" is about the efficient use of time for certain types of working environments and specific types of workers:

> [When you focus on unproductive emotions,] you lose a phenomenal amount of time. You lose thirty to forty percent of your day. There is only so much time and you lose. When you have to produce you don't have time to lose, so I try and help [my clients] find their voice and their confidence. Emotional intelligence isn't a necessary skill for every working person, but for those people who have goals related to their employment.

Typically, Claire works with men in middle management all the way up to CEOs in various North American companies. More recently she has started traveling to Western Europe and South Asia. She tells me she is "going global with emotional intelligence." At the time of my visit, Claire has just been invited to work at a call center in India. She explains that she "does not do knowledge management or time management on the call center floor, where there are three thousand operators, because they are there for the money, so they don't really need it." Time management is reserved for workers whose time is of qualitative concern or whose productive capacity is not measured in units of time that correspond to a going rate of pay, or wage. This subtle comment reflects exactly how the differential biopolitical economy of time operates. Labor time is understood qualitatively for some populations in the labor force, not purely in labor time's productive capacity; "quality" time can only exist for those whose time does not literally equal (company) money.

Claire works "eight days a week, depending on what you call a day." When she is on the road, her day can begin at four thirty in the morning and end after dinner, when she "still has to be 'on.'" When Claire is not traveling for work, she feels more in control of her time: "I come and go. I know the rhythm of work. I know there are times I can't think and I forget it. And when I'm in a mature mood, I'll say screw it and I'll take off and go play. But when I'm not in a mature mood I'll sit and struggle to produce." For Claire, "knowing the limits is part of having emotional intelligence." She jokes that though she is in the business of time management "for others," she still needs better balance for herself.

DARRYL

Work-life balance for Darryl, a married father of two in his mid-fifties, is a nagging tension. He is an executive specializing in human resources for a high-tech firm, and Darryl says: "There is no separation of work and life until retirement. I think about business twenty-four hours a day, seven days a week." Quite candidly, Darryl admits: "I just can't relax." But the alternative, as he sees it, would be "a middle-range income, which means debt and less freedom in the future." Citing a weekly business magazine on the "toxic workplace," Darryl contends that "the whole value and the way people work has made it very difficult to find job satisfaction, unless you are at the top of the house." Darryl is extremely proficient in the corporate discourse surrounding retirement and time management. An important aspect of his job includes running workshops to train managers to better supervise the "time of their employees" and to "meet the demands of changing technologies." He works in and out of the various global offices of his company to "standardize the efficiency and the methods of time management." He also advises and consults with individual employees on their retirement and future goals.

I meet Darryl in his home in Toronto. He recently relocated in order to be closer to his two grown children. He greets me in a golf shirt embroidered with his company's insignia. Darryl has been an executive for numerous high-tech firms in Malaysia, Hong Kong, and Canada. He has traveled internationally and nationally for business for more than two decades. At one point, he estimates, he was traveling 240 days of the year. In the past three years, Darryl has significantly cut down on his travel to "about once every two weeks for a few days or once a month if it's a weeklong trip overseas." Adding it all up, Darryl figures that he has probably spent more time in hotels, airport lounges, and in the air than at home.

More recently, Darryl has made a shift in his travel habits to try and make the journey more comfortable. He now chooses boutique hotels over chains. He expresses a preference for train travel in Europe; whether knowingly or not, Darryl cites a popular Canadian National Railway advertisement, saying that the train is "a much more human way to travel." For Darryl, his new focus on comfort is an effort to become, citing another piece of business literature,[7] "high touch in an increasingly high-tech world." When I inquire as to what this phrase means to him, Darryl explains that "'high touch' is face-to-face and more personal in relation to a highly transactional and technology-driven type of work environment." Darryl is worried that "people have lost the human touch in the increasingly fast-paced information-driven world." Darryl is a voracious reader of business literature. As I spend a few hours with him, he relays an extensive knowledge of the different anxieties in workplace culture over the past three decades. He is on top of every global business strategy that has been disseminated in the popular press.

KEN

Significantly, Ken also senses a lost humanity in a work culture he finds saturated by technology and too much travel. He is the owner and operator of a major recreational and leisure resort outside Toronto. He is also a leisure consultant for corporate offices. Ken was born in Trinidad, where his family owned and operated a beach resort. Ken merged his interests in hospitality and tourism with a degree in business. He then opened up a company that specializes in corporate leisure, including corporate outdoor recreation. Ken touches on a similar vein as Darryl; in recent years Ken has decided to take more buses and trains as often as possible in order "to slow it down and have some time." But, much to his chagrin, he is most often at the airport. He stays plugged in to his BlackBerry and earpiece at all times: "It is almost permanently attached to me at all times except for sleep." I meet Ken when he is in Toronto for a convention. He keeps his earpiece on during our entire two-hour conversation. The blue light flickers several times but Ken reaches into his pocket, looks at the caller ID, and presses a button that sends the call to voice mail. He insists that "face-to-face conversations are increasingly rare in his world." By traveling in what he calls a form of "slow business travel," Ken feels that he "encounters the best of both worlds," where he can be productive but also relax. He enjoys being restricted in a space, such as a bus or a train, because there he "cannot rush around" and can "enjoy the view and be around people." Travel time is "Ken's time."

Ken's business travel is by no means routine. He travels at least once every two months for a week at a time and, quite frequently, ten days out of every month, depending on the "new demands" he creates for himself and the business. He recognizes the ironic context in which he works. He travels to travel conventions and consults for the hospitality and tourism industry on issues related to the culture of corporate travel. He explains to me that the corporations he consults for are interested in how their employees vacation: "How people spend their vacation time is of interest to the places they work." Ken tells me that he thinks most people would find it surprising that "different corporations have a stake in the travel and tourism industry." Ken consults on time management in corporations and how to create relaxation for employees. One of the more interesting elements of Ken's profession are his training workshops to create "leisure therapists" who then help people plan their vacations to maximize relaxation. Leisure therapists are hired to come speak to employees. Like Claire and Darryl, Ken is in the business of work-life balance while trying to maintain his own work-life balance.

While Darryl might be the most proficient and knowledgeable about relevant business literature, all three of these frequent business travelers relay an almost identical set of concepts to describe the contemporary moment. They speak of work-life balance, humanizing travel, emotional intelligence, time maximization, and, most important, the increasing speed of life. Moreover, their labor is directed toward these descriptors of the moment: leisure therapists, early-retirement counseling, emotional management in the name of time saving, and creating corporate recreation. They imagine speedup as an economic condition that requires increasing amounts of self-sufficiency. Yet they are highly commodified bodies; the market and the corporate world have invested in them. They are extremely hard workers but they are not necessarily self-sufficient in a world of speed. Instead they are ushered along by a temporal infrastructure of time maintenance.

Road Warriors on Speed

In the late 1990s a new icon emerged in business literature aimed at the frequent business traveler. "Road warrior" survival guidebooks hit the market with tag lines that promise some combination of time management and meaning in one's life. Guides written exclusively for women espouse soaring lessons for the woman road warrior to help her find her travel style. Fashion advice on where to purchase airport-friendly clothing and shoes are geared to women. In 2001 a "frequent-flyer bra" guaranteed to pass through metal detectors hit the market.[8] Christian road-warrior guides preach "how to keep your faith, relationships and integrity when away from home."[9] The book gives tips for dealing with infidelity, such as bringing pictures of your spouse on the road, keeping a rigorous calling schedule, developing an accountability partner who is a person of your gender, as well as blocking adult channels that lead to temptation. *The Way of the Road Warrior* offers many "lessons in business and life from the road most traveled."[10] An indication of the enduring cultural salience of the term *road warrior* is the amount of real-time warrior advice available online for any destination.[11]

The online guides serve as maps of the temporal infrastructure, but they are also a key part of this architecture of time maintenance.

In the same way that my anonymous airport interlocutor claimed the liquid man as a description of his existence, the road warrior is a trope that these three frequent business travelers claim. From Darryl I learned that the road warrior is someone who is always on the go, plugged in, connected to "the network," and ready to do business. Characteristics of the road warrior include a certain technological savvy, knowledge of the latest, smallest, and fastest personal technologies to manage his or her time, and preparedness for the culture, politics, and values of his or her destination. Darryl explains, "You have to make the right choices to suit your needs in order to balance while traveling for business; what time is good to travel, places you are most comfortable. You have to know your body clock, and you have to be self-sufficient. In other words you need to be a road warrior." In fact, Darryl uses the term as a self-diagnostic: "He's the gadget guy in commercials—he's sitting at the airport and he has everything, he probably hasn't had a secretary in years—he's a very self-sufficient person. They don't have secretaries. Me, I'm probably an eight out of ten on the road-warrior scale—because I have no need for a secretary." Darryl explains that the road warrior should have an armament of time-saving strategies just in case the mode of transport, whether plane or train, is late or if an upgrade is required for a hotel room. Darryl confirms another expectation I find in the literature on road warriors: one must be knowledgeable of the limits of his or her body. This includes dietary needs, patterns of sleep, special drugs, and any other jet-lag requirements. These should all be worked out and properly managed prior to a trip. Katherine Ameche's *The Woman Road Warrior* is filled with not so much technological know-how but issues related to bodily comfort and safety. It is obvious that this management of time takes on highly gendered nuances.[12] Claire confirms this important detail as she explains how her travel plans were once methodically organized according to her cycle. Lately, because of menopause, she finds it more difficult to plan ahead. Business travel is also cited as a reason why some woman are taking "control of their menstruation" and "forgoing" their periods altogether.[13]

While discussing perceptions of speed and the acceleration of everyday life with all three frequent business travelers, I saw a general consensus: acceleration is simply a fact of life. Their responses to the topic of speedup are much like reflexes: "of course the world is getting faster" (Darryl), "the cycles of production are tighter and you have to be fast" (Claire), "humans thrive off of speed" (Ken). For road warriors, speed emerges not only as an inevitable fact of everyday life but also as part of their labor, a challenge to their ever-advancing business agility. For the frequent business traveler, terms such as *time-space compression* and *the cycles of capitalist production* are not abstract academic lingo or even postmodern jargon. It was interesting to note how often these phrases peppered my conversations with these private-sector professionals.

To a great extent speed is the basis on which these folks' livelihoods thrive. When I first ask them to relay their thoughts on the idea that "things were getting faster," they each immediately discuss the implications on their careers. Speed, for them, is more than just the pace of life, it is an ever-present potential that they have to be on top of. Speed is a problem their labor is oriented around. Speed looms. If they stay on top of their time, then they will not have to deal with its consequences. They perceive a good part of their labor and lifestyle as pursuing time control. In my conversations with them it became quite apparent that so much of their work is understood in the context of maintaining the speed of life, including keeping other people "up to speed."

For Claire it is the tighter cycles of production that require people to have "emotional intelligence" to "get what needs to get done done fast, in a healthy and efficient way." Her consulting techniques are oriented toward the new emotional needs of a sped-up corporate culture. Darryl doesn't think the world is so much faster as it is smaller: "Because of technology you have more access to it—faster—in shorter time frames." To Darryl, speed is a "condition of modern living." And this condition requires him to pay attention to getting "the various global constituents of [his] company up to speed because everything is connected." Speed is something to which Darryl's human-resource management must tend and accommodate. Darryl compares companies across the globe and explains that his company is buying all of them out: "These other companies aren't able to make it; they run out of money." He explains, "They [other companies] put us through to their secretaries to make appointments and by the time we get a meeting it is too late and decisions are already made and they've lost out." For Ken evidence of an accelerated society comes by way of his "tired and overworked vacationers who just don't know how to relax on their own." Ken thinks that speed is an inevitable part of contemporary life. "It is just the way it is when you live in any advanced capitalist society," he says, and goes on to exclaim, "lucky for me, there will always be tired and overworked people who need a vacation!"

When pressed further about their personal feelings regarding time, all of the frequent business travelers correlate feelings of imbalance with speed. In other words, living effectively in sped-up culture and balancing work and life are synonymous. Balance and being out of time are major sources of anxiety in their daily lives. Claire describes how she feels: "Most people won't balance unless someone tells them to. People need to be reminded to slow down. I have a friend who checks in with me and just tells me to breathe, and I realize in those instances that she tells me this that I do forget to breathe. But you have to make the choice to slow yourself down." When I ask Darryl what he thinks of the expression "time is money," he responds:

> Time isn't money in the sense that it is dollars and cents, but rather something that has to be structured in order to reach your goal. I'm very goal directed and sometimes it [my life] is not structured enough from a work-life-balance perspective, but nonetheless I am very results driven. So I think of time as a very precious commodity and I want to make the best use of my time. And with things getting faster, this is more important. But the bottom line is that it means I don't really know how to relax.

Darryl's bottom line is striking and provides insight into how the discursive power of speed is helpful to capitalist reproduction. To a great extent business travelers *need* to believe in speed as a defining characteristic of the contemporary moment because it justifies their existence and extremely tiring days. They are not materially impoverished workers and they are not working just to get by. Moreover, they each indicate during our interviews that, in one way or another, they don't necessarily need to be working any more. "I don't know how not to work," exclaims Claire. "I could stop all this, but I'm just getting going and I like being out there part of things," Ken tells me.

But as much as they are in it, they are out of it. The frequent business travelers discuss an overriding sense of living in an exceptional time; one that they imagine is quite different than other people's time. A key theme in our discussions is how they felt outside of the parameters of a normalized day. Claire, Ken, and Darryl relay how often they feel both out of place and out of time. Darryl explains how he often wakes up and has no idea where he is, what day it is, or if it is day or night: "Especially in those new rooms where all light is blocked out, I've woken up and almost had to call [the] front desk. You sort of panic, and it's a strange feeling. You do feel alone." Pico Iyer, the author of *Global Soul*, writes, "You feel like you're an exile, a fugitive of sorts, as you walk along the hotel corridor at four in the morning, while all good souls are in their beds, and then you begin to yawn as everyone around you goes to work."[14] But one comfort in all of this disorientation has always been the airport lounge. Darryl finds that airport lounges offer a home away from home:

> You walk into the business lounges, and the first thing they'll have is if you are first-class passenger, you go one way, [and] if you are a business traveler, you go another way. First class is like a first-class hotel—the top-notch ones will actually have a separate door that you can go through with your ticket; some will actually take you there and check your bags for you and then when you get there you can get hot towels, [and they] sit you down for free champagne, hot food, top-notch everything, a leather chair—it's just like home.

When frequent business travelers are feeling out of it, airports function as a comfortable space, a second home. To return to Darryl's language, the high-tech world is increasingly replete with high-touch solutions.

As out of time as the frequent business travelers think they are, in another sense they couldn't be more firmly entrenched within the time demands of global capital. Road warriors are subjects of immense value, and their labor cannot be easily replaced. There is no room in this economy for a reserve labor force of traveling businesspeople. Instead, reserve labor must be extracted from their bodies.

The Soldiers of Jet Lag

In December 2005, the *New York Times* ran an exposé on business travel, reporting 41 percent of business travelers complained of not sleeping enough and 29 percent complained of not sleeping well.[15] Instead of focusing on the downside of fatigue the article focused on how business travelers downplay their tiredness. One of the interviewees concluded: "A business trip is not about sleep. Nobody comes out of any business meeting and says, 'You did best today because you look freshest.' Clients couldn't care less if I am fresh as a daisy. They just want to know that when

I, or my team, comes to the table, we've got a big idea."[16] As subjects of value within global capital, the time of the frequent business traveler is an important object of biopolitical regulation. The sleepy body of the business traveler, perhaps comparable only to the military soldier, is therefore also a significant object of knowledge production.[17] The problem of sleep is an area of scientific research shared by both the military and pharmaceutical companies. In fact, one military researcher who refers to sleep as "sleep architecture" maintains: "There is a quiet revolution going on in sleep medicine."[18] Chronobiologists contend, "We are living in a time famine where there isn't enough time in our waking periods to accomplish all that is expected of us."[19] Data on the productive aptitudes of tired workers are accumulating. Sleep specialists and other medical researchers are investigating how the body reacts to shift work, long-distance driving, jet lag, and even space travel. Business travel tends to be at the center of these experiments on temporal management—subject to medical testing, corporate surveys, and sleep-institute interventions. The Time Isolation Research Unit was built as part of the A$10 million colocation of the Woolcock Institute of Medical Research in Sydney. It opened in February of 2009 to house more than a hundred test subjects who will live in complete isolation, including from externalities like sunlight and noise.[20] The isolation rooms are set up like hotel rooms, but volunteers are monitored twenty-four hours a day.

In the 1970s, health specialists and journalists charted the arrival of a medical condition at the gates of the international airport. Understood at the time as a health hazard, the flying body was positioned as fragile and weak in relation to the harsh environment of air travel and far-off exotic places. Diana Fairechild, a jet-lag activist fighting for flight attendants, pilots, and citizen flyers everywhere, chronicles her life lived in the air as a former flight attendant in the 1970s. Her list of the perils of air travel is exhaustive: there are shifts in time zones, alterations in magnetic fields, modifications in climate, and the need to contend with diversities of cultures. Passengers are deprived of air and humidity, and exposed to re-circulated germs, chemicals, radiation, pesticides, noise, and dehydration.[21] Symptoms of jet lag include dehydration, deep vein thrombosis, cardiovascular and circulatory problems, insomnia, headaches, cramps, and nausea.

Body-temperature controls, techniques for staying hydrated, where one should sit in the plane, how one should breathe during takeoff and landing, the types of foods that should be avoided, and how many hours of sunlight are necessary before and after the flight are all topics that fill up travel guides, advice columns, and brochures found in doctors' offices and travel agencies from the 1970s. Here the requisite techniques for the care of the self are being deployed. As Foucault explicates in *Care of the Self*:

> Between the individual and his environs, one imagined a whole web of interferences such that a certain disposition, a certain event, a certain change in things would induce morbid effects on the body. Conversely, a weak constitution of the body would be favorably or unfavorably affected by such and such a circumstance. Hence there was a constant and detailed problematization of the environment with regard to the body, and a positing of the body as a fragile entity in relation to its surroundings.[22]

But this discourse has changed in the past decade as jet lag has shifted from a specifically located medical problem or even mindset to a generalized condition of working and living in fast times.

In popular discourses today, *jet lag* rarely refers to the time spent in the air. It is now referred to as a byproduct of the fast-paced tempo of modern living for a particular socioeconomic demographic.[23] Jet lag is a new "problem of living." Once known solely as desynchronosis in the medical world, chronic jet lag is now an accidental side effect of living as a subject of value in the global economy. Chronic jet lag was formerly a medical malady associated with flying east of the point of embarkation, but it has now become a general social phenomenon termed *social jet lag* by marketers working in business tourism. The vice president of Westin Hotels and Resorts promoted a new jet-lag concept room at the Westin River North location in Chicago: "It will be useful not just to our road warriors, but to sufferers of 'social jetlag' as well. Our incredibly busy lives interfere with our bodies' natural rhythms, causing widespread symptoms of lethargy, grogginess, insomnia and headaches."[24] The term *social jet lag* describes the bodily and social consequences of living in a harried world on the go, perpetually unable to catch up. It refers to biological life and lifestyle. The concept room also speaks to the rather vogue status of being socially jet-lagged.

With the shift from jet lag as a medical condition to the socially jet-lagged body, there is a change in how the relationship between the body and its environment is understood. The body, once a weak and fragile entity to which the environment posed a danger, becomes potentially limitless given the right technological care. The body is no longer limited in its ability to adapt to change. Its ability to labor longer depends on assembling the right program of time control. Time is integral to this process. But it is no longer an issue of socially necessary labor time, as in Marxist critiques of time and labor. Nor is the issue about turnover time, as in the focus of scientific management. Instead, it is about the expansion of value into the realm of meaning making where labor is oriented around making qualitative adjustments to the problem of time. The body's labor time has no foreseeable limit.

The limitless potential of the productive temporality of a technologically managed body is nowhere more evident than in the scope of sleep technologies that have been devised in collaboration with the military and pharmaceutical companies. Sleep technologies, as they are called, go beyond specific programs and commodities that deal with tiredness. The eradication of sleep itself is the ultimate goal. Modafinil, for example, is issued for "sustained military operations."[25] Known in the military as the "go pill," it has also been used by narcoleptics for the past decade and a half. However, its more socially appropriate term is a *wakefulness promoting agent.* In 2001 Americans spent US$150 million on Modafinil.[26] It is important to note that three-fourths of the pills were taken neither by narcoleptics nor soldiers. So far, tales from the trenches of Modafinil come from young corporate types and journalists with deadlines. The pill that "cuts sleep debt in half" and allows you to stay awake for forty-eight hours currently awaits FDA approval for wider use. DARPA, the Defense Advanced Research Projects Agency, is searching for ways to create the "metabolically dominant soldier." Among the projects it is pursuing is the creation of a warrior who can fight twenty-four hours a day, seven days straight. "Eliminating the need for sleep while maintaining the high level of both cognitive and physical performance of the individual will create a fundamental change in warfighting," says the Defense Sciences Office, the unit of DARPA responsible for bridging any potential gap between new technology and the military.[27] The corporate front has similar expectations of its warriors.

The discourse surrounding Modafinil attests to a particular way of living and regulation of conduct that alters how time is managed and stretches the limits of the body. As Foucault argues, medicine is not conceived only as an intervention or cure: "It was also supposed to define, in the form of a corpus of knowledge and rules, a way of living, a reflective mode to oneself, to one's body, to wakefulness and sleep, to the various activities and the environment."[28] The capitalistic potential of Modafinil is realized by the fact that the drug only really works when you are working. According to a test subject, in an interview titled "Get Ready for 24-Hour Living" in *The New Scientist*: "I wouldn't say it makes me feel more alert or less sleepy. It's just that thoughts of tiredness don't occur to me. If there's a job at hand that I should be doing, I'm focused, but if I'm watching a movie or something, there is no effect."[29] The last line of the article reads: "To all intents and purposes we are already too far down the road of the 24-hour society to turn back. For millions of people, good sleep and productive wakefulness are already elusive, night work or nightlife a reality, and the 'stimulant-sedative' loop all too familiar."[30] As wakefulness increases among certain populations and night productivity becomes the norm, the already overworked and overconsuming have more to do. Instead of sleep, the business traveler is offered an elaborate cocktail of military tactics, spa services, pharmaceuticals, technological gadgets, and commodities. Being tired is a requirement of labor, but being tired *and* unproductive is not a viable option. Within this temporal infrastructure, it is difficult to set a limit to the body's productive capacity for work. The jet-lagged and time-zone-jumping bodies of contemporaneity are instead invited to enter into the architecture of time maintenance. This architecture is designed to meld their physiological ability and the ideological necessity to stay in time.

Temporal Architectures to the Rescue

The modern airport appears to be haunted by the specter of public space. Simulacra of town squares with street lamps, murals, and park benches fill the concourse halls and gates of the international airport. In Paris's Charles de Gaulle airport, mock plazas with chrome benches, gaslights, and graffiti can be found throughout the departure zones. At the Charlotte Douglas airport in North Carolina, white rocking chairs are scattered across the terminal byways and walkways, signifying the neighborly porch culture of Southern aspirations. At the Amsterdam Schiphol Airport there is a deliberate nonpolicing of the homeless who find shelter and other means of survival at the airport.[31] Here urban planners have encouraged city officials to consider the airport as a central space of civic life rather than demarcated and gated off from the rest of the city. In many ways the public-space decor at the airport reflects the anxiety over the diminishing of virtuous and sacred space as well as the realization that the airport, though privatized and exclusive space, is still more public than most other places.

The faux public spaces seem to beckon, to promise a prefab community, saying: "Here we are, strangers in shared space. We offer an instant public, while you wait." It is hard to tell if these installations that signify a vibrant public are invitations to reconvene and to gather, to recognize a mutual humanity in the context of a world that feels elusive and full of missed connections, or nostalgic curiosities, memorials to something that has long passed. Either way, the installations' existence speaks to the persistence of democracy's spatial imaginary: the need for open and accessible space. Against the hustle and bustle of the movements of the travelers and the airport laborers through time, these spatial markers of democracy stand still, most often deserted.

Along with public-space decor—an immersive environment oriented around time maintenance—an elaborate temporal infrastructure has arrived at the airport. It combines technologies and human labor that allow frequent business travelers to recalibrate and get resituated within the particular time demands of global capital. The airport's temporal infrastructure attends to accidents and risks within a biopolitical economy of time. It does the reproductive work to enhance, activate, and affectively transform the body's capacity to produce as well as alter the subject's experience of time to match the rhythm of a capitalist work ethic. This temporal infrastructure maintains highly structured temporal experiences and normalizes a set of mutually reinforcing conceptions of time: (1) time management is the individual's responsibility; (2) one must work harder to stay in time; and (3) being tired is a slow person's excuse for being unproductive.

There are at least two contradictory yet intertwined attributes that mark these technologies of time maintenance. First, they are what Patricia Clough calls "affective technologies," those technologies that work on the physical body to produce capacities beyond one's organic-physiological constraints.[32] Second, the temporal infrastructure incorporates a component of care that is meaningfully linked to traditional forms of women's work or feminized labor. These technologies offer care in the most maternal of ways by rocking jet-lagged bodies to sleep, massaging backs, and providing aroma-therapeutic mists and gentle touch (see figure 1.1). The masculine force of speed is tempered with a feminized form of maternal care.[33] With special sheets, night-lights, and bathing routines, the subjects of value are coddled through time managing interventions, while more of their labor time is extracted via a qualitative form of time control. Bio-

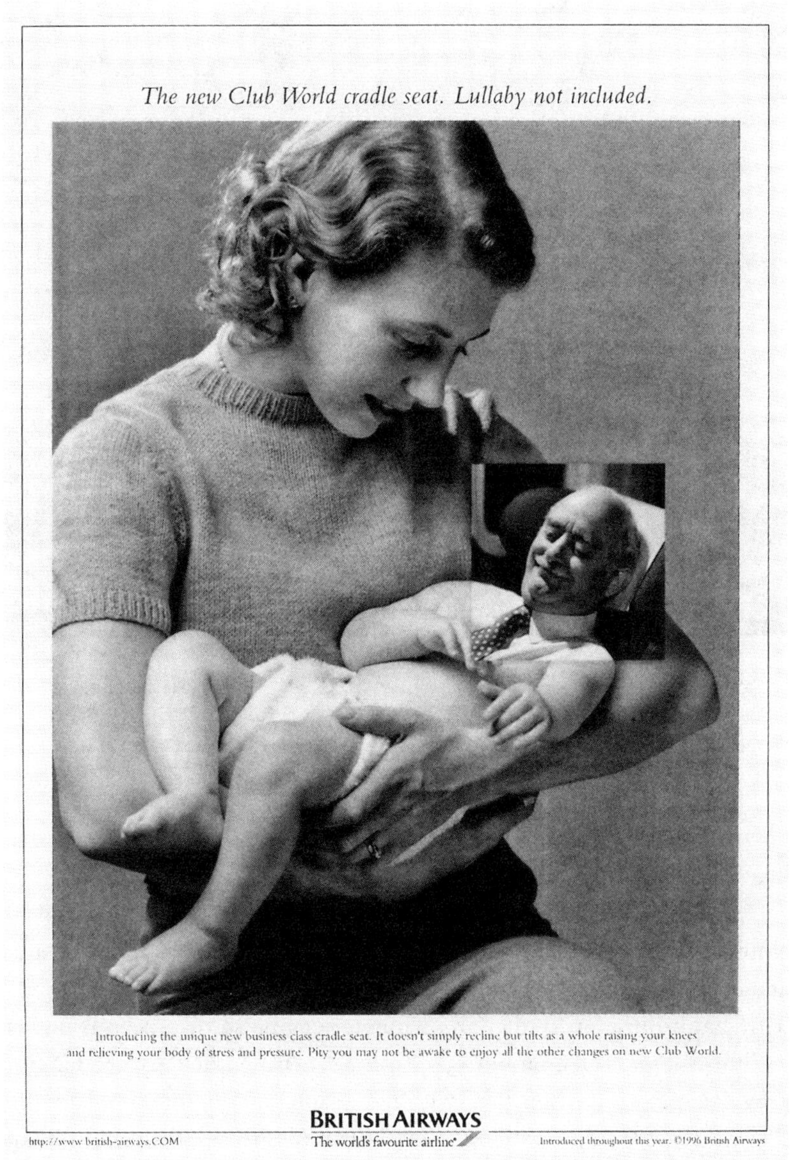

FIGURE 1.1. A British Airways advertisement from 1996 for the New Club World Cradle Seat. June 10, 1996. *New Yorker* 4/5.

FIGURE 1.2. The Boeing Dreamliner interior was designed to fight jet lag. Image retrieved from http://newlantern.com/innovation-economy/boeings-dreamliner-is-no-longer-a-dream/.

power is exceptionally high touch. The temporal infrastructure operates like a cradle, but its ultimate form arrives as a jet.

The Boeing 787 Dreamliner, "the plane that fights jet-lag," is said to eliminate the major factors that cause jet lag by reducing cabin pressure and controlling cabin humidity (see figure 1.2).[34] The jet is also equipped with an air-filtration system and a quieter engine so that sleep is not as easily disrupted. The Emirates A380 that flies between New York and Dubai provides "time-zone transition" within the cabin interior that simulates the time of day at the destination.[35] As the flight progresses, the cabin ceiling emulates a night sky with a blue hue and the sparkle of stars. As time passes the light changes to indicate the rising sun. The Emirates is flaunted as a "hotel in the sky," offering private cabins, showers, and massages.

Back on the ground, Hotel Okura in Amsterdam offers a complete customized jet-lag program. Time spent at the hotel is referred to as a "program" instead of a "stay," thus reflecting the programmatic nature of neoliberal projects for self-maximization.[36] The program at Hotel Okura includes exercise, light therapy, and carefully planned meals to combat jet lag through nutrition. The hotel's website instructs travelers to "take the active route to reducing jet lag effects. . . . You'll be tired from traveling but you will be surprised how well you perform at that next business meeting."[37] The "jet-lag concept room," designed by the Starwood Hotels and Resorts, offers an entirely new environment for the jet-lagged and overextended individual living in the fast lane. Starwood and Philips Lighting have designed the room with blue lights for phototherapy. Reebok, another investor in the room, designed exercise routines and equipment. Beyond lighting and fitness, the hotel group has created its own line of bedding, which includes a mattress with ten layers, sheets and pillows, and a range of aromatherapy products. There are blacked-out window shades to turn day into night. A light box situated above the desk provides light therapy while one is working. In the shower an aromatic mix of lavender and eucalyptus mists are released straight out of the showerhead. The shower also boasts a high-intensity lamp that purportedly activates the "third receptor" of the retina and enhances wakefulness. Starwood Hotels and Resorts has also teamed up with Meditainment media company, which is working on a lineup of what it calls "media meditation," a genre that blurs the medical, meditation, and mediation. The company has created SleepTV, a channel that hotel patrons can turn to for guided meditation. The room is equipped with a sound box of fifty different noises that can fill up the room, including rainfall or waves. Beside the bed are "sleep vials" filled with essential oils that trigger the olfactory senses to provide calm and relaxation.

The Park Hyatt in Toronto, specifically its Stillwater Spa, also advertises its services as fixing the road warrior's body and soul, and fingertips. Stillwater offers "the high-tech hand massage" to ease "blue thumb" tenderness that results from the use of miniaturized technologies.[38] While labor and leisure already blur in this example, increasingly spas are designed as spaces to replace the boardroom, providing treatments while power brokers meet.[39]

At Charles de Gaulle, light therapy is also on offer in a specially designed structure that allows travelers to walk right in and lie down. "Journey management" is a service offered by a "fatigue risk" management firm called Circadian Technologies, which coordinates companies' travel when employees are flying from different time zones. In the line of fatigue risk comes MetroNaps, whose clients include Google, PricewaterhouseCoopers, and

Procter & Gamble. MetroNaps has created a few different versions of the Energy Pod. The pods are found in private offices as well as public places, such as Vancouver International Airport and the Empire State Building (see figure 1.3). Customers can enter the pod for a quick nap in guaranteed privacy under a protective cover. The pod will rock back and forth to aid in sleep and provide an aromatic mist for a peaceful wake-up call. Attendants service the pod by wiping it down after every customer. Nemorelax is another company that offers pods for "an oasis of calm in busy, transit, crowded, and stressful environments" for thirty minutes at a time. The pods are for working, watching (films), sleeping, or talking (on the phone). A Nemorelax suite consists of six pods and covers a minimum of 110 square feet, with an encircling cocoon for extra tranquility.[40] While pods appear in public spaces, there are also full-service napping spas. YeloSpa in Manhattan offers midday naps that are sold for five dollars a minute (see figure 1.4).

Sleeping in public is often considered illegal in the context of antihomeless laws. But it depends on who is falling asleep and how they sleep. Tokyo is interesting in this light, as sleeping in public on the subway is an act of creative and productive time maintenance. It indicates hard work rather than laziness or transgression from social norms. A dark business suit absolves a sleepyhead from regulation. Napping in public is sanctioned insofar as it is a power nap. Likewise, the frequent business traveler at the airport is absolved from the feminized, lazy, slovenly connotation of nap taking when a technological device or the labor of others is present. The advertisement of the motherly figure cradling the business traveler doesn't leave the impression that the frequent business traveler is a baby. Instead, it works to reinforce the frequent business traveler's status as a subject of enhanced value while maintaining an ideology of gendered time and labor. Everyone in the area is reminded that the frequent business traveler is a hard worker. The temporal privilege of business travelers is most apparent in the fact that the management of their time occurs as public spectacle. Their retreat is advertised, made public (see figure 1.5).

Public napping pods also indicate that sleep is both a new space and time, amenable to direct market and corporate intervention. Sleep time is treated as a transit space for the redistribution of temporal power, a site of traction for capital. Shut-eye is no longer the dreaming hour, free from trading, transactions, and being productive. Time (and space) for sleep is present in the capitalist grid, and is therefore able to be bought and sold.

The infrastructure of time is not devised of technological parts only. The

FIGURE 1.3. (top) The MetroNap pod. The founder and CEO of MetroNaps, Arshad Chowdry, is in one of his own creations. Image retrieved from the biography page of Chowdry's website, http://arshadchowdhury.com/biography/.
FIGURE 1.4. (bottom) YeloSpa Napping Chair at the YeloSpa in Midtown Manhattan. http://www.yelonyc.com/.

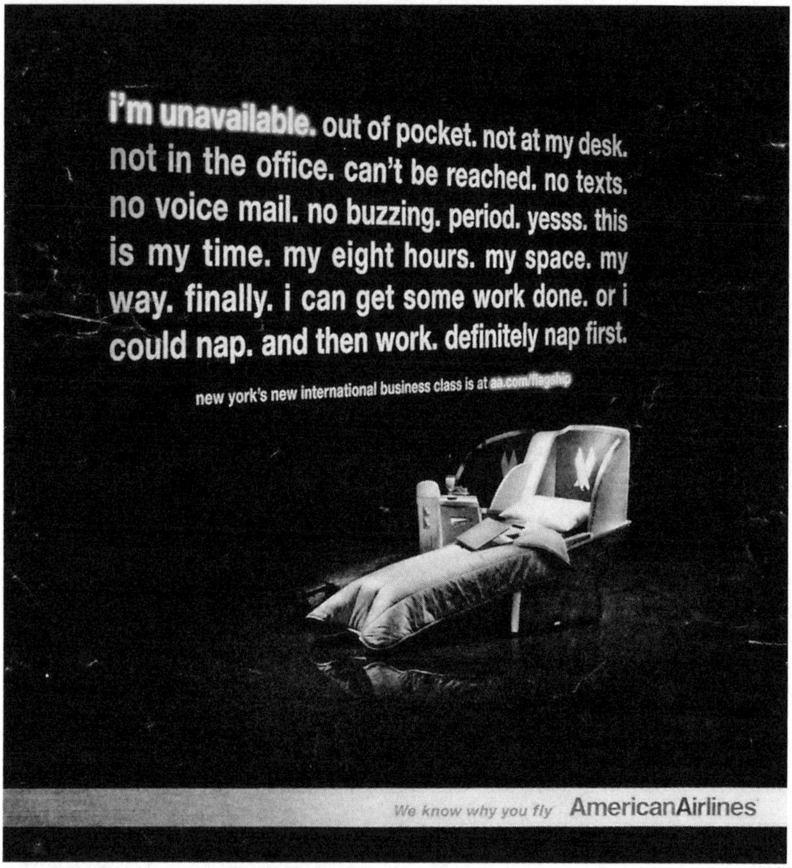

FIGURE 1.5. "This is my time." An American Airlines advertisement from 2011 for the new international business class air bed. Images such as these increasingly fill the terminals of international airports to distinguish the business class as a particularly busy and tired class in need of rest.

labor of others is also a significant part of the frequent business traveler's temporal infrastructure. In fact, frequent business travelers themselves quite often orchestrate a system of labor support in order to maintain their exceptional temporality. Claire explains her network of support:

> I have certain hotels. I have a driver. I have hired help at home. I have a person who would drive me to and from the airport. I had people who knew my routine and made it easy as possible for me. I went to the same hotel, same drivers. I don't have to think. I can

try and focus on what I have to do. If I was teaching, working, one on one, my mind and space could be focused just on that. I have a network of people, places, comfortable to me, and I can just sit back and relax, work, sleep, and it is very helpful.

In his self-help guide for business travelers, Robert L. Jolles gives many examples of employing labor in order to stay en route and in time. He directs: "Stop taking your car to the airport, and use a taxi. If you are in Washington DC, you can use Sam, my driver. He'd love your business. If not, find a Sam in your city."[41] The labor support for the harried on-the-go business traveler may no longer include "secretaries," as Darryl indicated earlier, but temporal architectures require workers. The frequent business traveler's labor demands also reorganizes the time of others. People are needed to drive at all hours of the night. Front desks need to be occupied overnight. Security guards are needed to stand in the foyers of corporations during the night hours. Offices are cleaned while employees are at home sleeping. Homes are cleaned while the same people are at work. Maids are trained under the circadian-rhythm standard to accommodate the jet-lagged traveler.[42] Remote assistants are hired to take care of menial tasks while frequent business travelers and other entrepreneurial types are asleep or in the air. While capital develops at the expense of bodies, it makes clear which bodies will be taken care of. These technologies of time maintenance reinforce the idea that subjects of value—here the frequent business travelers—cannot be easily replaced, but the secondary labor they depend on can. The commodity market and lifestyle industry are one step ahead of their self-acknowledged alienation. The technologies of time maintenance are machines for the social reproduction of a particular temporality and their value, that of the frequent business traveler. But at the same time there is also the social reproduction of other temporalities, ones that are increasingly devalued.

Speed Waiting

Airports keep capital and bodies on time and on track.[43] After 9/11 international business travel slowed for a short period, but "let's roll" meant "let's fly"—keep working. Since 9/11, airport waiting times have increased—people are expected to spend more time at the gates. The eighty-six minutes of time that passengers average between clearing security and waiting for takeoff is an unaccounted for time, open to investment by retailers and other machinations of global capital.[44] Waiting is a differential temporal experience for the frequent business traveler. In fact, airport waiting is said to cost businesses billions in lost productivity.[45] Even in the context of this deliberate slowing down, it is telling that business travelers still encounter their worlds as unparalleled speed. In the airport, the typically slow experience of waiting is transformed, for the business traveler, into yet another element of life in the fast lane.

As Ameche confirms in *The Woman Road Warrior*, "no business traveler wanted to spend any more time than was absolutely necessary either in the airport or in the plane before departure."[46] Waiting is not a universal condition or experience. Jeremy Rifkin's *Time Wars*, published in 1987, considers the politics of waiting to be a class matter, where the past aligns to the masses and the future to the elites. He argues, "A monopoly in every society begins with severing people from control of their own future, making them prisoners of the present. Unable to gain access to the future, people become pawns in the hands of the temporal pyramid."[47] In *Pascalian Meditations*, Pierre Bourdieu also explains the politics of waiting in relation to the economic and social conditions of possibility: "The empty time that has to be killed is opposed to the full (or well-filled) time of the busy person who, as we say, does not notice time passing—whereas paradoxically, powerlessness, which breaks the relation of immersion in the imminent, makes one conscious of the passage of time, as when waiting."[48] Temporal power takes on a performative element. The frantic colonization of the seats at the gate by the business travelers after they've departed from the business lounge speaks to the unacceptable status of waiting. (That is, of course, if they weren't able to bypass the gate altogether with expedited boarding rights.) As they sit for a short time, undifferentiated from the economy classes accustomed to waiting, you'll often hear the businessman take to his phone. His taking up of space is gendered as well; he disregards the fact that he is sharing the gate with others, and assumes that his time takes precedence in the ostensibly communal space. He talks loudly in codes and acronyms, "tell Jim I got his APR file and I'm just waiting on BRT to get back with the 145 before I send it off to PR." In this otherwise empty time, the business traveler has had his waiting legitimized by the closing of the deal, by spending empty time wisely. The frequent business travelers can make themselves matter in otherwise uneventful time, reaffirming that waiting is a temporal condition reserved for others. For them, life is full.

The rise of a temporal architecture elevates the cultural significance of waiting from the dead time of doing nothing to a time of self-improvement and a privileged moment of reprieve. Everyone manages time in one way or the other, for better or for worse. But for most populations, the management of time is more or less internal or at least invisible—hidden from the view of others. And even for the frequent business traveler, waiting is not always a public act. It is often done in exclusive lounges with other temporally compatible subjects. But the emerging architecture of time designed for the business traveler offers a public display of busyness where the frequent business traveler, and other members of the socially jet-lagged, retreat privately in public view. It signals both the need for the frequent business traveler to take their time management into their own hands without diminishing their sense of temporal worth.

Departing Terminal Time

The technologies of care and outsourced forms of time management described here are evidence of an emerging culture of re-temporalization. They signal the fact that the very institutions that drain life are also in the business of providing extra energy. In the end, the limits of the individual body, a tired and potentially resistant body, are overcome through enhancing the subject's experience of time with commodified technologies and the labor of others. The institutional governance of time is embraced rather than rejected. There is no dead time of labor, and this is by design. The temporal infrastructure is a technological solution and a corporate response to the time of the frequent business traveler, one that produces new social relations of time across the social fabric while maintaining the uneven distribution of time.

What surfaces in consideration of these interviews, these discourses of speed that permeate the world of the frequent business traveler, and the incipient temporal infrastructure, is that being tired by the contemporary speed of life is a specific kind of tired. There is no uniform fatigue in this world full of tired people. Claire, Darryl, and Ken admit that they don't really need to work solely for financial reasons any more. How fast is this world, then, where it is acknowledged that they do not even need to keep up? The discursive power of speed is nearly irresistible.

Belief in speedup enables the business traveler to both feel independent and self-sufficient while allowing for biopolitical interventions that keep him or her within a pace and path commensurate with global capital. Speed is by no means a generalized cultural or economic phenomenon. In the case of the business traveler, speed is not a pace of life but an experience of time, one temporality in the multiple and interdependent constellations of time.

The tired body of the frequent business traveler is a grave economic risk for global capital. The run-down body of the business traveler is in danger of drifting off; the travelers are not materially impoverished but are increasingly and exceptionally fatigued. The body of the frequent business traveler operates as a very particular circulatory site, a point of transfer and exchange within the global economy. It is a human node in the network of information and capital, a potentially blocked source of energy and capitalist accumulation. Thus, the emotions and bodily states that result from this labor are those to which biopower must directly respond. These worked-upon subjects, however, often welcome biopolitical interventions. Within the biopolitical economy of time, for subjects of temporal worth, biopower is high touch. It can often feel good.

Chapter Two

TEMPORAL LABOR AND THE TAXICAB

Maintaining the Time of Others

The front seat of a taxicab offers a rare glimpse into the taxi driver's relationship to time. The taxi driver in most major metropolitan cities in North America is almost always newly immigrated and waiting for accreditation papers. Many drivers are seeking asylum. The taxi driver straddles multiple temporalities, both personally (the offset clocks of time zones that dictate phone calls home, the slow progress of work-visa applications, the movement of their children through the U.S. school system) and professionally (the tempos of those they must transport, the slow traffic, night and day, the ticking of the clock and the running meter).

The front seat is a private space for the taxi driver. Rarely are fares invited to sit in the front when there is room in the back. It is where drivers keep their personal belongings that help them get through the day. There are coffee mugs, packages of khat, cigarettes, pillows, eye masks, blankets, cell phones, water, hand sanitizer, and half-eaten meals. Overhead on the visor, there are pictures of family members, CDs, business cards, and picture postcards of elsewhere. Hailing a cab with a large group of people, when everyone won't fit in the backseat, often results in frenetic scurrying. The driver quickly pushes the belongings to the floor, stuffs things into the glove compartment and the sides of the doors, or collects it all in a pile to dump in the trunk.

But these scattered front-seat objects are hardly just things. Together they compose the taxi driver's daily rituals of time management. Unlike the jet-lagged traveler in the previous chapter, whose life unfolds within an elaborate temporal architecture, the taxi driver navigates an entirely different infrastructure of time. In the front seat of the taxi there are stimulants for staying awake and negotiating stress (coffee, music, khat, and cigarettes). There is also a range of items for breaking from work in order to sleep, rest, and eat (the eye mask, pillows, and blankets). The pictures and postcards on the visor can be likened to the screen savers or minimized Facebook windows of desk workers—reminders of life outside of work.

The taxi driver is connected to a central unit via the radio, camera, the meter, and a GPS. Their routes and paths are never uniform or known in advance. Nor are the hours they will spend working each day determined from the outset. The absence of a precise and knowable parameter of the day indicates some freedom in time—the ability to control the length of the working day. But the taxi driver does not just submit to the ebb and flow of time. Instead, his or her daily life is structured by the constant tension of being out of time while responding to and maintaining the time of others.

Unlike the frequent business traveler, the taxi driver is not a subject of great economic value whose temporal well-being is a site of growing investment. And the market (the companies that drivers work for) and the people the drivers service do not provide ways to enhance their productive capacities. Taxi drivers must create their own strategies of survival in order to stay in time. But the lack of investment is also entirely biopolitical. As the expendable bodies of a labor force that can easily be replenished, there is no need for the structures of capital to endow the taxi driver's time with importance. Biopower rears its head through divestment as well as regulation. Biopower is made incarnate through the police, tow-truck drivers, parking officers, fares, dispatchers, and fleet owners. These different entities hover over taxi drivers' long days. Police and tow-truck drivers chase taxi drivers out of parking spots when they break to use restrooms.

They are yelled at and treated like second-class citizens by both fares and dispatchers. They are disciplined verbally, or abused for that matter, for missing fares, getting lost, not answering immediately, or taking allegedly wrong routes. They are subject to racist tirades, acts of violence, backseat interrogations, and bad directions.[1] In the midst of all of this, their labor is confounded by an intense competition to catch fares.

Speed theorists configure the politics of temporal difference through the binary of fast classes and slow classes. A biopolitical perspective offers a more complex, and politicized, framework for understanding social differences as they relate to time. In *Homo Sacer: Sovereign Power and Bare Life*, Giorgio Agamben argues that bare life is a form of contemporary subjectivity, and we must learn to recognize its many forms.[2] Bare life accounts for those lives abandoned by the institutions of modern power and forced to live as outliers in the very order their existence works to maintain.[3] Agamben is useful for thinking about the contemporary biopolitics of time. The taxi driver is much more akin to life in the state of temporal exception, closer to bare life, than the protected and much valued temporality of the jet-lagged.

An exploration of the politics of temporal labor provides a more complex understanding of temporal difference and is a means for understanding contemporary theoretical debates that revolve around labor and biopower. I use the term *temporal labor* to account for the experience of laboring within a temporal infrastructure while being cast outside it.[4] The taxi driver is constituted in time in a way that is structurally related to the time of the business traveler. There are different struggles over time that occur when one's labor entails directly synchronizing to the time demands of other populations' temporalities.

I begin with accounts of three taxi drivers and their reflections on the "speed of life" and their experiences of time. The case studies are followed by a deeper look at the taxi driver's infrastructure of time maintenance. What becomes most evident is that there is a temporal order against which cab drivers measure their time. The order is alluded to in their choice of words to explain their labor and their time practices. Their attempts to stay in time, and the processes and struggles that this entails, are just as significant as whether they succeed. Taxi drivers' time is tied to many of the busy and tired populations' temporalities, produced by contemporary capital, but how taxi drivers experience being out of time is by no means analogous.

Itineraries: The Taxi Drivers

ABRAHAM: SIX YEARS

When I meet Abraham for our interview on a cold winter evening at a Tim Hortons coffee shop on Bloor Street in downtown Toronto, he has been driving cabs in Toronto for six years. As soon as I walk through the door, Abraham greets me frantically and explains that we have to leave right away. He can't find a parking space anywhere and is parked illegally and worried about getting fined. This is a usual predicament for Abraham when he wants a cup of coffee or needs to use the restroom—there is nowhere to park his cab unless he wants to pay. Leaving his car for even a minute could result in a fine. "Cabs are an especially easy target for the police," he explains. He tells me of another place around the corner, a "coffee shop for taxi drivers that has a parking lot and is open twenty-four hours a day." He doesn't know the name of it and thought I wouldn't have known how to find it on my own, as "only other taxi drivers, homeless, and prostitutes go there." I get in the taxi with Abraham and we drive around the block to the "coffee shop for taxi drivers." He's right, there appears to be no name for the shop—the sign is blurry and the awning has the remnants of at least three other previous establishments' emblems. The parking lot is full of taxicabs, and the drivers are all sitting outside drinking their coffees. Some are smoking. Most are conversing eagerly with each other. The sound of dispatchers and the static from the radios of the parked taxis fill the air. Abraham moved to Toronto ten years ago from Eritrea, seeking asylum. His father had come to Toronto years before him under the same conditions of civil unrest to try and "set up for the family." Abraham's father started driving a taxi within months of arriving in Canada. After years of being unable to create adequate conditions in which to support his wife and children, he encouraged Abraham to seek asylum and join him in Toronto. They thought that together the two of them could save up enough money to send back to support his family in Eritrea. Abraham arrived in the city for what he thought would be a "very temporary thing," but six years after his arrival, Abraham's father died of a heart attack. His mother remains in Eritrea with his youngest brother.

Abraham is a shift worker, which means he rents his cab from a taxi-fleet owner on a daily basis. He might drive the same car, but he shares it with other drivers, and he must pay for the rental time. He typically works 4:30 p.m. to 4:30 a.m., except for Sunday. He arrives home from work on

Sunday at 4:30 a.m. and starts again Monday at 4:30 p.m. On Sundays he cooks a big "healthy type of meal" for himself, goes to church, and does laundry. For Abraham, what is good about driving is that "you get to choose when you want to work." Abraham has not taken a holiday or an extra day off except for four years ago, when he visited Eritrea for four months. He expresses his desire to take the same kind of trip very soon. In fact, what keeps him going every day is his "dream of going back home and not having to work." But Abraham doesn't expect that to happen for another few years: "Maybe in two or three years I can afford to go home for a visit and take a break from this." He started going to a trade school to become a mechanic but "gave up because it would take too long to start over" and "make enough to live and go to school." Between taking time off and changing careers, Abraham feels better off just getting by in the instant. The difficulty lies in the fact that after a twelve-hour shift Abraham hardly makes close to minimum wage, which at the time of our discussion is seven dollars and seventy-five cents in Canadian dollars. He is "just living" and "putting a few away here and there to visit [his] mother."

An excellent day for Abraham is when minimum wage is met, but an average day is more likely to result in a net of five dollars an hour. At the end of a typical shift, he gets home after gassing up and parking the car around five in the morning. He shares the car with a "day driver," who lives in the same block of flats in the northern part of Toronto. Prior to this arrangement, when Abraham first started driving and was living with a group of newly emigrated people from Eritrea, he struggled to get home every night after parking his cab in the garage. Driving the cab home would mean that Abraham was paying rent for his cab even though he wasn't driving it. Instead, he would park the car downtown and would sleep on a cot in a friend's house in the garage. Abraham would pay his friend up to fifty dollars any given week to stay. After a year of this "homeless feeling," he befriended another driver, and they now live in the same apartment building and share a cab. He chuckles and says, they "might as well share the apartment, too."

Abraham typically falls asleep with the television set on at six or seven in the morning after "winding down." He wakes up at one or two in the afternoon, eats, showers, and gets back on the road. He begins his shift in the heart of the city, usually a main train station or bus terminal. He says, "I always think it is temporary—I think all of us think it is temporary—but people end up doing this for thirty years."

JUDY: THIRTY YEARS

Thirty years is exactly how long Judy, a fifty-four-year-old single mother, has been driving a cab in Toronto. Judy moved to Toronto from Trinidad thirty years ago and has been driving a cab ever since. When I set up a meeting time and place with Judy, she offers to pick me up from my apartment since she lives close by. She requests that we meet well before three in the afternoon so that she "can still be out there for the rush hour." Judy picks me up and we settle into a café in the neighborhood we both share. As soon as we are sitting down, Judy informs me that she is "one of probably about only twelve women cab drivers in a city of eight thousand cab drivers." Thirty years ago, when she first arrived in Toronto, she enrolled in a community college, taking classes to become an accountant. She took a part-time retail job to cover tuition and the costs of raising a son on her own. After a few months of "waiting for paychecks," Judy took the advice of her friend, another one of the twelve women cab drivers in Toronto, and started driving cabs to make "instant cash." While accounting continues to be her "dream job," the struggle to raise her son, work part-time, and be in school part-time proved too difficult. Judy left school altogether and began driving full-time. She continues to drive, she explains, because of the "flexibility and not having to deal with the anxiety of waiting for a paycheck since there aren't any savings."

Judy has been an "ambassador" driver in the city for the past three years. The ambassador program allows Toronto taxi drivers to own their own cars and plates after taking a forty-hour course on customer service and safe driving. Ambassadors give 10 percent of their meter earnings to the leasing company for insurance and are not expected to pay for their own repairs as other cab drivers who own their cars do, like Billie (who we will meet next), or shift drivers who rent from a lease owner, like Abraham. Judy's cab had been in the shop for two days, and although she didn't have to pay for the repairs, she lost serious wages. After she drops me off, she will drive through the night until "six in the morning or so, even though it is a Tuesday."

Judy works "about five days a week for fourteen hours a day between 10 a.m. and 12 a.m. She gets home after her day on the road and typically falls asleep at 2 or 3 a.m. and is up again at 7 a.m. In the mornings she does a Pilates DVD, makes a big lunch, and prepares food to eat after her shift. Judy explains that she doesn't take "real" breaks. Her breaks are when she's "just sitting in [her] cab reading [her] newspaper waiting for a fare." On Friday and Saturday nights Judy is "on the road until 4 a.m., starting at three in the afternoon." She takes off Mondays and Tuesdays because they are the "slow days." There are not as many fares, and those are "the good days for banks, doctors, dentist" and when places such as the "Laundromat and grocery store aren't busy."

BILLIE: THIRTEEN YEARS

One driver's slow day is another driver's opportunity. Billie, a fifty-five-year-old father of three who lives in a suburb north of Toronto, owns his own cab and treats it like a limousine service. Billie and I arrange a meeting at his home in North Toronto. His youngest son picks me up from the subway station. When we arrive at the family home, the taxi is sitting in the driveway. He mentions that there are other taxi drivers in the neighborhood, but many of them take the taxi signs off of the car when it is in the driveway.

Like Abraham, Billie moved to Toronto with an asylum program eighteen years ago. An engineer in Iran, he entered Canada under a professional placement program for immigrants. It is clear from talking to Billie that, first and foremost, he is still an engineer; he is "an engineer that drives a taxi." In discussing his life in Iran before moving to Canada, Billie fondly reminisces about his past affiliations with the Left literati and socialist movements in Iran. He laments that he has little time now for local politics in the city because of the hours and nature of his work as a full-time taxi driver.

Unable to find work after the internship, and no longer "patient [enough to wait for better work], with three children to support," Billie started working as a delivery person for a chain restaurant. After a few months, he felt limited by a job where his hours were "dictated by someone else's hours." He really needed to be working more to make ends meet. He began driving cabs on top of keeping the delivery job. He worked as a cab driver from 4:30 a.m. to 4:00 p.m. and would deliver food at the restaurant between 5 p.m. and 11 p.m. Billie reflects on those early years, during which he balanced two jobs, six days a week, "without sleep and never seeing the family." It took approximately six years for Billie to save up and buy his own taxi plate in order to begin his own taxi business. Billie prefers to drive "mostly the business crowd around."

Billie now works six days a week on what he terms the "business hours."

This includes Friday and Saturday "until two or four in the morning, if it is busy enough." He will occasionally work into the night on a weekday if one of the "children needs money for school or the house needs some repairing." He has not taken a break of more than one day for the past five years. Billie is less forthcoming about talking about his wages. He says, "There is no way to really say how much money I make. At the end of the year it is always the same. On a daily and weekly basis it is not even. And, I just have to keep going thinking that in the end of the year it will be the same as the year before." He goes on to say, "You just have to work more when it doesn't even out. And if you keep working, it will even out. But you need new strategies and have to drive the right people." The taxi belongs to Billie. He doesn't rely on a central dispatcher. Instead, Billie keeps a cell phone, gives out business cards, and relies on a network of business people who frequent the city. This, he imagines, gives him control over his workday. His usual route during "the usual business hours" moves between hotels, the financial district, industrial parks, and the airport. Billie's taxi, except for the night revelers on Friday and Saturday, is in the service of businesspeople. He goes out every day with the intention of establishing connections to ensure that his taxi circulates within this larger flow. He quite often is booked days in advance or will meet a "person in town for business" and set up a few days of transportation arrangements. If he hasn't already established a fare to start his day, he drives for approximately twenty-five minutes to the city center and waits outside the hotels where businesspeople are most likely to stay. On a bad day he could be waiting "up to one hour for a first customer." This waiting is also Billie's "break time."

As with the other two drivers I've described, Billie has hope that this job is still temporary. He is open to trying something else, ideally working as an engineer or a job closely related to engineering. One of the reasons he prefers to drive businesspeople is that it could lead to making a business connection beyond his taxi business. Billie takes the element of chance that the taxi provides seriously: "You never know who you might pick up and how they might be able to help."

Speed Takes the Backseat

The notion that the world is getting faster has little to do with the taxi driver's experience of time. Drivers fully recognize that certain populations live in their own fast worlds. The taxi driver's experience of time is recognized as one lived on the margins of a temporality. The fact that taxi drivers are always trying to keep up with the time of others structures the drivers' horizon of possibility on a daily basis; this affects how they understand time in terms of their lifetimes. When I asked if a change in tempo or speed of life was noticed, all three took some time answering the question. In various ways, they responded that they had not experienced acceleration. In fact, the common thread running through the interviews was that if there was any transformation in tempo, it was slowing down.

In the past decade, the city of Toronto has been flooded with cabs, their numbers doubling in five years from three thousand to six thousand, and the city plans to have ten thousand on the road within the next few years. Couple this with the economic crisis, and these are slow times for cab drivers. Abraham laments, "Life is slow, business is slow, things have never been this slow before, and it is only going to get slower for us; it is harder to make money than ever." Judy and Billie explain how business is so slow and uncertain that they no longer take breaks because they spend so much time parking and waiting. Billie, who prefers to start his day from a hotel in the financial district, exclaims: "I spend sometimes an hour outside a hotel waiting for a fare at the beginning of every shift in the morning." These breaks are fraught with anxiety, as Abraham explains: "You're just waiting and you're looking everywhere for someone to pick up. Sometimes you drive around aimlessly and when you see someone you speed up to them." The drivers' first reflections on changes of tempo were related to their own labor. When probed further, I found that their perceptions of speed were relative to the tempos and demands of their fares.

Speed has always frequented the cab. It comes dressed in suits, talking on cell phones, late for appointments, or about to miss a flight. Abraham says, "People in the day are always in a hurry. They take cabs because they are late. And I feel so stressed when they do this." Billie maintains the same level of frustration regarding "day people" and their temporal demands:

> They think the taxi is going to make magic, like a magic carpet flying over the city. They have a job interview, a business meeting to close a million-dollar deal, a flight. Friday I had a customer at six at Yonge and Bloor and his flight was at seven. So the time he gets into my cab is the time he should have been going through security at the airport. He says he has a security pass but that doesn't do anything for me! It is a forty-five-minute drive. He is transferring his stress to

> me immediately. The minute he gets in the cab. That is the service you are doing for this customer. You're a doctor and he has a pain and you want to help him because this is your job. You have to do something.

For Billie "making time" is part of his labor. A taxi may appear to be a liminal space within the nodes of global capital—in other words, another non-place that people traverse and travel through rather than live in and make meaning. But cabs are only liminal in the back; there is a living subject in the front. It is the driver whose heart rate accelerates and adrenalin increases due to the diminishing time the passenger has left to catch a flight. The taxi driver exposes the singular gaze of acceleration and liminal spaces, and considering his or her position can help us understand the contemporary moment. Some populations, like taxi drivers, are in motion but are inexorably tied to a structural position within capital. They are treated as mechanical pieces of the technology that "cradle" the valuable and producing subject, the frequent business traveler.

Judy's comments on the speed of life make an important link between speed and power as particular to social and political contexts. Judy realizes that different experiences of time are linked to greater structural inequalities. In her case, the difference is gender. I ask Judy if she feels stressed out when her fare asks her to go faster, as I had learned that Abraham and Billie were. She surprises me in her response:

> You know you aren't going to believe this, but rarely have I heard "go faster." And do you want to know why? It is because I am a woman driver. Men get scared of women drivers, you know. Do you know that almost every day I have had to hear a man tell me to "slow down"? They say, "I'm in no hurry, SLOW DOWN." And I'm not even going fast, but they don't feel comfortable because I'm a woman. This has to be why. Have you ever heard of someone getting in a cab and wanting a slow ride? I see them. They get in. And they don't say anything. But they looked freaked out and they hold on to the handles, and they aren't relaxed. My last fare I drove to the airport, was like this. I never say anything. But once in a while I say "relax, I'm not going to kill you." But I have to slow down if they say so.

Her tempo is dictated by her fares, like Abraham and Billie. However, with Judy, that tempo cannot be disarticulated from male dominance and the fares' gendered understanding of appropriate pace and mechanical competence.

Significantly, in discussions about time and the conditions of their labor, the drivers share a comforting notion that, overall, they are in control of their time—perhaps not their tempo, but their time spent on the job. This belief appears to work almost as a technology of the self. Foucault defined technologies of the self as consisting of the various techniques that allow individuals to exercise, by their own individual means, operations on their own bodies and minds in order to work upon themselves to achieve a state of being, such as happiness, or a sense of well-being and quality of life.[5] The practice of controlling time works here via specific strategies but also through the repetition of a discursive statement: "I control my time." This statement works like a mantra. It is repeated over and over and mentioned several times by all the drivers as an aside or a *but* to everything else they endure. The sense of—and belief in—control permeates the way these drivers see themselves existing in space and time. Abraham's wish to soon return home again is supported by the fact that "there will always be a cab to drive," since he can leave and come back when he wants to. For Billie, like Judy, the instant cash means that he has the option to make more money if he works longer or later if something comes up. When Billie's children have to pay their tuition, he is most likely to spend more hours on the road—he can "control" his income. Judy tells me, "I can go out whenever I want; if I don't feel like working then I can just stay home or do something else or go out at night with people." In the next breath, though, Judy admits: "But I'm afraid if I do go out, I won't have a good time. And then I'll be thinking the whole time that I should be driving. That's what happens, too, when I decide to stay home and take it easy. I can't." Abraham explains why drivers keep driving: "There is one thing that keeps you driving and that is that you make your own hours, no boss over your shoulder, but it is like gambling. Today I don't make any money and I say 'That's it! I'm going to quit this shitty job.' But the next day you make money and it gives you hope. And I think I can save up to get to my country." Billie expresses the gamble in terms of fishing: "You got to know what time, where to go, otherwise it is like fishing. This job is like fishing. There is no fixed salary. It is all about timing. You have to try and catch a fish, but you'll go again tomorrow to try again because that is what you do." Later in the conversation, Billie shifts the focus of the metaphor and refers to himself as the fish, lost in the current: "I'm like a fish caught in a stream and I have to go the way the river takes me." But Billie's animal-ecology analogy runs through Judy's and Abraham's sentiments as well. "It is a dog-eat-dog world for us drivers," says Judy. Abraham claims, "I'm like a hyena. When the daylight comes, I need to get off the road and home." Each of these animal analogies casts the driver in a subordinate role to another dominant rhythm somewhere higher up the food chain: the fish is pushed around by the stream, the dogs compete for scraps from the master's table, and the hyena patrols the night for the lions' leavings. When talking about temporality, the drivers first reflected on their own labor and the temporal demands associated with driving. As the conversations continued, they considered their own lives within the larger structures of time. All in all, they understood their time as being dominated and relative to a dominant temporality. The taxi driver's time is structured around the instant. This fact is not merely representative of a sped-up world. It is an experience of time that is constantly oriented toward the temporal needs of other populations and individuals—the experience of the subordinate subject, a piece of the machine.

Regardless of their material wealth, career orientations, and social positions, time is a problem for both the taxi driver and the business traveler. Michael Hardt's rumination on prison time is particularly compelling here as a route toward the next section of analysis.[6] For Hardt, the ultimate form of punishment in much of contemporary society is "doing time." The fact that a temporal nothingness, a great void in living a life, exists as a punishment automatically necessitates the questions: "How could one redeem time? How could one live a full time?"[7] According to Hardt, cultural anxieties over filling time exist, in part, because prison exists as a reminder of a full life, rich in time. However, prison is not the alternative to society; rather it is "a focal point, the site of the highest concentration of a logic of power that is generally diffused through the world. Prison in our society is [that logic's] most realized form."[8] Where one stands in relation to the attainability of temporal fullness (the *opposite* of a prison sentence) determines ones temporal horizon of possibility. Such horizons are partially determined by modern institutions of power that promise to work out and manage quality time for different populations.

The control of time is a problem for both frequent business travelers and taxi drivers. Both populations must orchestrate and make personal choices to navigate their time and maintain themselves in a certain order of time. However, they are met with different biopolitical investment. For the frequent business traveler, quality time is made to order, right down to the pillow menus at hotels that promise to match sleeping styles with designer head-cushioning technologies. Frequent business travelers imagine themselves as self-sufficient and independent, well versed in the limits of their bodies. They describe themselves as being solitary navigators of their own roads. However, their time is almost entirely dependent on the time of others. Their leisure and labor demand an infrastructure of temporal maintenance made up of a host of timekeepers and time makers whose time is not their own. The logic of prison time extends into the realm of labor. There is a demand for the fullness of time, but it must also be a time of productivity and efficiency.

Mean Time

Abraham told me:

> You know your mind is set for nights. If you sleep day and work nights, time is different. You wouldn't believe me. When I see the sun come out, I feel like I'm a hyena. I run to my house because when you see the light and you are used to the dark, you don't feel too comfortable. I can't explain how it feels, but I feel like I'm stuck and I can't do anything about it.

Soon after 9/11 the municipal government in Toronto began increasing the number of cab licenses and changing the driving requirements for taxi drivers. One of the major changes was the expectation that drivers would go to Taxi-U (Taxi University). There drivers would learn cultural sensitivity and basic issues in professionalism, such as how to open doors for people with disabilities. As of 2013, drivers are expected to pay $750 for the course or no license will be provided. As Abraham understands it: "Basically it was a way to make money—I already know that I'm supposed to smile and be nice to people even if I don't feel like it, just like all those people who work in restaurants who have to give service with a smile."

At the time of my interviews with the taxi drivers, tourism in Toronto had significantly waned—it was a post-9/11, post-SARS, post–global economic crisis Toronto. Hotels, theme parks, theaters, and restaurants were unusually empty. The ethos behind increasing the number of cabs was to make sure no one had to wait for a cab. It is important to note that the impetus to make cabs overavailable stands in direct contradiction to a wider city initiative to make the city more bikeable, walkable, and green. The drivers I interviewed, as well as the discussions I followed in *Taxi News*, generally pointed to one explanation: the changes in cab policies were an initiative for the city to make quick and easy money off of immigrants without a concern for the drivers' economic equality. Driving a cab is the one available job for people waiting for papers under the asylum-seeker program.

Each plate is worth approximately $80,000 on the market. If a plate owner controls sixty plates, the investment is worth $5 million at current market prices. Plate owners do not typically own the cars themselves. Instead the taxis are usually owned by somebody else. At current rates, obviously, the $80,000 plate is worth three to five times the value of the taxi. The cars and plates are then rented out on a shift basis to itinerant drivers, who must hustle for long hours to make up the cost of the regulatory apparatus before they get paid themselves. The lease owners are large conglomerates. Eight owners control most of the licenses in Toronto. None of the eight owners are drivers themselves, nor have they ever driven a cab. The drivers I spoke to also claimed that most of these owners live outside the country.

The drivers who do not own their own plates make anywhere from thirty to a hundred dollars a night after gassing up, paying the car rent, and getting something to eat. The average cost of rent for a plate is $1,000 a month. This is usually 30–50 percent of a driver's income. For the drivers, there is a direct correlation between their temporality and government licensing initiatives. The investment in the city's image by providing more cabs is a disinvestment to existing taxi drivers' time. They endure a slower pace of life, which for them means fewer fares and longer hours. And, more important, this change in labor time means the drivers have even less time to take care of their own lives outside the cab.

Pico Iyer, a popular travel writer and the author of *Global Soul*, is best described as an advocate for the precarity of the well-heeled and jet-set classes of a globalizing world. He gets it so mistakenly wrong when he asserts: "The 'borderless economy' we hear trumpeted so often means that today's businessmen and women have to live everywhere at once, and the speed of global communications means that they can be anywhere tomorrow. Frequent business travelers are the new breed for which 'globalization' takes root in the stomach and the heart."[9] The affective dimensions of laboring in the global economy cannot be leveled out in such a way as to argue for the precarious position of the privileged when we know that there is so much invested in rescuing these bodies. A consideration of the stomachs, hearts, and living lives of city cab drivers reveals a condition of labor only superficially analogous to sufferers of frequent-flyer fatigue. True, both are tired and overworked. And even though drivers don't travel through geographical time zones where the continents drift, they do travel through many dislocating zones of time. Cab drivers' (ironically immobile) travel includes webs of other people's temporalities. It includes excessively long hours with little pay and the particular demands of "night people" and their rhythms, as well as a different kind of stress during the rhythms of the day. However, unlike the jet cradles and nap oases in place for the frequent flyer, there are no technologies of care or temporal infrastructures to keep drivers in time. The cab driver relies on his or her own devised temporal strategies and technologies of the self to navigate the road and maintain his or her time. These technologies of the self result in an alternative architecture of time. The absence of external and infrastructural temporal investments into the life of the taxi driver is where we can best locate how globalization may take root "in the stomach and the heart." More specifically, the absence of temporal investments reveals how a taxi driver's life is lived in a "state of exception" to the temporal order.

For example, Judy expresses frustration over a lack of adequate health insurance and benefits: "We have to do everything ourselves—I mean take care of ourselves. Many drivers don't do anything. They die from heart attacks." Judy explains how she makes time to work out at home in the morning before her shift with a Pilates DVD. Abraham compares driving the day shift to "smoking ten packs of cigarettes a day" because of the exhaust fumes. He says, "When I blew my nose it would be black, and I would cough up stuff at night." He also reiterates Judy's stories of casualties in the driver's seat. They don't result from crashes, but rather strokes, heart attacks, and high blood pressure. Abraham feels that even a few years ago he could have had a little more time to take care of himself. He reminisces about playing soccer some days: "I used to be more active. You know, I'm pretty young. I'm thirty-five and I have trouble walking. I can hardly run. Now driving for years and living in the city, I basically sleep, drive the cab, eat. I don't exercise. I park the car right by my house and I walk to the door—less than eight meters." Judy tells me: "Being on the road all day is just bad for your heart—all the near misses. My heart is skipping beats all day." As for being aware of the limits of her body, unlike the "woman road warrior," who is told to be aware of her menstrual cycle for scheduling travel, no potential for such adjustments exist for Judy. She points to her left eye, which is extremely puffy and red. She explains that this winter she is going through menopause and has to keep her window slightly open to keep herself cooled down while the heat blasts for her fares that "need the cab to be warm." The skin around her eye has become swollen from the stream of cold air it gets from her window, coupled with her "hot, flushed body and the extra heat in the cab." Her body is at odds with the temperature controls, the season, the time of night, this time in her life cycle, and the climate all at once. Judy must provide a pleasant ride. Her labor is both immaterial and affective, but her labor materializes on her body.

Judy's experience provides an interesting counterpoint to the salience of *affective, precarious*, and *immaterial* labor as concepts with which to examine the production of the subject under global capital. Marxist theorists of globalization and neoliberalism such as Michael Hardt, Antonio Negri, and Jason Read use the terms *biopolitical production* and *real subsumption* interchangeably to refer to the elimination of any exteriority to capital.[10] All social relations become relations for capital. Thus, capital's confrontation with the body, the market, and the world becomes interiorized as the full realization of biopolitics. One familiar example of *formal subsumption* is automated bodies that work like robots and are fragmented by the dictates of the machine. Read defines *formal subsumption* as the encounter between capitalism and its outside—it is capital's confrontation with other modes of production: the machine, the body, the world, and the world market.[11] These theorists do not argue that formal subsumption no longer exists, but rather that real subsumption has become hegemonic. The end products of human labor in formal subsumption are generally material. The movement toward real subsumption depends on and creates immaterial labor through the production of knowledge, desire, information, and experience. While it still requires material bodies and materials, the immaterial quality of labor and production within real subsumption becomes the defining factor.

Even in the context of affective labor, it is *not* safe to say that we are all precarious laborers, all road warriors, in the same way in this era of empire, fast capital, global capital, real subsumption, and neoliberalism. These terms are most useful when recognized alongside an understanding of the differential biopolitical economy of time. Part of capital's transformative effect is maintaining a fiction of generalized effects. Being aware of temporality disrupts the tendency to generalize the conditions and effects of capital's transformations.

The business travelers I interviewed are in the trade of affective labor, producing an emotional and immaterial effect. Claire cultivates emotional intelligence in a large corporation so that employees don't waste time. Darryl trains managers to cultivate the most productive use of time. But for taxi drivers, affective labor is about creating a connection in space and creating time for another person. Their job is to get a passenger somewhere on time, by the fastest means possible, and even "making time" if possible. They learn in Taxi-U that they are in the business of producing a pleasurable ride, bridging the distance between point A and point B. From the outside, this is not affective labor. They are not producing an emotion, knowledge, or information but rather a destination. Yet they are producing time. But if we shift gears and look inside the vehicle, then driving a cab does become a recognizable form of affective labor.

Drivers talk of accommodating the mood of the fare and quote their Taxi-U manuals that state: "The fare has the right to a silent ride and the drivers should also be ready and willing to converse as they are 'ambassadors of the city.'" All three drivers explain how they have to be cheerful even if they don't feel like it, even when they encounter racism, sexism, or intruding questions about their nationalities, their immigration status, or religions. Billie explains how he always starts off the ride with a question: "How is your day going?" He goes on: "It means you are caring about this guy—and I really care—he's a customer. This is customer service. The guy gets a chance to empty himself from the stress he has. Or if he is happy, he is expressing more and may get even more happy about it. And when they are upset sometimes you tell them a story about another fare and maybe they will get more relaxed." Significantly, there is also the element of confession. Random strangers enter a cab and divulge secrets and intimate details of their private lives to the driver. Like a bartender, the cab driver doubles as a therapist, a willing ear. Whether or not the driver cares, and many do, providing this willing ear is part of their customer service.

To a large extent, the drivers also share an entrepreneurial ethos with frequent business travelers. They take pride in their labor as if they were solitary and independent businesspeople. The drivers recognize the competitive climate in which they labor. The drivers significantly valorize their control over their own time and ability to be affective laborers. Billie is a particularly interesting example. He sees himself and his cab driving as a business first and foremost. Billie explains that, after years of experience, he has become discerning. He prefers only to drive people with an education or people like him. Billie will start his day at a downtown hotel even if that means waiting an hour for his first fare. Through his discussions with passengers, he learns when the next big conference, meeting, or training workshop will be and what areas may be requiring a connection to the financial district. He explains that his strategy is often to give them a tour of the area en route and explain things about Toronto while getting the fare to the destination faster: "I have made business cards so that I can hand them out to good fares. And many times out of the year, I'll have a whole month where I work with one group of people." Billie's strategy of only driving during business hours is an example of an attempt to normalize his time to a legitimized time frame.

Sharing time with the business traveler gives Billie some sense of legitimacy, not only within the business world but also with the general public. Further, it offers a potential opportunity and a sentiment of hope for his future. Later in our discussion Billie explains his hope:

> If I work these hours and meet these types of people, the educated who have some power, I just might meet someone who can help. Like one guy will ask you and feel sorry for you. He'll say, "you don't look like a taxi driver, what are you doing?" And you tell him your story. And maybe he can do something for you—like give you a card or a phone number or he can talk to a recruiter for you. So you feel okay . . . sometimes.

Billie recognizes a looming temporal order, and he works very hard to not be cast as one of the outliers of time. The night people, he claims, "are the scum of the earth. These people have no life. Anyone out after ten on a weekday or 2 a.m. on the weekend is a person with no life." His experiences with racist tirades from fares and a social system that doesn't recognize his engineering credentials and has him delivering food and people instead has made him sensitive to when and where he works in the city. That there is a temporal order of things, and that a certain dominant temporal order should be maintained, is entrenched in his speech and his actions. Time becomes the arbiter of exclusion and inclusion. It is a measure of what it means to be a worthy human. Billie works to maintain the temporal order in more ways than by labor alone.

Feeling out of time in an alternative temporal plane is a common state of being for the taxi drivers. It is significant that the drivers don't refer to themselves as warriors trying to balance their lives. Instead they talk of themselves as fish floating in a stream, dogs in a dog-eat-dog world, and hyenas that can't stand the daylight. Feeling out of time and exiled from a "normal time" is exactly how Abraham explains his life: "I know it is really bad, but I can't change it. I've lived in this building for four years and I don't even know my next-door neighbor because of my night shifts. I come home; they're gone to work. While they're gone I'm going to leave for work. When you do this six days a week, you just won't know a lot of people." They are out of time in terms of the normal order of the day, but they also feel out of time when they are expelled to a state of exception in their interactions with fares. In a relationship of subservient time, the "state of exception" is not a space they enter, but it is constituted in time when momentary and fleeting interactions with fares reinforce their lives as outside of the order.

Quite often, exchanges of racism, sexism, and class violence are not so fleeting. Abraham tells me that "you cabbies" is something he hears every other day. When that happens, what he hears is a general statement that lumps all drivers into "pieces of shit and stupid immigrants." Abraham explains that racial violence is a consistent part of his interactions with the public. Billie tells a story of a businessperson he picked up from the financial district who asked him some personal questions: Where are you from? Why are you driving a cab? Do you have a family? Do you own a house? When Billie explained that his kids were in university and that he was recently able to afford a small house for the family, the fare responded by saying that Billie was a good example of someone who had made it on his own. The government, said the fare, doesn't need to help immigrants. Billie goes on to say: "I couldn't work after that. I went home in the afternoon. I felt it was an intention to stop immigrants from doing their own jobs because the guy said he had been at a meeting and said, 'no matter what we do to them, they will make it, so why not leave them alone from the beginning.'" Billie gets angrier when he recounts this story. He exclaims,

> What is this? We bring people here to stop them. What is the reason? The guy has an education. The poor, back home, culture spends all this money to make him a healthy guy with education and he comes here 100 percent in your hands and is ready to use it. So why stop him from doing what he was doing and push him to do low-level

> jobs? When we can't get the job we want, we are supposed to deliver pizza.

Judy shares a disparaging interaction with a female fare. She recalls driving into the financial district at ten at night, where a young woman in "a power suit and a briefcase, obviously burning the candle at both ends" flagged her. Judy couldn't afford a babysitter for her son and would sometimes have to bring him along during her night shifts. He would sleep in the front seat while she worked through the night. On this night:

> The woman looked into the car and then asked me, "What kind of mother are you, running your babysitting business at the same time?" I drove away really upset and this was the worst time of my life I think. It was this time when my son was too young to stay on his own. This is really bad. You might think this is horrible, but sometimes I would leave him alone and I would drive by every hour to check on him.

Billie, Abraham, and Judy may be the true road warriors in the sense of being solitary, self-sufficient, and independent. There isn't a time-maintenance infrastructure to support their time needs and to help keep things in order. There are only strategies of survival and technologies of the self.

The Subarchitectures of Time Maintenance

Pierre Bourdieu suggests that "waiting is one of the privileged ways of experiencing the effect of power." In order to dissect the relationship between time and power, Bourdieu outlines an ethnography that must "catalogue and analyze all the behaviors associated with the exercise of power over other people's time both on the side of the powerful (adjourning, deferring, delaying, raising false hopes, or conversely, rushing, taking by surprise) and on the other side of the 'patient' as they say in the medical universe, one of the sites par excellence of anxious, powerless waiting."[12] The taxi driver's temporal labor is a form of labor that consists almost solely of waiting. As Bourdieu writes, "It follows that the art of taking one's time[,] . . . of making people wait[,] . . . of adjourning[,] . . . is an integral part of the exercises of power."[13] The lack of time control over one's own immediate and long-term bodily needs in the cab driver's life includes increased heart palpitations, black phlegm, having a full bladder, falling asleep at the wheel, and overheating. These are a few of the most common side effects for the drivers, who are synchronizing to the tempo of structural "backseat" relations and constantly waiting to be necessary to others' time needs.

Judy, Billie, and Abraham each recount stories of falling asleep at the wheel. When drivers are in the car typically twelve hours a day, and in some cases sixteen hours, staying awake is a struggle. Judy says, "I catch myself dozing off here and there, but I can catch myself." Abraham tells of the time he fell asleep while he was stopped at an intersection in the day. His fare angrily got out of the car. Abraham mentions khat, a bitter green leaf that is chewed on but not swallowed and is usually lodged in one side of the mouth. Khat leaves produce cathine as a stimulant. Chewing khat "makes you stay awake and stay full of energy. It is good for a Friday or Saturday," explains Abraham. He goes on to say: "Some drivers can work twenty-four hours on it, and I would take it more often if it wasn't so expensive." All of the drivers attest to drinking "too much coffee." They express frustration with being unable to take bathroom breaks because of parking or having a fare that is going far. Billie rhetorically asks, "Can you imagine not drinking something you wanted because you were thirsty, because you might have to go the bathroom? It is like being a child."

While places of rest are not always convenient, they do constitute an alternative temporal architecture necessary for drivers' needs. Informal but established rest areas provide places for bathroom breaks and naps, or a parking space to be able to stand and stretch. The drivers' temporal infrastructures are both ad hoc and get established over time. Quite often, breaks are spent with congregations of drivers from the same ethnic communities, another testament to how the geopolitical and chronopolitical are mutually imbricated. Billie explains that drivers of the same ethnic communities will frequently drive the same kinds of hours. The circumstances of why taxi drivers moved to Toronto in the first place often determines the type of hours they work. Their reasons for being cab drivers are historically contingent. (Generally, most drivers are immigrants, except for a few older men who have been driving for more than fifty years.)

Billie explains that Middle Eastern drivers are quite often educated fathers who are less likely to work through the night and into the morning hours because they have families. Billie's earlier ruminations on keeping a normal routine fit this profile: "I try and make life close to the way it was before we left. I like to dress well for work and come home at a decent hour as much as possible." Abraham confirms that the temporal choices of drivers are linked to ethnic communities during a discussion of his own circumstances: "Most people from my country and the African continent that are driving are waiting for papers for asylum and are in between things. So they don't need to be free at night. And I actually feel more comfortable with night people." Judy will go to a certain bar where drivers from her community will be out at particular times. And while it is uncommon to take breaks, the drivers relay the particulars of where these breaks are taken. According to Abraham, "We meet at the bus station, that's our stand." And for Billie there is a particular stand at an intersection north of the financial district. Billie exclaims, "Look! When we are all immigrants, we come to this town and you get to know each other and destinations where you feel relaxed and okay. You know what time, where to be."

"The Indian house by the airport" is an attempt by Sikh taxi drivers and their wives to provide a place of rest. A South Asian driver tells me about a house close to the airport that a particular taxi fleet owns. The house has been made accessible for the fleet's drivers. It is part of their infrastructure of time maintenance. Like Darryl, whose airport lounge "is like home," this driver says: "[The house by the airport] is like home; it has a bed. There are old and new Indian movies, Indian food, and newspapers from back home." He goes on to say, "We usually work sixteen hours, and we go to this place to take breaks because it is between the highway for the city and the airport. And we can't go home to rest. And we are Aerofleet [a fleet tied to the airport], so we can't pick up passengers in the city. So some of us have organized this place for us." The fact that the house is sustained and supported by the labor of the wives of the drivers and fleet owner adds another dimension to the temporal layering and politics of maintaining and nurturing dominating tempos. In this context, the women are temporal labor within a subalternative architecture of time—two levels removed from dominant temporalities. Because these drivers rest in a space created by their fleet owners, it might seem possible to also conclude here that this is an indentured relation of the body to the company—a cab driver's company store. However, what complicates this type of conclusion is the comfort the drivers feel being in a space where they aren't treated as bare and expendable life, but as members of a community. The space also serves the basic bodily needs of the drivers who work just to get by.

Other material structures within the urban landscape reflect the biopolitical economy of time for populations who wait differently. The proposal published in *Designing the Taxi* by the Design Trust for Public Space

Figure 2.1. A STRETCHfence designed for taxi drivers. The Design Trust for Public Space in New York City asked Truck Product Architecture in New York City to draw up plans for a rest station for taxi drivers at Houston Street and First Avenue. Megan Canning, Savannah Gorton, Deborah Marton *Designing the Taxi* (New York: Design Trust for Public Space, 2005), 30.

includes designs for waiting stands for taxi drivers and passengers.[14] The design group consists of architects, leading interior designers, public-space advocates, and two representatives from New York Taxi—a fleet owner and a driver. Two specific design initiatives that the group has put forward to city planners involve two types of taxi stands. One is for fares at the airport who need to wait for cabs. The other is for taxi drivers in the public space of the city (see figure 2.1). The open-air relief stands, resembling children's monkey bars, are public spaces in which drivers can sit, stretch, rest, and use the restroom. The space offers the bare minimum of resources and is designed for "relief" (see figure 2.2). The waiting stand at the airport for fares, on the other hand, adds modern glamour to waiting with television screens, outlets for laptops, and shelter from the weather (see figure 2.3). Passengers can plug in and (literally) recharge their batteries while the drivers stretch in order to (figuratively) recharge their bodies for their shifts. Both are forms of recalibration within diametric architectures of time. Both are responses to the time demands of drivers' labor.

FIGURE 2.2. (top) Another view of the STRETCHfence from *Designing the Taxi*, 30.
FIGURE 2.3. (bottom) A taxi stand for waiting fares designed by Weis and Yoes for the Design Trust for Public Space in New York City. The stand is promoted by *Designing the Taxi* as "bringing glamour to the wait for a taxi," 32.

I can't argue that these relief stands won't provide any respite, nor can I deny that, without a doubt, they are much needed demarcated zones in cities where drivers are fined for quick stops to use restrooms. But it is important to point out that these two design initiatives reveal the disparity between investments in the time of drivers and fares. Relief stands do not overcome the low wages and inhumane hours necessary for taxi drivers to make a living wage. The different vision of what constitutes relief for different populations speaks volumes to how the time of the drivers and passengers are differentially imagined, regulated, and practiced. It is not so much about whether these technologies for waiting work or not, whether they actually provide relief or not, but what they indicate about the politics of uneven temporal orders and architectures.

Cab-Lagged at the Margins of Time

Over the course of their days, as part of their livelihoods, the drivers' technologies of the self include synchronizing to the time of others. How they understand time is in large part structured and controlled by the time of others. Attention to synchronicity as a relation of power forefronts disjunctive temporal differences in a world that too often claims to be working in organic temporal unity. While there is a rhythm to social life, it is neither an equitable nor egalitarian rhythm. The micropolitics of maintaining rhythm is such that the temporality of the frequent business travelers ultimately governs the time practices of the cab drivers.

This chapter has explored what it means to be out of time from the perspective of living and laboring on the margins of the temporal order. If jet lag captures the temporality of those living life in the fast lane, *cab lag* is a potentially productive term that evokes the materially impoverished relationship to time that is exacerbated by the sped-up lives that others choose. Cab-lagged temporalities, those servicing the privileged itineraries, exist on the boundaries of time, falling in and out of time without the safety net of a temporal architecture to keep them in time. Cab lag, then, refers to a condition of labor of where people exist in a differential and inequitable temporal relation with another group with whom they are expected to synch up. The cab-lagged temporality includes hotel maids whose labor now requires them to lift luxury mattresses for the socially jet-lagged and clean on a night shift so that business travelers can sleep during the day.[15] The cab-lagged temporality includes city workers paving over highways in the morning before the rush hour. It includes women who work in call centers and answer the phone with a cheerful "good morning," preferably without an Indian accent, even though they are working in Delhi late at night.[16] The cab-lagged class includes aging security officers from privatized companies who work in skyscrapers and airports. The cab-lagged may include nannies and housecleaners. Cab-lagged populations do have a relationship to the dominant temporal infrastructure. They clean, service, secure, and maintain it.

The different workers I describe will find and enact a distinctive architecture of time of their own making. The experience of being out of time is differential. It depends on where one is positioned within the larger biopolitical economy of time. And the maintenance of the body is at the center of the struggle for life for some and imbricated in the maintenance of a certain lifestyle for others. The cultivation of differential temporal regimes is not an autonomous practice, free from modes of production and institutions of modern power. Rather, it is conditioned and disciplined by this power. Taxi drivers and frequent business travelers are just one incarnation of the mutual imbrication of time. The relationships among these temporalities are not simple temporal binaries—fast classes and slow classes—with one floating high above and the other stalled on the ground. Their difference is not spatial. It is temporal. All populations under global capital are at once out of time but firmly grounded in time. The point is that time, as it is constructed in terms of power, must be acknowledged as differential, relational, and tangled.

Chapter Three

DHARMA AT THE DESK

Recalibrating the Sedentary Worker

Several years ago I worked "trade" at a yoga studio in Toronto. If I cleaned the studio twice a week, I could have unlimited yoga classes for that period. My work took about three hours to complete. A single class cost fifteen Canadian dollars. I had time, not money. My duties included sweeping and mopping the studio floors, scrubbing toilets, filling up soap containers, wiping mirrors, and disinfecting the yoga mats. After a morning of cleaning, I would take the first available class. This tended to be the new forty-five-minute "lunchtime express yoga class," an initiative of the studio owner. She advertised to nearby office workers in the hopes of reaching out to people who would trade their lunch breaks for yoga.

The atmosphere in the studio during these express classes was quite different than any other yoga class I had taken. By "different," I do not mean the difference between Kundalini and Ashtanga. Men and women came in smelling of perfume and cologne, a huge taboo in any yoga studio. Next to their yoga mats lay their cell phones, usually forbidden. Their ringers were off, but the vibrations could be felt across the bamboo floors. People rushed into the studio at a frantic pace, quickly changed, and then entered the practice room with just enough time to tear out their mats and get situated. As soon as the class was over, I was often the only one left in the room for Savasana, also called dead man's pose, the cherished last and languorous pose of any yoga class.

The most striking aspect of the class for me was the yogic mantras devised by the instructor. She had created a one-way dialogue full of aphorisms about the speed of the world "out there," the hectic pace of life, and the benefits of yoga practice for getting through these time-starved days. Over and over again she would repeat such statements such as: "You can take this yoga back to your desk with you. It is so great that you are doing this for yourself because nobody can take this away from you. Nothing else matters other than what you are doing here right now." Classes would end with her repeating in a hushed tone something to the effect of: "Life is not more than this. Life is not more than this." Of course, as a graduate student with a flexible schedule and more time to spare than dollars to my name, the mantras were not necessarily for me. Nonetheless, being mindful and present, balancing life and work, seems like a valuable skill no matter your itinerary. But is it?

Standing at the elevator at a corporate building in downtown Vancouver, I came across an advertisement for on-site yoga. This ad called me back to my trade days and the express-hour yoga class. It read, "Do you ever wonder if your life could be more than this? Do you wake up in the morning and dread going into your office? Do you come home after work exhausted wishing your life could be different? Well it can be, with Synergy Yoga." Yoga classes were being offered twice a week from noon to 12:45 p.m. for fifteen dollars a person in a conference room somewhere in the skyscraper. I flipped the brochure over to find that there was copy for a different population, the managers. "For every 1$ invested in workplace wellness," it claimed, "a company can expect 3$ in cost savings or benefits."

There are millions and millions of industrious desk workers toiling at the workstations of contemporary capitalism's nine-to-five days. The desk worker is not on the margins of a temporal order, as are taxi drivers. Nor do they exist within the privileged architectures of time built to maintain the temporal needs of the itinerant business traveler. What is significant about the temporality of desk workers is that they live within the auspices of what is most often conceived of as the most normal time, the most structured of temporalities. The nine-to-five job encompasses a range of temporal normalcy, or temporal normativity that extends beyond a typical workday. Along with the nine-to-five, one expects to find weekends, retirement, TGIF, happy hour, the daily commute, and the two-week holiday. Television scheduling also reflects a nine-to-five normalized rhythm of the day.[1] By evening, expository television programs fill prime time directed to nine-to-five workers, warning about the dangers of the sedentary life. The sedentary life is a slow and silent killer associated with multiple cardiovascular problems, cancers, and obesity. It is a physical byproduct of a life structured around electronic and mobile speed, the dashboard, the computer at the desk, and the television set.[2] Life can be more than this. Life is not more than this. Nine-to-fivers are in time and out of time simultaneously.

In response to the newly discovered dangers of a sedentary existence in the past decade, wellness and lifestyle management have become incorporated into the health plans of many companies. These include on-site gyms, walking clubs, golf retreats, and cafeterias stocked with low-sodium low-calorie foods. Harvard Business School uses MRI scans to study Tibetan monks on loan from the Dalai Lama to prove the benefits of meditation for the corporate work environment.[3] Programs found in how-to guides such as *Yoga for the Desk Jockey* instruct desk workers to incorporate yoga and meditation from the moment they slip out of bed in the morning to their commute back home. After a few breathing techniques to get you ready to face the day, "you can build up a reservoir of energy as you drive, ride, or walk to work, or even while standing on the bus."[4] The introduction of yoga, massage, and spiritual healing is one of the latest additions to corporate wellness. In the United Kingdom corporations offer spiritual options like Reiki for their employees as part a "fitness for work" benefit plan, similar to corporate wellness initiatives in the United States and LifeWorks in Canada. Within the repetitive temporal unfolding of workdays, weekends, and annual holidays, corporate yoga appears as an alternative temporality, one purportedly counter to the normalized tempo of the workaday world.

It is no great Marxist revelation that yoga in the office might benefit capital. As Marx argues, "We may read on one page the worker owes a debt of gratitude to capital for developing productivity, because the necessary labor time is thereby shortened, and on the next page must prove his gratitude by working in the future for 15 hours instead of 10."[5] Further, in *On Belief*, Slavoj Žižek argues that western Buddhism is the perfect ideological companion to global capitalism: "The 'Western Buddhist' meditative stance is arguably the most efficient way for us to fully participate in capitalist dynamics while retaining the appearance of mental sanity. If Max Weber were alive today, he would definitely write a second, supplementary, volume to his *Protestant Ethic*, entitled *The Taoist Ethic and the Spirit of Global Capitalism*."[6] An overwork ethic is normalized, and the body becomes happily indentured to a company and economic system that cares about workers' total selves—physical, material, and spiritual well-being. Yoga in the office is certainly reducible to another set of cultural technologies for capitalism to produce docile and productive bodies. But this is, at best, half of the story.

The sedentary body is both a sped-up subject of global capital who needs to slow down and a slowed down body who needs to get up to speed. The sedentary life is not just the physical byproduct of sitting all day; it is a systemic location. The sedentary life is a structural position where individuals and populations occupy the various stations of global capital. I read the emergence of yoga instructors in the corporate setting as indicative of the importance of maintaining time sensibilities as a form of social control. The yoga instructor is a roving infrastructural technician of time maintenance who extends the sedentary tradition through recalibration, a form of temporal regulation and disciplining of labor.

At first, this particular form of recalibration may appear as resistance to the corporate structuring of everyday life. The offering of time at work—free time or time out—seems antithetical to the aims of corporate capitalism. But recalibration, no matter what its form, is never resistant—it is a generalized form of temporal management that is administered and incorporated differentially. Recalibration as a form of social control is hard to recognize because it is discipline *in space* that is commonly recognized as the oppressive arrangement. Moreover, recalibration appears to be resistant to this spatial disciplining because it appears across workplaces as a form of free time. But time is neither freed from the structures of power nor free in and of itself. The time of the desk worker, how he or she is brought in and out of time, is worked upon in a very particular way. The desk worker is offered a new experience of time within the confines of a sedentary life. They are fixed firm, so to speak. The idea is that the at-work yogi will keep working but with a renewed sense of time. Such renewal makes the sedentary life palatable. Yoga helps capital produce the sedentary body by working upon the time sensibility of workers, by creating and managing sedentary time.

Yoga gains easy entry into corporate life precisely because the discourse of speed can be mobilized for different ends. For employers, yoga promises to maintain the speed of work and rates of efficiency. Yet for employees, yoga is experienced as a form of slowing down. The yoga instructors imagine themselves as independent entities, bystanders, or even rebels against an economic system they have nothing to do with. They enter this sphere with their own understanding that yoga is a resistant practice that not only benefits everyone involved but also is a form of social change. But the yoga instructor has a parasitic role within the biopolitical economy of time. Armed with a concomitant mix of esoteric knowledge consisting of wild aphorisms about technology and speed, the mobile yoga instructor turns the imperiled desk worker into a renewed temporal subject better adapted to a life spent at the desk.

Mobile yoga instructors and holistic healers travel from office to office on a daily basis. Many work for large wellness organizations. The typical mobile yoga instructor espouses a strong entrepreneurial ethos along with a spiritual mélange of Buddhism, Hinduism, and Chinese medicine. They are deployed to a host of offices by a central operator-owner. Some instructors contact companies on their own, depend on word of mouth, and have websites to advertise their services. Full-time instructors teach anywhere from seven to fifteen classes a week in office settings. Classes in offices tend to last between forty-five minutes and an hour. The classes take place in ad hoc, makeshift spaces cleared for the class, such as basements or conference rooms. Employees generally pay for the classes themselves, somewhere in the range of ten to fifteen dollars per class, and the instructor can make up to two hundred dollars per class or as little as fifty. Management teams will often take afternoon sessions or half-day retreats, with bigger yoga companies charging anywhere from two hundred to eight hundred dollars per afternoon depending on the services offered, instructors required, and number of participants. When a company regularly offers yoga for its employees, desk workers are generally given the option of these classes once or twice a week.

Speed Therapists in the Temporal Order

Lydia is the owner of a yoga corporation based in Vancouver, British Columbia. She has more than two hundred yoga instructors working for her. I ask Lydia how she approaches potential clients. Lydia explains "the sell" she gives to office managers and human resources: "I tell them yoga in the office will save them money and their employees will work better, et cetera, et cetera." She hands me a sample script that she uses when talking to human resources managers: "I can say something different to the employees once I get there, but to get in the door it is all about productivity. It has to be." She goes on to say: "Managers already know about going to the gym and blowing off steam or running and endorphins, but yoga is different." Lydia reveals, "I have several talking points." The first bullet point on the script reads: "Job stress creates up to 60% of employee absenteeism." She maintains, "The point is to get the managers to see how yoga will benefit the company as well as the employees." She continues, "It isn't something you can really prove or measure just like that, so I have to be really convincing."

While productivity might be key to gaining entry into the workplace, not all instructors prioritize productivity. I meet Kendra at a coffee shop close to Research Triangle Park in the Raleigh-Durham area of North Carolina. She has just finished a class at the headquarters of a major U.S. pharmaceutical company. Kendra has been a yoga instructor for a decade and has been in the corporate setting for five years. She offers a workshop on "desk yoga" in Raleigh on Sunday afternoons once a month. The class is set up with yoga mats and chairs to simulate the office setting. In my conversation with Kendra, I show her Lydia's materials. By her reaction, I sense that Lydia's practice seems at odds with Kendra's approach. "Oh wow," she exclaims. "This is all about increased productivity. I don't talk about that. I don't think about that. I come at it from a yoga standpoint, not a business standpoint." I inquire further about what she means by a "yoga standpoint."

Kendra thinks of yoga practice in the office setting as a "time out from it all." For her, the yoga time and space is outside of the spatial and temporal order of the workday. While Kendra is adamant that yoga is just yoga, in the next breath she shares how she has been asked to "tone down the om" when coming into an office. Kat, another instructor based in Vancouver, teaches yoga in prisons, schools, and corporations throughout the lower mainland. She too makes the claim that the practice does not differ from place to place. The overwhelming sense of their practice is that yoga is always a transcendence of time and space. Kat speaks in universals: "Yoga is about yoking mind and body. You can do that anywhere and for anyone. Everyone needs it." For Kat, "It does not matter where I teach. It should be taught everywhere." But even Kat admits that she tones down the "spiritual stuff" in the workplace. She maintains, "As a yoga teacher it is my responsibility to plant seeds, but you do it in a way that is sensitive to cultures and the corporation." Navina, who practices reflexology, Reiki, hypnotherapy, and Indian head massage in a temporary office space in the headquarters of a major British Columbia corporation, thinks of her relationship to the company as a much needed service that just happens to be on-site for the purposes of saving time:

> Our working lives are such that we go go go and even eat lunch at our desks with a phone glued to our ears. I would love to see more people use my services in my private studio away from their work space, but having lived in the corporate world for many years I understand that the work environment doesn't allow much time for off-site care of the body, mind, and soul. Living at the speed we live at, I am perfectly happy to provide it at work for my clients because at least they are thinking of themselves for a brief thirty [minutes].

But Navina also points out the shortened time she has to work with when employees visit the Reiki room at the corporate office versus a regular session: "At the company, I can only do express Reiki and reflexology." Lydia most concretely suggests that yoga in the office is "very different" because people are "more stressed. They are under some surveillance about if they choose to go to class or not. The time of the class is a pretty discrete fifty-five minutes."

I ask the instructors how employees were able to take the classes in the first place. Was it their lunch hour? Did the classes take place before work? Is it compensated time? Except for Lydia, who owns a yoga corporation, there was generalized disinterest. In fact, there was an aversion to the question. There was a common unwillingness to engage with the economic conditions of yoga practice. It was as if my questions were getting off the topic of the true purpose of yoga. They were not wrong.

Kat asserted, "You can go down that road but then you aren't thinking like a yogi. We're not at a place in the yoga world where we should be critical of it. People just need to do it and see for themselves." When I pressed further there was great hesitancy to assert, even though it was completely obvious, that their classes were most often during employees' lunch hours. Lydia, who is quite open about the business-venture aspect of yoga in the office, explained: "Managers aren't just offering yoga for their employees' midday classes as a break from work, but it is a break at work that they can take. If they take it at lunch, then they eat lunch later at their desks." In fact, she explains how right after class there is a scurrying of employees from their mats, rushing back to their desks, "which is quite different than yoga in the studio outside of the office." The disengagement with the issue of *when* the office workers were "able" to take a yoga class is consistent with the general sense of disconnect that the yoga instructors shared with the actual sites and time arrangements in which their students work. They acknowledge a spatial and temporal order, one that they even find oppressive, but they consider themselves outside it.

The yoga instructor claims a relationship to time that is entirely different from the time of his or her clients—both the students and the corporations. The instructors understand their life and labor as being free agents in a world that is revving up to detrimental speeds. My discussions with yoga teachers were laden with phrases like "in this fast-paced world," "in these sped-up times," and "now with things going faster." "This is a culture of speed" is their universal mantra. When I ask my interlocutors how they see themselves in the context of the larger world out there, without ever once mentioning speed or pace, their responses are quite similar.

> NAVINA: I see my role as someone who is providing a much-needed service to everyone. It is crucial in our fast-paced lifestyles that we stop and take a moment to breathe and decompress. These modalities help the person to do just that.
>
> KENDRA: People have forgotten how to breathe with the speed of everything, and I'm teaching them that, and with that comes mind-body awareness. I want to create a bubble from that fast pace.
>
> LYDIA: Speed and the nature of work are never going to change, but what we can do is take little moments to rest our minds. I am providing a service by giving people the space to have these moments while at work. We can make these choices *but* also be in these fast-paced times.
>
> MAGGIE: With the pace of life, [people] are spending more time in these poses that are unnatural and not good for them. I see myself as bringing to my students a way to counter these poses with new poses. You can be in a better position in your daily life, so to speak.

KAT: You just look around and you can see people are not doing well. They can't deal with the speed of life and yoga is going to continue to catch on. I feel good that I am part of the planting of seeds.

Yoga teachers are self-identified speed therapists. Speed is an inevitable fact; it is totalizing and irreversible. It requires new modalities to counter its effects. Yoga practitioners maintain a stance of expertise about issues concerning speed, technology, and changes in the workplace.

In our discussions, the instructors relied mostly on neologisms about technology and anecdotal evidence framed as empirical facts to support their claims. Kat tells me, "Scientifically, they have proven that, vibrationally, the period of time in twenty-four hours has increased today in comparison to fifty years ago." When I inquire about the "vibrational" evidence, Kat exclaims, "Ask any scientist!" She continued to explain that the "vibrational pull" was evident by looking at children today: "You look at kids today and they are so plugged in. Life isn't as simple as it was fifty years ago. We have way more to think about. Everything goes in cycles and we are at the end of a sped-up cycle. Things might start to slow down now with people taking care of themselves." Navina describes the energy that is culled from overworked workers and transformed "from a very negative energy to a smart energy by the time they leave [her] office and get back to their desk." I ask her what a "smart" energy is. Navina explains that smart energy derives from a type of emotional intelligence: "When you are at peace with yourself and whole, then you direct your energy appropriately, so you will waste less time at your desk thinking about how you can't wait for the day to be over." For the most part, the instructors spoke from a perspective of experience with this type of alienation.

Entering the building and leaving after an hour of "doing something [she loves] feels so good," Lydia says. "I shudder when I think about having to work there. I can just come and go and leave after an hour of teaching." Many of the instructors relayed a single monumental breaking point where they "charged out" of their previous lives as unhappy office workers to what they see now as a life in the "service" of healing. Kat, who worked long hours with difficult people, cites an incidence of road rage that was her turning point. Lydia broke down and cried after her first yoga class and realized that she wanted to teach people this rather than be a journalist. She said, "When I was working for this newspaper, I always felt like I was bothering people for information with all of my questions, and I didn't feel

I was having an impact on anything or doing any good. But with yoga, I feel like I am helping people." Lydia, Kat, and Navina think about what their lives were like and how much they would have wanted these "services" when they were "stuck in cubicles" and "chained to their desks." Navina, now a full-time independently employed Reiki master, maintains an office in the same corporation for which she worked for more than twenty years, and she espouses this sentiment: "I enjoy working here in this capacity. I do remember what my working life was like and how I probably needed to have some of these therapies back then. I feel that they are lucky to be working here now. I mean to have these options of on-site wellness programs available to them." Yoga instructors are there to spread the word and to offer help in the taking care of the self.[7] All of them have made it out of the rat race but find it an unrealistic expectation that others will as well.

I asked Lydia if she believes her own materials; that is, does yoga really make people more productive and save money for the company? She replied, "Yes, of course, but it isn't really why I do it. I'm not really concerned for the company but with making these people at work feel better." She then adds, "And this is my business now. I need to do this for my career." Lydia is savvy and explains, "It is what they [management] want to hear. Plus, you have to make it sound like something for the company and not just a bunch of ladies that want to do yoga. It is what they need to hear in order to offer this to their employees: They need a way to rationalize it."

The mobile yoga instructors are critical of "the system": of consumption, technology, and the fast pace of life. Yet these corporate healers are in the business of recalibration. Their work is oriented toward making sure workers become psychically and physically more secure within the sedentary life and the normalizing temporal order. As Nikolas Rose has argued of the neoliberal workplace, the responsible citizen is self-enterprising and will work on the self while at work: "The worker is an individual in search of meaning, responsibility, a sense of personal achievement, a maximized quality of life, and hence of work. Thus the individual is not to be emancipated from work, perceived as merely a task or a means to an end, but to be fulfilled *in* work, now construed as an activity through which we produce, discover, and experience ourselves."[8] What is being produced is a rat race that never ends, one that is always renewable, thanks to the presence of a yoga mat.

As a mobile entity independently invested in corporate life, the yoga instructor is emblematic of Gilles Deleuze's theorizing of the diffusion of control and discipline away from centralized or hierarchical organizations of power.[9] Flexible workers who feed off of businesses reenter the field of corporate relations as experts and authorities on self-responsibility and work to instruct subjects to choose wisely, sit properly, and assemble their daily choices accordingly in order to better endure the sedentary life. While promulgating a neoliberal ethos of learning to make the right choices in order to protect and enhance the self, the instructors carry a notion that they, like yoga, are outside of any networks of power. They have no stake in workers' productivity. They are there mostly out of good will and genuine interest in people's well-being. The instructors think that they offer a new take on time in an accelerated, out-of-control world.

While the instructors are excited to have escaped the corporate world, they have hardly taken leave. Autonomist Marxists refer to the collective act of exodus, or leave taking from capital, as a third way beyond the dialectical, but these yoga instructors' imagined resistance is little more than revulsion with the corporate world. In fact, revulsion rather than resistance simply means that life at the desk isn't for them. They are unsuited for *that type of work*. They are no longer under the control of a single company, but they are low-paid workers who have to cobble together several jobs in order to make ends meet. They claim to have less of an affective investment in a corporate identity. It is more apt, then, to see the instructors as having changed positions within the same structures of corporate capital. And it is a mistake to think that they are not invested. While they claim to be outside of the networks of power in which they teach yoga, it becomes clear that the desk is central to their practice.

Kat and Kendra both explain how they focus more on shoulders, backs, and other injuries specifically related to sedentary culture. Maggie, whom I meet at a local coffee shop in Durham, North Carolina, where she teaches in both corporate and nonprofit sectors, explains how even in her studio classes she gears her language and postures toward individuals she imagines have been sitting all day—in the car, at work, and in front of the television. Yoga, she argues, "is the great counterpose to modern living." In other words, for Maggie, yoga denormalizes: "Yoga is really about creating a counterpose if you think about how people generally go through life: sitting, or driving, [or] at a computer. [Yoga] is also a very protective pose." But really, this yin for the yang is not so much a counterstance. They key lies in her use of the term *protective*. Yoga in this context doesn't oppose as much as it ameliorates. Moreover, it seems quite obvious that yoga practice can hail bodies in a normalizing way that reconfirms their relationships to the disciplinary and institutional spaces in which they spend their days. Bodies on yoga mats are referred to in very culturally and institutionally specific ways. The yoga instructors refer to the body of the yoga student in quite generic terms—it is a body that sits, drives, watches television, and is hunched over with slouched shoulders. The assumptions that guide classes assume a nine-to-five working day. The rest of the world is understood as systemically tied to the workplace. Maggie explains how even when she's not in the office setting she looks out over the sea of contorted bodies on yoga mats and recognizes that many of them have indeed come from desk jobs.

Yoga in the office is already twice removed from its roots in classical yoga, where breath work is central. In other words, yoga is already specifically geared to the sedentary life. In the office setting, yoga is an extension of modern postural yoga, which is itself a set of counterpostures designed to maintain the postures of modern living: sitting and repetitive motions that put strain on necks and back. Underlying modern postural yoga is an ethos that defies Western linear conceptions of time, including clock time. In many ways, to practice yoga is already to shift one's temporal perspective beyond measureable time. Fundamental to yoga is a concept known as samsara: "a conditioned existence, bounded-ness, and the yoking of spirit to spatial and temporal confinement."[10] Western concepts of time are regarded as repressive in their linearity.[11] Samsara encompasses a notion of time as cyclical between "birth, life, death, and rebirth."[12] Time is understood as "both creator and destroyer of all worlds; for as we know, time favors nothing in its relentless movement. It offers up the beginnings of all things and at the same moment rips asunder all order, all life, all seemingly unchanging forms, and in so doing begins again to create. The astounding realization is this power also lies within our grasp."[13] One must escape time in order to achieve timelessness.

Fundamental to these yogic principles is the problem of attachment. Intrinsic to Western conceptions of time is the condition of remaining beholden to events, the charting of time by birth and death, beginnings and endings. Linear time is a denial of the cycle of rebirth that, according to the philosophy that accepts samsara as a cycle of repetitions, allows one to shed attachment to the heavy burden of linear time. To detach is to release oneself from the burden of life's dualities of birth and death, of mind and body. It is to recognize that to exist in time without attachment is to be free of events. The boundaries of birth and death, memories, and a situational understanding of time that limits life's possibilities are let go. To travel through time and shed linear temporality is to gain a new freedom and confront life outside of the conditioned reflexes prescribed by ordinary time. Such an understanding is put into practice by TAKE5MOMENT, an online wellness program that desk workers complete in five-minute intervals. TAKE5MOMENT's informational website states: "It is our desire to have office workers, the unemployed, the retired, the social networkers . . . to take 5 minutes every day to check-out and take care of their health."[14] Five minutes can be eternal. Five minutes is enough of a time-out.

Kat enthuses, "Yoga expands the moment. That's precisely what the classes in the office are about. They are about letting go and becoming present at a place where you aren't often able to be present in your own life. When you become present there is an expansion of time and you come back to a place of stillness. This helps you deal." I ask her, "Deal with what?" and she replies, "Deal with the fact that you work at a job that doesn't express or define you. Being that way is not being present. Yoga, being in union with you, is present, a way of yoking yourself to something." Kat elaborates further on the relationship between yoga and the present as a temporal mode of practice, a stance every yogi should take in everyday life: "When you are not present you are in the past or worried about the future. That is so debilitating. People shouldn't live like this. They should only live in the present. If you think about the past and the future all the time, then you just can't do anything with your life." The yoga instructors' task, then, is to do precisely this: teach employees how to "expand the moment" while staying at their desks.

From Discipline in Space to Recalibration in Time

Theoretical interventions regarding labor in the new knowledge or informational economy have been more or less occupied with outlining the exploitative conditions of labor for wireless populations. The immaterial laborer, the entrepreneurial worker, free-labor netizens, the creative worker, or the knowledge worker animates most theoretical debates within contemporary Marxism concerned with new flexible arrangements of labor and the production of precarity.[15] When sedentary life is broached, the concern is how bodies are in motion even when they are still. Even while sitting in front of screens, bodies are transmitting information: moving, sharing, connecting, and creating it.[16] The focus of such critical perspectives continues to be on the mobile, the migrating, and the telecommuting, which are all spatially oriented understandings of contemporary labor practices.

While changes in the conditions of labor for much of the creative sector have surely taken place, sedentary work and the sedentary life continue to be one of the most normalizing temporalities within global capital. The sedentary body is important to the contemporary moment not because it teletravels or produces a particular affective output, but because a stationary life is a significant conduit for capitalism's dream of an unfettered flow. Sedentary life is a form of stillness not chosen but actually required by global capital. And the body's capacity to sit and work as well as the growing need to foster a particular meaning of time for workers while at work require techniques of recalibration.

Recalibration troubles the temporal and spatial bounds of how discipline at work is traditionally conceived and theorized. Discipline's scope is typically understood as spatial.[17] Within this framework the problem of time tends to be spatial too. It is a framework concerned with the body's movements in space or quantities of time. Thus, Marx's concern with the "working day" is a concern about time, but time is ultimately translated into the "boundaries," a spatial marker, of the day.[18] Frederick Taylor's scientific management and Frank and Lillian Gilbreth's time-motion studies conceive of time in quantifiable units that are measured.[19] Time is about output. For example, in *Discipline and Punish* Foucault argues that disciplinary control is not about imposing a series of gestures but about the best gesture for the particular position of the body in order to create conditions of efficiency and speed. He argues, "In the correct use of the body, which makes possible a correct use of time, nothing must remain idle or useless; everything must be called upon to form the support of the act required."[20] If we continue to conceive of discipline solely as spatial, then recalibration appears to be a resistant practice because it is not about movement in time but about a seemingly free use of time, or the cultivation of a new sense of time, while at work.

For example, the company Yoga in Business promises the employer that "through a sequence of yoga poses created for office employees they can reduce sick days, time off, and create calmness of mind in the work place so that employees naturally work more productively."[21] Here the yoga company is inviting the employer to take further disciplinary control over the worker's body by mobilizing time differently. According to Foucault, exercise, part of the docility-utility regime of disciplinary power, "served to economize the time of life, to accumulate it in useful form and to exercise power over men through the mediation of time arranged in this way."[22] For Foucault, alterations in pace establish control. Speeding up and slowing down are both fundamental to the political anatomy of disciplinary control. On the one hand, Foucault offers a framework for understanding how time and space are used as disciplinary mechanisms of control. But the ways in which time is mobilized exceed the simple conceptual equation of *time* with *pace*.

Yoga at the desk is an extension of a set of previously calculated, strategic initiatives used in offices for keeping workers at the desk all day. But the strategy does not revolve around a conception of time as pace. Instead, the strategy works through recalibration. In his *Labor and Monopoly Capital*, published in 1974, Henry Braverman explains how office work had been subjected to similar rationalizations and disciplinary controls found in factory work. Braverman contends that it proved much easier to control workers once the volume of work grew large enough and once a search for methods of rationalization was seriously undertaken. Office layout was not only an aesthetic issue; it was a matter of time management. The location of water fountains, use of pneumatic tubes for sending messages between desks, and the type of pens and ink used were all strategic choices for the efficient and productive use of the office space. These seemingly minute decisions were important for saving time and extracting as much labor out of the employee as possible. Braverman elucidates how managers calculated the placement of water fountains. "That each clerk walked, on the average, a mere hundred feet for a drink would cause the clerical workers in one office to walk an aggregate of fifty thousand miles each year just to drink an adequate amount of water, with a corresponding loss of time for the employer (this represents the walking time of a thousand clerks, each of whom walked only a few hundred yards a day)."[23] Braverman stresses how these sorts of arrangements gave "birth to the sedentary tradition which shackles the clerical worker as the factory worker is shackled" since everything gets placed "within easy reach so that the clerks not only have no need, but dare not, be too long away from the desk."[24] He reveals the disciplinary logic of the work environment always-already embedded in office design: cubicles, workstations, and the entire work floor. Significantly, this sedentary spatial rationalization is precisely what is currently being problematized as injurious to the physical well-being of the employee and the quarterly reports of the companies they work for, creating the need for recalibration. Contra Foucault, the sedentary body has reached its limit. New forms of time discipline must be devised.

Enter yoga. Yoga in the office is a form of qualitative time control that revolves around recalibrating the desk worker's body and disposition. It depends on discourses, bodily interventions, and breathing techniques as much as the ticking of the clock does. The worker's pace is not controlled through deliberate attempts to speed up or slow down his or her movements. Instead the speed of the world "out there" becomes a way to rationalize interventions into workers' sense of meaningful time. The incorporation of yoga in the office indicates that time and discipline within the postindustrial workplace is not so much about the control of bodies under the governance of a single technology in a particular place that makes capital "work" faster, but rather a diffuse decentralization of power, where the meaning of time becomes central to time management. The desk worker's place at the desk is reestablished by the temporal mandate espoused in office yoga that he or she live in the "now." It is not just a set of ideological precepts that are operating here. Bodies are physically worked upon to produce a particular temporal outlook and comportment.

The images in figures 3.1–3.5 are a collection of advertisements for corporate yoga classes aimed at both employers and employees. The images show workers exerting control over their own time while at work. There are several ways to read these images, but most significant for my argument here is a focus on how the images mobilize the time of labor for different ends. From the employer's perspective, these people are still working, on the clock, and mostly fixed in place. They are professionally attired, serious, and healthy. The employees see themselves doing yoga, bouncing on balls, and meditating while at work. They defy the clocks behind them. The desk workers are rising above the hectic demands of work, transcending time and space, floating above the places they work. They have shut it all out. In each image, however, the worker is still properly stationed. The workstations represented in the figures, then, double as places to work and places to work on the self. While time is malleable, it is clear that one's place at a desk is not.

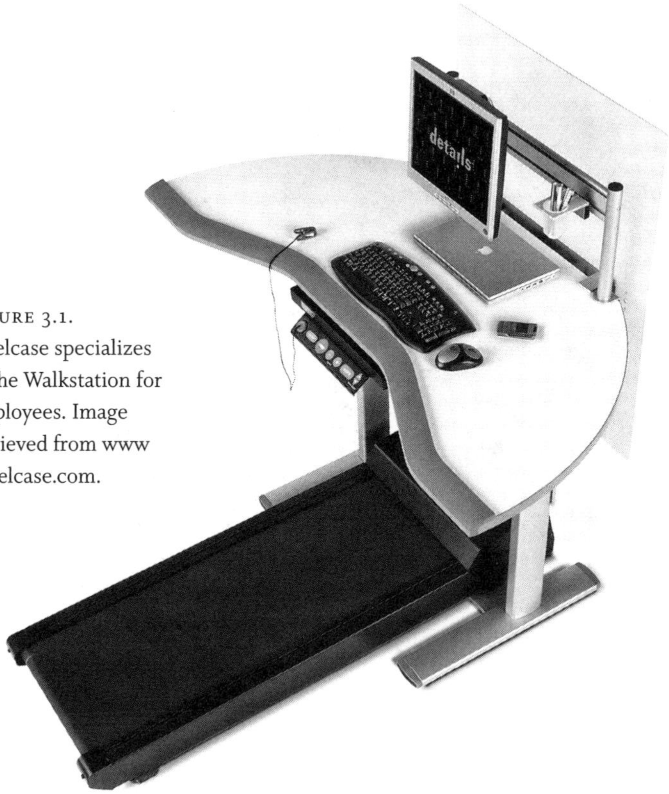

FIGURE 3.1. Steelcase specializes in the Walkstation for employees. Image retrieved from www.steelcase.com.

Mantras for Materializing Sedentary Time

Sedentary time is a constructed sensibility attendant to the sedentary life. It is the eternal present of sedentary life. The integration of spiritual healing in the office draws on two antithetical processes within modern life: financial profit for the company on the one hand and transformation, enlightenment, awareness of one's place in the world on the other. The yoga instructor's repertoire in an office class works to relieve this tension. The tenor of the classes is completely different from any other time of day. The yogis rush in, the class lasts only forty-five minutes, and the yogis rush out again. The fact that the majority of students are in the midst of the workday is absolutely central to the dialogue in class, revealing that yoga is site specific. The workers are led through a series of postures and mantras that espouse a sentiment of emancipation from workday lives, as a life spent at work is made endurable. The subjects are repeatedly told that their lives

FIGURE 3.2. (top) Executives at the desk. Advertisement for the "Introductory Office Yoga" class for Shiv Yog Sadhna (The Science of Living and Self Realization), based in Chandigarh, India. http://www.shivyogsadhna.com/news.php?news_id=13.
FIGURE 3.3. (bottom) Office-yoga advertisement for Yoganonymous, an informational website for those interested in "practical yoga" without the "lavender oil and granola" across the globe. Image retrieved from http://www.yoganonymous.com.

FIGURE 3.4. (top) Promotional material for Intercase, a private, full-service corporate insurance brokerage and consulting firm for employee wellness based in San Francisco. Image retrieved from http://view.intercaresolutions.com/?s=yoga.
FIGURE 3.5. (bottom) Promotional materials for Performance Enhancement Consultants in the United Kingdom. http://www.anicecupoftea.co.uk/page/5/.

are not reducible to the desk or the companies they work for, yet surreptitiously their place at the desk is constantly affirmed—this is where they are, this is who they are, they are here and nowhere else.

The first essential mantra echoed in every modern postural yoga class, whether in the office or in the studio, is that you must listen to your body; do not push. Kendra explains that her primary goal is to teach people how to achieve "mind-body awareness." Part of this awareness, Kendra asserts, "is to know when to stop, when you've reached your limit." "And that should be okay," she maintains, "there should be limits! People need to recognize this." Kat shares this sentiment: "People need to listen to their bodies. And in fact, with stress in the workplace, people will have physical injuries as a way to get a break to do nothing." The yoga instructor identifies the source of the problem as the sitting body, for them a result of the inevitable speeding up of global capital that requires individuals to work longer and harder. But ultimately the matter is one of workers' ignorance of their bodies. The Lotus Exchange in London beckons the desk worker: "The human body was never designed to sit in 'computer pose' for up to eight hours a day and now too many people pay the price for this; our advice is to repay your body for the effort it makes on your behalf."[25] The concern is not the system's negation of the body but the individual's inattentiveness to how the body labors for him or her. While the limits of the body are to be recognized, the body needs to be trained and treated well in order to develop a form of capitalistic endurance. Ultimately, one of the aims of at-work yoga practice is to extend the limits of capitalism via a limitless body.

Pierre Bourdieu and Marx both argue that the body bears the social conditions of the material world that it inhabits. The body is in the social world, but the social world is also in the body.[26] "Listen to your body," the yoga instructor instructs. But to really listen to the body is a privilege reserved for few workers. Jean-Luc Nancy remarks in *Corpus*: "Capital means: a body marketed, transported, displaced, replaced, superseded, assigned to a post and a posture to the point of ruin, unemployment, famine."[27] The commodified, disciplined body is a consistent reminder that bodies are subjected into the process of laboring. However, sedentary workers are hailed as if their bodies were laboring as the bodies of construction workers, cleaners, and sweatshop employees. One of the interesting aspects of the contradictory place of sedentary life is the role of the corporeal.

The body is cast as central to the laboring process. It is understood as increasingly precarious and in need of attention in affective workplace environments. In fact, autonomist Marxists refer to "the social factory" as the current configuration of social life under contemporary capitalism, wherein the factory has become a generalized condition of labor and living.[28] The office worker is in pain—suffering from carpal tunnel syndrome, backaches, and fatigue, as well as depression and lack of sleep. The way the body is hailed in a yoga class as if it were engaged in manual or factory work, when such interventions do not take place in factory settings, indicates that the social factory has become central to not only the critical Marxist imaginary, which considers mostly manual labor, but also to the contemporary corporate world. The social factory becomes a corporate strategy, a useful concept for the proprietors of capital to extract more labor from tired bodies.

The innovative impulse in these places of work that revolve around immaterial labor is to rematerialize the body, make it resurface. This way, the body continues to be the ultimate site of investment, subject to control. But the form of discipline that responds is also temporal. As the factory extends, so too does the meditation hall, it would seem. In an interview in Beliefnet.com about the place of spirituality in the corporate workplace, Lewis Richmond, author of *Work as Spiritual Practice*, argues one should not even attempt to transform the company they work for: "You have to let the business be a business and operate within that framework with a sense of individual responsibility. There's a subtle balancing act. . . . It's a real challenge."[29] In the same piece, a corporate public-relations manager who is also a former Zen monk relays, "One of the teachings I took from my Zen days is that everything is the meditation hall. There's only now, and that doesn't change whether you are in a spiritual environment or a normal environment." There is a deliberate attempt to make the workplace a meditation hall in order to deal with problematic conditions of labor—namely long hours and a pained body and soul. Yet, it is an individualistic pursuit. Alienation is not a condition that workers recognize as a shared experience. It is dealt with individually. As such, alienation seeps deeper and deeper into the core of one's existence.

In workplaces best described as "immaterial"—workplaces that produce ideas, information, or experiences—the productive capacities of labor occur through communication and the production of knowledge. These are both the condition and product of labor. The supposed energy flow between ideas and colleagues becomes another key focus of corporate yoga classes. Interestingly, the language in a yoga class resembles the way information technologies are often described. There is attention to the flow of energy and information and their ephemeral nature. In *Digital Sensations*, for example, Ken Hillis characterizes virtual reality: "People cannot see into, much less physically enter, the conduits and data flows that are now the ironically rhizomelike centers of power." He continues: "If invisible data flows have become a nexus of power, then many people will be drawn to find the means to experience these flows of information-as-knowledge in a sensual fashion by conceptually merging with on-line VEs [virtual environments] and other as-of-yet unimagined optical procedures."[30] A corporate yoga class will reference the "the moment," "real time," "instant," and "the now." Lotus Exchange is one such U.K.-based company that promises employers that they can "unlock people's energy and full potential."[31] The Cartesian tensions of disembodiment and embodiment are in constant reformulation, depending on what can reestablish a productive temporal relationship to work.

"Bonding through Bending" is a class offered by the London Lotus Exchange. It is advertised as "a fun sequence of partner-based yoga poses which not only deliver the regular benefits of yoga, but also promote trust and communication between individuals."[32] But most important in this business literature is an overwhelming focus on untapped energy sources. The term *energy* comes up frequently to refer to the renewable resource of the working body—an immaterial quality of labor that can be harnessed and is relied on by contemporary capitalism. The body is treated as having a hidden reserve of energy that can be unleashed with a little hard work. The focus on energy implies an ongoing timeless quality, a renewable resource that can be expended but also saved. It does not have to run out. An expansive temporal disposition becomes the goal. Yoga can create an employee whose energy is boundless, endless, and shareable.

The yogic opportunity to listen to the body and respond to it is an uneven privilege. Many bodies are in constant pain with no relief as part of their labor while other bodies are invited, and increasingly forced, to enter into preventive practices such as company supported smoking cessation, corporate wellness, and yoga at the desk. Significantly, we do not see yoga-healing packages offered to manual laborers who clean, secure, and serve sedentary spaces. I ask all my yoga instructors if any lower-level employees of the company take yoga. Lydia tells me, "Not really. We haven't advertised much in the cafeterias or the maintenance staff, but we could." In some sense, these workers do not need a reminder that they are physical laborers. They don't need to listen to their bodies or gain mind-body awareness in order to register that there is a toll on their bodies in the process of hard labor. This is an effect of their place within the temporal order and their relationship to the biopolitical economy of time. Manual laborers who can be found in the same spaces where corporate yoga classes are taught exist well outside of the normalized temporal order of the nine-to-five. Even if they clock in the same amount of hours, enter and exit the building at roughly the same time, these lower-level employees are more like the taxi drivers than their fellow company employees.

Another popular mantra extols the necessity of repaying the body for the effort it makes on the worker's behalf: "this is your life, accept it." Yoga is a psychotherapeutic intervention that leads to better mind-body awareness, but it is not a critical awareness of the structure that ties the worker to the desk in the first place. Instead, it is an intervention that is intended to lead individuals to accept structural conditions and make themselves responsible for their own well-being: "Forget about the world out there; nothing else matters but you being here right now." To be negative about work or critical of pain-inducing labor practices is treated as a toxic mentality. Resistance to work is cast as a type of negative thinking and an unhealthy fixation on unhappiness. Taking on a healthy disposition while at work means you must avoid being a victim of time. *Awake at Work*, a Buddhist self-help book for nonbelievers to incorporate Buddhist principles into the chaotic and accelerated workaday world, wants the desk worker to take control of his or her life: "By simply observing the speed mindfully, we have tapped the brakes, so to speak, and slowed down just a bit."[33] The bodhisattva reminds Buddhists to work diligently because time waits for no one. If time is inevitably spent working, then wiser still is to work well. *Awake at Work* is concerned with desk workers' inability to deal with the speed of life. It advises, "We have noticed there is a speedometer in the car; we have noticed that we are here for just a moment. By deliberately acknowledging our restlessness, we get the first hint that maybe we are the authors of our speed, not just a victim of an out-of-control job."[34] What is an author of speed? In the context of work, an author of speed is one who decides to become responsible for his or her time. The onus is on one's own relationship to time. Individuals are made to be aware of their places in the flow of time and their places at work. When workers are at their desks, they are where they are meant to be. To think otherwise is a waste of time.

When in doubt, it is important to recognize that life is not more than this. It is not supposed to be different. The only thing you can do is breathe. When work is painful, when being a circuit in the production of capital causes physical and mental strain, listen to your body. Realize that this moment will pass. There is nothing you need to change. You are where you are supposed to be: at your desk.

Modern postural yoga is about dealing and coping. It is not about transforming objective social conditions or social relations but transforming how one relates to this social reality. Nothing else matters; you have no control over the world. Instead, postural yoga motivates individuals to not feel so discouraged, depressed, or exploited by invoking a new sense of time. Pain, stress, and fatigue are merely reactions that must be rechanneled elsewhere. The negative feelings that would lead to structural critique are massaged away, replaced by the transcendent present of sedentary time.

Marx's description of capital's endless drive for surplus labor, without regard for the limits of the body, is especially significant to this new workplace practice. He writes: "[Capital's need for labor] usurps the time for growth, development and healthy maintenance of the body. It steals the time required for the consumption of fresh air and sunlight. It haggles over meal-times, where possible incorporating them into the production process itself, so that food is added to the worker as a mere means of production, as coal is supplied to the boiler and grease and oil to the machinery."[35] Yoga practice in the office integrates deep breathing, meditation, and spiritual awareness to produce an experience and emotional response such as calmness, focus, and clarity. Such responses are extracted from the body and reintegrated into the mode of production. Massage, yoga, and spiritual healing occur through touch and are extremely nurturing practices that connote care and calm. It is difficult to acknowledge these corporate packages and perks as a means to keep the body and the meaning of time indentured to labor. Individuals are taught how to better care for the sedentary body, rather than recognize, turn against, or deplore the structural conditions that depend on the sedentary body. Far from indicating a culture of wellness, yoga is an example of extreme alienation cast as enlightened empowerment. Further still, yoga's resistance to the spatial disciplining of the laboring body in the office is an example of how investments into time incorporate alienation into the flow of production. Alienated labor becomes a place to define the self. The overcoming of alienation *at work* becomes the thing that binds the worker to work.

Resisting Work-Life Balance

When discussing this topic in various settings with friends, at conferences, and with colleagues, it has been suggested to me more than once that yoga is better than nothing. After one conference presentation, someone in the audience quipped, "Well, isn't this better than a whip?" Another peer chimed in, "Why would you want to deprive tired employees of yoga? It is better than nothing. It might create more positive changes." My interlocutors were convinced that yoga at work was a form of worker resistance to capital.

To reiterate my argument: Yoga can only appear to be a resistant workplace practice if one has an entirely *spatial* conception of *time* control. Moreover, yoga in the office in the absence of a nuanced conception of the temporal—that is, without an awareness of how time is a site of material struggle, subject to biopolitical intervention and experienced differentially—may appear to be a liberating temporal practice. The very offering of time for the self for the worker while at work *is* a biopolitical intervention. Far from indicating a new time free from the corporatization of everyday life, yoga in the office indicates that time control is exceeding its spatial boundaries into the zone of the temporal. Experiences of time are tied to inequitable horizons of political possibility. As such, we need a political understanding of time that doesn't rely on contractual notions of time, time as a mode of occupying political space, or time reduced to a disciplinary mechanism of control.

Today we are witnessing the proliferation of techniques of recalibration that revive temporal subjects stuck in otherwise confining spatial arrangements. The office is one node in the composition of spaces dictating how time is normally spent: at the office, in the shopping mall, in front of the television set, behind the wheel. Although such yogic techniques promise that the confining and normalizing spatial arrangements that normalize daily life will be broken with, they are in fact reinforced. The addition of yoga and spiritual healing to the office makes life at the desk temporally maintainable.

The banal working day has long been denigrated as the doldrums of human existence. Popular culture is replete with television shows that represent office work as soul deadening, mundane, and dull. But nine-to-five working days and holiday times have been fought for and remain significant sites of struggle, including different national struggles across Europe, for example, to shorten the working week to thirty-five hours. Even in the context of a culture of overwork, the parameters of a legal working day are the result of tremendous labor struggles by unions, workers' rights agitations, child-labor laws, women's reproductive rights in the workplace, and so forth. This struggle is nowhere near over. The fact that the advent of yoga at work may make a shorter workweek harder to fight for is worth thinking about. The corporate control over the time of life is so diffuse that even the mechanisms used to fight against it are futile unless the temporal is taken seriously.

For example, if the temporal is taken seriously, then work-life balance is a potentially limited goal. Work-life balance is an idea about the time of work and the time of life that sees no alternative temporal order beyond the corporate control of bodies. Work-life balance itself is a way of giving meaning to time precisely to manage time. It is important to consider how the cultivation of temporal dispositions is a form of biopolitical investment by the structures of modern power. The unquestioned virtues of work-life balance can often keep individuals in place, manning the various stations assigned within capital. Work-life balance, as attractive as it sounds, is a time claim that further institutionalizes the space and time of work as being fundamental to a person's identity. It makes alienation normal and institutionally recognized and managed, nothing extraordinary or worth fighting against.

And we must recognize work-life balance as a specific form of women's temporality and a dominant theme of women's movements in the 1970s and 1980s. But women's work lives also have a power-chronography that needs to be acknowledged—a normalizing temporal construct differentiated by race and economics. Women's temporal empowerment was (and still is, most would argue) based on their ability to recalibrate to the normalized structures of white male patriarchal capitalist time. Women's work-life balance is a practice of time management that can also further imbed vulnerable individuals into the normative time demands of governing institutions.

The incorporation of yoga legitimizes normative temporal frames as central to the balancing of work and life. Desk workers reset to the expectations of work and internalize a new time clock by way of yoga and its nonlinear temporality. They remain in the nine-to-five, but with a new temporal disposition. Even in the imagined context of a 24/7 day, nine-to-five's claims on time remain powerful. After all, it is the separation of discrete spheres of work and life, home and work, labor and leisure, and production and consumption that are protected by the nine-to-five. The nine-to-five is a spatial treatment of time that refers to a temporal frontier that corresponds to an ideological notion of when one is supposed to be at work. Its hold on our temporal imaginaries is astounding. The nine-to-five is the foundation upon which alternative temporalities resist, revolt, or recalibrate. It is the base from which so many time claims of busyness, speed, and accelerated living are waged. The social gains made to create the nine-to-five should not be abandoned, but neither should the nine-to-five be made more palatable, as if the struggle were over. The normalizing temporal order is at risk of becoming sediment within the political imaginary: invisible, seemingly innocuous, but actually insidious—an ache behind the eyes, a pain between the shoulder blades.

Chapter Four

SLOW SPACE

Another Pace and Time

A few days before January 1, 2012, a New Year's resolution about changing temporal orders appeared in the *New York Times*. An op-ed by Pico Iyer titled the "The Joy of Quiet" caused quite a buzz on Facebook and Twitter because of Iyer's proclamation that the "black hole resort" was bound to become the ultimate tourist destination in this fast-paced world. Black hole resorts are off-the-grid getaways without telephones, Internet, Wi-Fi, or even radios, where people essentially pay large sums to unplug.[1] Iyer quotes Blaise Pascal, Henry David Thoreau, Thomas Merton, and Marshall McLuhan to legitimate the virtues of doing nothing—of taking time out. Iyer points out that the "urgency of slowing down—to find the time and space to think—is nothing new." Yet, he warns, it is extremely imperative today because there are fewer reminders of its necessity: "We barely have enough time to see how little time we have." By the end of the piece, Iyer describes a stroll through a Benedictine hermitage located in Big Sur, California, only a few miles away from one of these black hole resorts. Slowing down need not be so expensive, he suggests. It is an essential and attainable ideal.

Iyer's article is merely one of many to appear over the years in the *New York Times* that instructs individuals how to unplug and take it slow.[2] Slowness is featured in lifestyle magazines, cookbooks, and corporate wellness materials. Within the popular imaginary, the turn to slowness is fast becoming the new mark of the moment. Cultural theorists and proponents of "slow living" argue that slowness will create "joy, wonder, and generosity towards others," as well as "intensify civic engagement and global responsibility."[3] Let us not forget, however, that McLuhan also proclaimed that speed was the mark of his time, and "his time" was almost fifty years ago.

In 1967 McLuhan prophesized that electronic technology would alter the pace, pattern, and scale of human connection, and that the technoteleology would culminate in a global village. In McLuhan's view, racial violence and economic inequality was symptomatic of unconnected cultures and their technologies of social division. A society dominated by print fostered linear conceptions of time that led to the fragmentation and categorization of other places and populations. Before the speed of electronic communication, the world was nonimmersive, and social groupings were far too distant and different for individuals to empathize with the Other. For McLuhan, the new electronic environment would usher in an era of global responsibility. Speed meant connection, deepening empathy, and the eradication of margins and centers on a planetary scale: "Electric speed, in bringing all social and political functions together in a sudden implosion, has heightened awareness of responsibility to an intense degree. It is no longer this implosive factor that alters the position of the Negro, the teen-ager. They can no longer be contained, in the political sense of limited association. They are now involved in our lives, as we in theirs, thanks to electric media."[4] According to McLuhan, the change to "electric" media was a change to a more rapid pace that would create "a sudden eagerness to have things and people declare their being totally."[5] Conversely, today slowness is said to accomplish similar democratic goals.

The Society for the Deceleration of Time in Austria is famous in "slow circles" for its publicity stunts, including confronting fast walkers with speeding tickets midstep or inviting them to walk a turtle. The Long Now Foundation in the United Kingdom is an organization founded by the musician Brian Eno and Stewart Brand in 1996.[6] Brand argues, "Society is revving up to a pathologically dangerous attention span."[7] Through The

Clock of the Long Now the foundation intends to remind civilization of "deep time"—the type of time sensibility required to act and think responsibly.[8] The Clock of the Long Now consists of a binary digital-mechanical system that will run ten thousand years, clocking time in long durations. The founders argue that the clock represents the "slower/better" over the "faster/cheaper" mentality that "governs today's society."[9] In 2000 the sloth movement began in Japan with an aim to emulate the sloth. Advocates of the sloth movement praise the sloth for its slowness as compared to the greedy, destructive, violent ways of humans.[10] The movement has since established sloth restaurants, sloth cafés, and guides for sloth living.

The slow life is also linked to efforts at sustainability across Japan, North America, Australia, Italy, and South Korea, such as chemical-free farming, animal rights, the protection of so-called local produce, traditions, and artisans, and the cultivation of edible gardens in inner-city schools. But slowness, as I've outlined it here, is also a consumer choice. Slow bloggers, slow hotels, slow sex, slow tourism, and slow e-mail are all iterations of the same.[11] The slow life literati are also gaining prominence. Carl Honore's *In Praise of Slow: How a Worldwide Movement Is Challenging the Cult of Speed* and Carlo Petrini's *Slow Food: The Case for Taste* are popular airport titles.[12] Armed with how-to-be-slow guides and slow self-help projects, slow-life proponents consist of the middle-aged and middle classed who are tiring but not yet retired from their respective rat races. Slow runs the gamut.

At the level of the individual, it may be true that everyone is time starved. In terms of democracy, it may also be the case that our political processes are suffocated by short-term thinking that renders life as we know it unsustainable. Nonetheless, without recognition of the multiple temporalities that underlie the social fabric or an understanding of how experiences of time are not just the outcome of individual choices, these intellectual responses and progressive social movements that respond to the problematic pace of life risk reproducing the very social inequalities they rail against. How time is conceived of and practiced has radical cultural implications that exceed simple exhortations or complaints about the pace of modern life.

Slowness is the privileged tempo within theories of democracy and the public sphere.[13] (But we've seen, with the example of the taxi drivers, that this theory should be complicated.) According to these theories, a contemplative and deliberative citizen is the valorized subject of properly democratic political public life. And according to Iyer, slowness offers a sort of distance from the world that makes it possible to assess one's place in it; a change in pace is required to take stock of one's place within the global order of things. The culturally driven forms of slowness that I've described are spatially, not temporally, organized. They assert spatial solutions to the problem of time. These spatial solutions do not actually address the temporal dimensions of power that have been described throughout this book. Having distance is a spatial relationship. Moreover, slowness appears to be about getting away, maintaining *distance* from the temporal and the complex multiplicity of time.

To see the power-chronography of it all, however, does not require slowness, or any change of pace. Instead, power-chronography charts the relevant infrastructures of time maintenance and the forms of recalibration, as well as the temporal labor and temporal architectures that make slowness desirable and possible for some but not for others. Slowness is not outside the normalizing temporal order. Slowness encompasses its own particular ideological time claims and beholds its own exclusive temporal practices.[14] The promotion of slowness occurs for different ends—procapital, anticapital, and often in between. In the following section, my examination of four instantiations of the slow life and the different claims on time that they embrace lead to the conclusion that slowness is suspect. The cultural turn to slowness is a depoliticization of time, one that demands the containment and pacification of time. Through a critical analysis of slow culture a normalizing relationship between time and democracy surfaces. We must re-think the contours of democratic time.

That slowness depends on the assertion of space for its own realization is symptomatic of the spatial bias that pervades global capitalist culture. As Harold Adams Innis reminds us, it is necessary to recover a sense of time in a present-minded culture where spatial conceptualizations of time dominate. That slowness arises as a response to speed speaks more to the continued absence of the temporal within the political imaginary. More space is not the solution to the problem of time. Rethinking time is an urgent need. Such urgency suggests a place for temporal politics grounded in an understanding of how social experiences of time are multiple and uneven. Slowing down does not necessarily change (and certainly does not ameliorate) the ways in which individuals and social groups are tangled together in time.

Bowen Island, British Columbia: Rhythm Change

Bowen Island is a small community of three thousand people in the Howe Sound of Vancouver. It is accessible to downtown Vancouver by water taxi and to North Vancouver by ferry. The island has a rehabilitation center, a small film school, a yoga studio, a few boutiques, a culinary school, a chocolatier, day spas, restaurants, and a smattering of bed and breakfasts. There are seasonal residents who spend summers on the island and rent their homes out to island laborers during the off-season. There are also year-round residents who are both professionals and manual laborers working in mainland Vancouver. A range of shift workers labor on the island and arrive every morning via ferry, while other residents leave for work. But in all this coming and going, there is a large population of Bowen Islanders who do not come and go. They have lived on Bowen their entire lives. They tend to the island itself: building and repairing houses, working maintenance, and staffing the restaurants, cafés, stores, and farms. The island is renowned for fostering the slow life.

There are two grocery stores on the island that both employ locals. One is organic (Ruddy Potato) and the other not (Snug Cove General Store). Ruddy Potato's website boasts, "The Ruddy is a gathering place for our community—a place to visit, discuss, hang out and enjoy all things food and Bowen. You'll often hear an in depth conversation about the latest issue, discussion about ingredients or the origins of a product, folks pondering what to have for dinner, or laughter over a story being told."[15] The rhythm of the season is well accounted for at the Ruddy Potato. The shelves are sparse, but that is because of a commitment to seasonal produce. The maintenance of healthy bodies and the importance of a time-out are a major part of the Ruddy Potato's commitment to the good life. The Ruddy Potato is also a center for wellness on the island. There you can find information about detoxification diets, yoga classes, and slow food cooking lessons. A section of the store is dedicated to wellness: tinctures, vitamins, oils, and aromatherapy. It is a quiet place. The Ruddy Potato is pricey, and it is definitely an important place of congregation, but only for a certain socioeconomic segment of the island. There are times—seasonal cycles when that social segment is absent—when you'll find yourself the only patron in the store.

Down the block at the general store, the same brands of sunscreen, diapers, and vitamins are sold at almost half the price. The general store is not luxurious in any way, nor is it cheaper than stores off the island, but it is much larger than the Ruddy Potato. The store bustles all day long as the rhythm of the day unfolds on Bowen Island. In the morning there is a mad rush for the daily newspapers, which are quite often sold out by late afternoon. People en route to mainland Vancouver grab two different papers at once. On Fridays they will grab three—local, provincial, and national. That's a die-hard public sphere, but then again, they have the entire ferry ride back and forth to read. Many of the locals sit and have coffee in the afternoon close to the grocery store and read the papers there.

I know a lot about the classed, gendered, and raced composition of the island from shopping at the general store. It stays open twelve hours a day, 365 days a year. A Korean Canadian family owns and operates the store. In the mornings, after the paper rush, mostly women and young children shop at the general store. It is clear that the island has a set of problematic town drunks—all middle-aged men. They rest in the parking lot of the Snug Cove General Store in the late afternoon. They are often hollering at each other and greeting the passersby. Over the summer I witness several heated conversations between local residents at the general store. They are arguing with one another over the plan to take down seven trees to put in a soccer field. There is also much consternation over the future of a park that may be subject to First Nations' land claims. Cases of beer and cigarettes move quickly out of the store every day starting at five in the afternoon. In the evening, like clockwork, at eight there is a last beer run. Every evening a roving bunch of rambunctious kids and bored teenagers collect bottles. They are bringing their parents' empties to the recycling depot in the store. There is also a pay phone outside the grocery store, an outdated icon of public space. It is an invitation for loitering without purchasing, an opportunity for secret conversations, and a good meeting place.

The organic, exclusive Ruddy Potato is a private attempt at building a public sphere on the island based on the consumer lifestyle. It is a deliberative space designed to foster a particular way of occupying time—mindful and contemplative. It also aims to protect the time of life in its dedication to the health of the human body and the planet. The Ruddy Potato's reasons for being are to provide a space on the island to foster a temporality conducive to community. The store espouses a notion of the time of nature as central to civic sociality. The general store, on the other hand, is just there. It asserts zero commitment to the slow, good life or a new public sphere. Yet at the general store, the temporal politics of Bowen Island are most visible. The general store is inextricably embedded in the pulse of the island. And it is this rhythm—multilayered, complicated, and messy—that the Ruddy Potato seems quite purposefully apart from. The Ruddy Potato represents a dream of a political public sphere free from entanglements with the temporal.

The Caretta Shiodome, Tokyo: Slow Living in the Sky

Many say that Tokyo is the fastest city in the world, with its Shinkansen bullet trains and the swiftest turnover of high street fashion. Everything moves fast. But in the same breath, those who find the city emblematic of the fast life would also attest that Tokyo, in many distinct ways, is also the great protector and creative producer of sacred time.[16] Tokyo contains a cornucopia of both inconspicuous and deliberate slow zones scattered all over the city. En route to Harajuku, the teen fashion Mecca of Japan, you can turn a corner and find yourself walking across the bridge of a koi pond on quaint temple grounds. Walk across the busiest intersection in the world, Hachiko crossing in Shibuya, and you'll see capsule hotels for the day-napping needs of businesspeople awake for the last thirty-six hours. In Tokyo it is easy to find manufactured and contemporary creations for slowing down and longstanding protected spaces of escape amid a hustle and bustle like no other.

When one envisions a deliberate architecture designed for slow living, the thought of a structure for slowness shooting up into the sky is an unlikely image. Slowness always seems much more horizontal, spilling out like molasses and extending outward, in an embrace. It should be down to earth, we think, rather than up in the air. But the Caretta Shiodome, a slow-living facility in the financial district of downtown Tokyo, nestled between Ginza, Shimbashi, and Hamamatsucho, quickly extends vertically into the sky, staking a claim in space.

You can live, work, play, rest, and even experience traditional Japanese "culture" in the Caretta Shiodome. Most of the office space belongs to Dentsu, a Japanese marketing firm. The remaining offices are largely composed of media firms. In fact, the Shiodome is also known as a media castle (*jokomachi*), the headquarters of Nippon Television and Kyoda News. But the complex is more than an office space; it is also a lifestyle community. The lifestyle complex makes no attempt to hide its ideological ethos. As you enter the building, a stack of brochures in Japanese and English introduce the facility: "Affluent living for those who want to live a slow lifestyle." The community's website promises the "slow simple life": "Caretta Shiodome, a town for adults looking for a place to dine, become stylish, and enjoy culture in a relaxing atmosphere. This 21st century skyscraper consists of four distinctive zones, each providing large-scale international facilities where people can meet and communicate with each other. Why don't you indulge in a comfortable space and leisurely pace at Caretta, a world totally secluded from that of business, where speed is everything?"[17] Caretta's slow space isn't just another fetish in Tokyo, such as the mayonnaise restaurants that serve mayonnaise milkshakes, the theme bars where service staff dress and behave like ninjas, or other forms of play you might find wandering throughout the city. Only a few years old, the Caretta Shiodome is still selling flats and business spaces. Inside it is busy, quietly pulsing in a slow but obviously productive way. The arrival of this slow lifestyle mall and living center signals the dawn of a larger movement in urban design and civic culture in Tokyo. The Caretta Shiodome is able to contain work, leisure, and play in a city that has little extra space to accommodate the desire to extend life out in space and time. In the Caretta Shiodome, all daily needs can be met in one space. But space and time are also services to be purchased and delivered, of course.

In the Caretta Shiodome, many apartments are full-service with a cleaning staff. The community boasts a dentist, a doctor, and a theater showing Broadway plays, a pharmacist, a bookstore, a popular advertising museum, a teashop, and a patisserie. Ironically, fast food options abound. In fact, a very prominent and busy McDonalds sits on the ground floor of the Caretta Shiodome (see figure 4.1). There are also slow food style restaurants, with traditional tea service and organic fare. The main floor is scattered with more than fifty modern chairs designed by the great furniture designers of the twentieth century, such as Charles Eames, Henry Bertoia, and Hans Wagner and manufactured by Knoll and Herman Miller. A legend for the variety of furniture is found close to the main entrance, with full details about the pieces one will encounter in the slow skyscraper. The chairs offer a self-consciously stylish place to sit.

As I walk through the main floor, I notice that all chairs are already occupied. Some are placed in a row and others are singularly positioned behind a labyrinth of walls, down hallways, and in the corners of the building. But people are not just sitting in the chairs. In fact, most of the seated Shiodomers are dozing off. In another area of the Shiodome there is a tiny

FIGURE 4.1. A busy McDonalds sits on the ground floor of the Caretta Shiodome, Tokyo. Photo by author.

plaza, a type of miniature public space, surrounded by wooden sculptures and benches that create an inner circle for about ten people. Outlets for cell phones are located next to every single seat; people are quietly talking on their phones (see figure 4.2). In the outdoor courtyard, wooden benches wrap around individual trees, allowing people to literally sit in the shade. In the middle of the courtyard sits a sculpture of a large sea turtle, the Caretta Shiodome's icon (see figure 4.3). The turtle represents two (seemingly) mutually exclusive visions of lifestyle and commerce in the Japanese endeavor. A manager of the Caretta Shiodome explains that the turtle has long been regarded as the god of commerce and also represents "the new 'slow life' concept, the new movement in urban lifestyle."[18]

The slow life in the Caretta Shiodome is organized around a slow monument designed for reflection. The sculpture becomes a water fountain every hour on the hour for twenty minutes. The twenty minutes operates as a timed break from work without the need for a watch. It also acts as a reminder of the passing of time and invites reflection on how to pace one's daily existence when time moves so quickly. The water fountain is not for making wishes but for reflecting on how to deal with and even overcome the nagging feeling of time passing beyond one's control. The different

FIGURE 4.2. (top) Cell-phone seating area at the Caretta Shiodome, Tokyo.
FIGURE 4.3. (bottom) The tortoise water fountain at the Caretta Shiodome, Tokyo.
Photos by author.

FIGURE 4.4. Taxis wait for slow lifers in the Caretta Shiodome, Tokyo. Photo by Jeremy Packer.

floors of the Caretta Shiodome are tightly controlled—some are for leisure, some for work, and others for living. Security guards stand next to the escalators and revolving glass doors that separate these spheres of living. The complex sits atop a busy metro station. A taxi stand with a sea of waiting taxis circles the structure. Inside their taxis, the drivers are sleeping, reading manga, or staring off into space (see figure 4.4). They await the signal from the dispatcher who controls the taxi stand. He indicates when a slow lifer is about to exit the Caretta Shiodome.

The fact that this affluent slow life is housed in a gigantic skyscraper pointing up into the sky indicates a particular kind of claim on time—a spatial one. The Caretta Shiodome is a spatial accommodation designed to uphold an ethos of slowness. Slowness, here, is something that can be contained, literally built from the ground up. From the various offerings in the Shiodome, it is hard to gather whether lines are drawn between what constitutes a slow practice or a fast practice. Instead, slowness is an entire lifestyle. It is the result of the complete orchestration of all of life's necessities within a single structure that has been built for the purpose of saving time. Life is easy, because it is full-service at all times. What makes life slow is the elimination of pursuits that might be considered a waste of time. The

Caretta Shiodome instructs the slow lifer, "don't waste your time" in fruitless pursuits such as waiting, rushing, commuting, cleaning, getting lost, or even hailing a cab. The Caretta Shiodome is about having time for time by eliminating things that get in the way. The imagined path of existence is one that should always be full and meaningful. In other words, slow lifers in the Caretta Shiodome are provided an opportunity to not have to make daily time-management choices themselves, nor be vigilant about how they spend their short time on earth. The underlying assumption in the Caretta Shiodome is that living there means living a life rich with extra time.

The Caretta Shiodome doesn't hide its investment in the lives of the wealthy with its tagline, "for those who *want* a slow life" (my emphasis). More important is the distinctive set of criteria for evaluating what makes a time-taking pursuit useless or meaningless. This evaluation of the "right practice of time" upholds and affirms the hierarchies of temporal power that establish difference across the social fabric. Living in the dome is itself a temporal practice. The only people wasting their time in the Shiodome, according to its slow-living ethos, are the nonresidents, the restaurant waitstaff, cleaners, security guards, and taxi drivers. These lives are not only *not affluent* but, under the terms and conditions of the facility's mantra, laden with unfortunate uses of time. To live a life devoted to service labor is not a great use of one's short time on earth. In many ways, to actually endure the reality of being short on time is an experience reserved for the laboring attendants, the temporal labor force.

Slow Food Nation, San Francisco: A Temporal Return

Late in the summer of 2008, I attended Slow Food Nation in San Francisco, a nonprofit subsidiary of Slow Food USA and the international slow food movement. Over Labor Day weekend, 85,000 people, mostly from the United States but with a notable international contingent, descended on the grounds outside the city courthouse to participate in conversation, lectures, meals, films, and taste experiences dedicated to reevaluating America's food system and its relationship to the culture of speed. The broad theme is encapsulated by these phrases that peppered the food halls, handouts, posters, and billboards (see figures 4.5 and 4.6): "Come to the table." "Let's go slow, eat together." "Get cooking." "Vote with your fork." "Drink from the tap." "Talk food politics." "Get to know your food." "Conserve, compost, and recycle."

FIGURE 4.5. (top) A liquor store supports Slow Food Nation with "slow food friendly" wine in San Francisco. "Slow food friendly" wine refers to organic grapes and sustainable-farming methods. FIGURE 4.6. (right) "Let's Go Slow" reminders at Slow Food Nation. Photos by author.

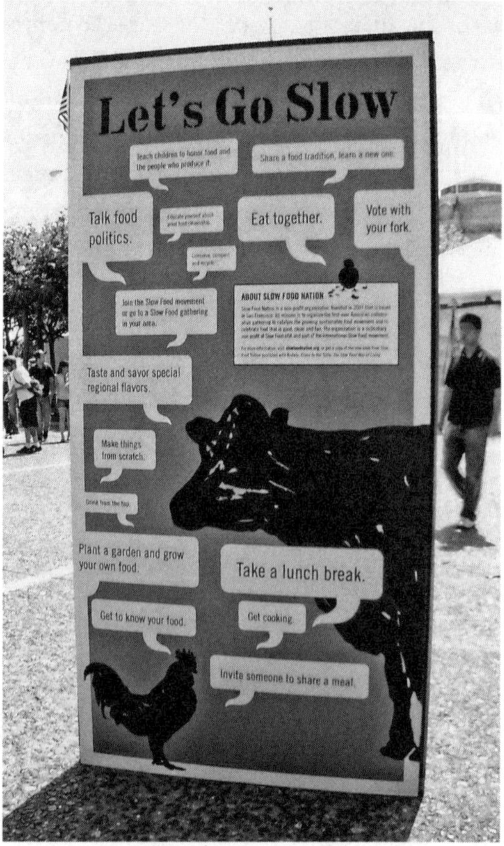

The international slow food movement began in 1986 as a protest in Italy outside a McDonalds at Piazza di Spagna in Rome. Several hundred protestors, organized by Carlo Petrini, a former culinary writer for the communist magazine *Il Manifesta* in the 1970s, marched outside the McDonalds with bowls of penne. Soon after, Petrini founded the international slow food movement. The slow food movement now has hundreds of thousands of members in more than 150 countries.[19] The slow food movement has become a vibrant global network composed of eco-gastronomers, restaurants, chefs, farmers, urban planners, grocers, agriculturalists, policymakers, and educators committed to cultivating social change around issues related to the dining table. They work at linking farmers to cooperatives while also encouraging biodiversity, opposing genetically modified foods, and protecting local food cultures. As such, this particular slow movement is a long-term effort, a slow revolution, for sustainability and policy change. Its mandate goes beyond a simple protest of the fast life as a vague cultural symptom and prescribes political changes, a practice that includes lobbyists pressuring the European Union on trade and agricultural policy in order to save farming and food traditions that are endangered.

One afternoon I attended the "Slow Food on a Budget" workshop. Upon entering the room I realized that the event was cosponsored by Whole Foods. The room was mostly made up of middle-aged women and young couples. The budget was announced as forty dollars for a dinner for four. The host enthused, "Slow food can show you how to have fun saving money because saving money is fun—isn't it?" The meal included truffle oil, sustainable wine, organic hen, arugula, and a peach compote for dessert (see figure 4.7). A representative from a California wine company extolled the wonders of sustainable wine, and we all had a try.

Petrini's slow food manifesto declares that a "firm defense of quiet material pleasure is the only way to oppose the universal folly of Fast Life."[20] He continues, "Technology has led us to forget what it means to be human."[21] For Petrini, the slow movement encourages "people to return to the natural rhythms enjoyed by previous generations."[22] Slow food has gained prominence by following a commercial model, but it calls itself a progressive social movement.

But the return to nature via natural rhythms of the body and eating seasonal fruits and vegetables will not change the fact that the largest group of low-wage workers in the world is farmworkers. Nor will it change the fact that in the United States, restaurant workers, in both fast-food and slow

FIGURE 4.7. Meal prepared for the "Slow Food on a Budget" workshop. Photo by author.

food establishments, continue to be paid less than a livable wage.[23] Toby Miller addresses the climate of food politics in the United States by pointing out how "'good taste' becomes a sign of, and a means toward, better citizenship."[24] But the relationship between slow food and the production of uneven time continues to be invisible. There is no doubt that slow food carries traces of a bourgeois endeavor that mistakes good taste for politics. A focus on the temporal could provide the necessary means to productively politicize the movement.

My experience at Slow Food Nation made it clear that slow food was less about a politics of time conducive to ethical relations than it was about learning the right individualistic practices of time made possible by particular spaces. The type of time that is valued by the slow food movement is "natural time," whether it is the time of the earth, the seasons, or the biological clock. It is imagined to be precapitalist and preindustrial. Individuals are expected to reclaim an "essential" experience of time, and such a reclamation is assumed to be possible. But the temporal politics of slow food recedes almost entirely from view because of this naturalized conception of time coupled with the privileging of space.

The main signifier for the movement captures the tension between space and time incredibly well. The icon for the international slow food movement is the snail—both a space and a tempo. The snail's survival in a fast world depends on its shell: "Cosmopolitan and thoughtful, it prefers nature to civilization, which it takes upon itself, with its own shell. It seemed that a creature so unaffected by the temptations of the modern world had something new to reveal, like an amulet against exasperation, against the malpractice of those who are too impatient to feel and taste, too greedy to remember what they had just devoured."[25] The iconography of the snail attests to a simpler time—a time when the snail didn't have to struggle to survive in the face of bigger and faster animals. The snail is not competitive but impervious. The shell offers a retreat into a protective casing, allowing for a protected space and an unaffected temporality. The snail is perfectly poised, patient, and calm—able to deal with its tremendous lack of power and control over its own fate. The snail weathers acceleration successfully. The shell allows it to balance speed. The snail can turn its back on the encroaching world and wait it out.

The slow food movement is oriented around a series of spaces that offer "shells"—protected spaces in which to deal with a range of sped-up forces—globalization, technology, automobiles, and fast-food restaurants. The resistant spaces that the movement focuses on include the dinner table, farms, fields, kitchens, slow food restaurants, urban gardens, Cittaslow (slow cities), and the local. At Slow Food Nation, an antiquated soapbox in a faux public square was the center point of the event. The hope was that people would step up to the soapbox to speak and draw a public. The main stage for the outdoor events at Slow Food Nation, called Come to the Table, literally had a dinner table placed in the middle of it for a series of scheduled debates and conversations (see figure 4.8).

The first Cittaslow groups were founded in Bra and Chianti, Italy, in 1999. There are now 120 slow cities in eighteen countries, including Japan, Finland, Australia, South Korea, Turkey, England, Canada, and Germany. Petrini and the mayors of these Bra and Chianti drew a charter for slow cities that includes the mandate that the population cannot exceed 55,000:

> We are looking for towns brought to life by people who make time to enjoy a quality of life. Towns blessed with the quality public spaces, theatres, shops, cafes, inns, historic buildings, and unspoiled land-

FIGURE 4.8. Slow Food Nation's slogan "come to the table" refers to sitting down to eat together, but it is also about the importance of the table to conviviality. Public debates and conversations were staged at a dinner table. Photo by author.

> scapes. Towns where traditional craft skills are in daily use and where the slow, beneficial succession of the seasons is reflected in the availability of local produce in season. Towns where healthy eating, healthy living, and enjoying life are central to the community.[26]

The Cittaslow groups form "an international network of cities where living is easy." These towns adhere to a mandate of slow living that is subject to reapproval every three years. Cittaslow has been described by Paul Knox, a scholar of urban planning and architecture, as "the true nature of community," and "towns where pedestrians can stroll, untroubled by the roaring traffic, towns with abundant and varied spaces in which people can run into each other, sit, talk, and enjoy communal life."[27]

Invoking the term *local* is a means for claiming something as natural and authentic. It is also the most dominant spatial marker of the slow good life. There is a fetishizing of local *space* as the ultimate site of a transformative *time* politics. All food is actually originally local, but slow food's attention to the place of production doesn't always mean that food is sourced locally. Instead, posters of "authentic locals" standing by their traditional foods filled the hall of Slow Food Nation's dining fair. There were myriad of stories about "traditional local foods." But a celebration of space ignored whole sets of other complicated conditions, including temporal power differentials.

For example, slow foodies celebrated local variations on the corn tortilla in Mexico with a featured documentary. The story it tells is of the women who wake up at four in the morning to start cooking. The narrative that captivates the slow food imagination is focused on these traditions, the authentic tortillas, rather than the fact that so-called traditional tortilla production is also strenuous gendered labor in impoverished working conditions. The making of the tortilla reflects a differential relationship to time structured by the particular gendered and classed context of the makers' (women's) lives. The local movement fetishizes Others such as the farmers, organic grape pickers, and tortilla makers, without a concern for how they actually negotiate their time. They are real people in locales whose fixity in space and arduous labor allows for slow lifers to imagine a possibility to make their own experience of time more "natural."

The slow food movement imagines that it provides another experience of time, resistant to both the speed of life and the notion of time as money. But members of the slow food movement operate with an economistic conception of quality time. They assume that better time management is all that is needed. They imagine that time is something everyone has, something everyone has access to, and something that can be shaped individually, given the right choices. The Slow Food USA website boasts: "Slow Food is also simply about *taking the time* to slow down and to enjoy life with family and friends. Everyday [*sic*] can be enriched by doing something slow—making pasta from scratch one night, *seductively squeezing* your own orange juice from the fresh fruit, *lingering* over a glass of wine and a slice of cheese—even *deciding* to eat lunch sitting down instead of standing up."[28] The movement is able to profess a politics of lifestyle since it is imagined that all slow actions link to better agricultural politics and practices of sustainability.

Interestingly, if we apply this logic to the other resource that slow food is invested in besides time—food—there is a vast difference in how the two are talked about. The uneven politics of food—starvation, contamination, and obesity, for example—are implicit. Water is a resource recognized as inequitably available, unfairly privatized. There are droughts.

Water gets polluted, becomes dangerous, and is wasted by those with leaky taps, swimming pools, and big green lawns.

In our discussion about budgeting for food at Slow Food Nation, a self-described "foodie activist" proclaims that slow food is about prioritizing time: "It is worth the money and time for me to drive to my favorite farm for two hours to get milk, cheese, and meat. I do that instead of watching TV." One needs to make trade-offs—driving for food rather than watching television is imagined as a more political practice. Cultural anthropologists call into question the discursive construction of the binary between slow food and fast food. For them, a false dichotomy lies at the heart of contemporary theorizing of food politics.[29] Ethnographic studies of slow food markets and McDonalds in Australia have revealed the contradictions within the movement's ecological project and the car-centered diet that slow food remains tied to. In fact, it is argued through comparative data that some slow food is actually far more car reliant than fast-food outlets. The problems associated with fast food and slow food must move beyond the issue of pace and toward what is considered unhealthy or unsustainable. As Miller argues, "Fast food encapsulates structural adjustments in search of efficiencies, as per the time discipline of capitalism."[30] A temporal perspective into the food system requires an understanding of the labor politics. More to the point, Miller argues, "casual labor and environmental degradation sustain fast food. It is a service-industry model of exploited workers and despoiled space."[31] To focus then on fast food versus slow food, which one is really slow and which one is really fast, is misguided. It draws attention away from the exploitative labor arrangements required for both food experiences. The production of slow food and fast food are predicated on an uneven temporal politics as a condition of their possibility.

In their mandates for slow living, proponents have collapsed all domains from agricultural politics, local politics, and a resistance to speed into an exclusive politicizing of time. There is no distinction between the political efficacies of their various projects. Everything begins to fall under "slow"—from squeezing oranges to resisting genetically modified foods. Speed is imagined to promote ill health and destroy the environment. As William Connolly argues in *Neuropolitics: Thinking, Culture, Speed*, "The resentment against speed and the refusal to challenge its most salient institutional sources combines to foster an accusatory culture."[32] In this case, sped-up people are treated as irresponsible, when in fact a sped-up body is quite often a condition of labor or results from larger structural differ-

FIGURE 4.9. A slow day at Slow Food Nation. An ice cream vendor waits for business outside the grounds of the event. Photo by author.

ences sutured along the lines of gender, race, class, and immigration status. One of the slowest bodies I encountered at Slow Food Nation was a fast-food vendor outside the venue. He asked me how much longer the event was going on as he had no business for the past two days and wasn't able to change locations (see figure 4.9). The only people eating at his stand were the workers inside the slow food pavilions who were not "part" of the event. These laborers, both the vendors and the cleaning staff inside Slow Food Nation, trouble the slow-fast dichotomy that the movement rests on. A labor organizer for farmworkers in California contended at a slow food event: "When farm workers work full-time, you don't even have time to be poor, you're screwed." But these aren't the time politics that the slow movement is concerned with.

The slow food critique of speed depends on a spatial understanding of time. Such a conception of time is detrimental to those individuals and social groups who are busy producing a slow culture, yet remain completely outside it. Energy is directed toward creating new spaces for slow living and lionizing iconic locals, not recognizing laborers. The focus is on beautiful and abundant farms rather than immigrant farmers. The slow food movement is concerned with the global locals (or authentic Others) rather than the global relations of dependence. Slow food eateries are celebrated rather than the service staff. In all of this, the time of nature is valued at the expense of those that deliver experiences of nature. It would seem that the workers in the farm fields are experiencing a different kind of closeness with nature. The spaces of slow food, its tables, kitchens, and various locales, depend on the recalibration of others across a range of spaces and temporalities far from San Francisco's own table.

The slow lifestyle is fraught with the neoliberal contradiction of demanding individual responsibility for how one spends one's time, as if the problem of time was really a matter of lifestyle choice, while advocating for slowness as an attainable public good. A temporal lifestyle is assembled through a series of well-thought-out choices, or time practices, that aren't available as public goods and will not translate time into a public good either. Living slowly will not become a form of radical activism until it acknowledges the truly temporal. The slow-living ethos problematically takes the position of a moral arbiter, making claims about how practitioners should spend time—as an ethical and mindful human being rather than mindless citizen of speed. Slow lifers, through community allegiances, learn how to eat right (local, organic, sitting with others and eating slowly while deliberating), consume right (local, grow your own food, or try slow food restaurants), be in time (contemplative, deliberative, and mindful), and best transport themselves in space (bicycles or feet). Slow living is mandated as correct yet reserved only for those who have time to make time. Proponents of the slow life need to examine their discursive terrain and the structural inequalities that might lead to speed as a condition of living; moreover, they should examine the ways in which their own lifestyle choices may simply displace speed onto the temporalities of less privileged populations.

Staycation, USA: Slowed to a Halt

In the summer of 2008, the financial crisis in the United States was met with public and privatized pronouncements of a larger slowdown. ABC invented National Stay at Home Week to encourage the American citizenry to use their travel days to stay home and watch television. The tagline read,

"With gas prices so high, the economy taking a nosedive, global warming, it's just better to stay in and enjoy great ABC TV." These were slow times. With a slowed-down market, life as many Americans knew it would also have to slow down. But living the slow life *at home* was an innovative economic directive fostered by corporate America—from the big television networks to big-box stores. With gas prices rising and the fear of terrorism still lingering, middle-class Americans were instructed to become temporarily immobile—to stay at home. While many were losing their homes thanks to the financial crisis, several others were being sold a version of homebound security, a new American Dream for the impending summer holiday.

Immobility was carefully elevated in status to meet the otherwise inevitable culture shock of staying at home in a nation where open roads, skies, and waterways are seen as a God-granted freedom. While traversing space is a public right in America, the closed interior of the private suburban home is also a sign of Americanness. The new undestination, the great American staycation, transpired in the summer of 2008 as a cultural and economic practice that merged the dual rites of passage (interior space and exteriorized extended space) into a revised American Dream. *Staycation* emerged as a neologism that refers to making a vacation out of staying at home.

Good Morning America first featured the staycation in spring of 2008 in a "parenting tips" segment that offered advice on how to deal with the impending slow summer. Here "slow" meant a summer stalled by impending financial restraints on international and domestic travel. *Good Morning America* continued with the theme for the entire summer. The other networks eventually weighed in with their own therapeutic interventions about how to stay at home staycation style. Between spring and fall of 2008, lifestyle experts, representatives from major retailers, and avid staycationers filled morning slots on ABC, NBC, Fox, CBS, and CNN with staycation tips. In a noteworthy lead story on CNN in June 2008, a father in South Windsor, Connecticut, was featured for his permanent staycation residence afforded by the money he saved by not going on vacation.[33] The palatial home was fitted with a basketball court, swimming pool, hot tub, gardening area, and volleyball court. In the same week (and for those without several acres), CBS's *The Early Show* featured the editor of BehindtheBuy.com, a company that specializes in informing the "time-starved consumer" about new commodities. The lifestyle consultant previewed the newest and most necessary items "so you could get away without leaving home." Key essentials included a family-size tent with an air-conditioning unit, a projector television screen made for the outdoors, a high-end snow-cone maker, a small beer keg, a minigolf kit, and a fast-setting swimming pool that attaches to garden hoses. The segment also extolled the virtues of the staycation, even when gas prices aren't so high. As one staycationer put it: "You have this stuff forever, if you go on vacation all you have is the pictures."[34] While people were distracted from the apparently pitiful lack of glamour that staying at home entails, the networks made staying home an issue of responsible citizenship.

Lynn Spigel has developed these themes extensively in *Make Room for TV* and *Welcome to the Dreamhouse*.[35] She offers a picture of the postwar domestic space in the 1950s "as a vehicle of transport through which [families] could imaginatively travel to an illicit place of passion while remaining in the safe space of the family home."[36] More than sixty years later, it is the staycationing home and undestinations that have become the products of creative affective interventions by marketers and advertisers. Yet another means to tap into the suburban anxiety between the interior domestic space and the exteriorized world "out there" had been found. The big home-building stores had staycation renovations and designs ready to go. Holiday Inns and local Hiltons were visited by ABC anchors to promote the experience of staying at a hotel in one's hometown—a staycation vacation. ABC Eyewitness News focused in on the retailers and the summer of the staycation. Target, Kohls, and Walmart were featured for "rolling back prices" on all things staycation. The list of staycationables included new patio furniture, grills, grilling meats, air fresheners, and scented candles. Staying home was not necessarily an inexpensive option.[37]

To put the staycation in context with U.S. vacation stipulations and practices, a recent report by the Center for Economic and Policy Research called *No-Vacation Nation* found that the United States is the only advanced economy in the world that does not guarantee its workers paid vacation.[38] Subsequently, without government standards, 25 percent of Americans have neither paid vacation nor paid holidays. The staycation was not for the working poor who were having difficulty even getting to work in the first place, nor for the unemployed, recently jobless, or the foreclosed-upon. The staycationers were middle-class suburbanites who had backyards and enough acreage for swimming pools and tents. By the summer of 2009,

Webster's Dictionary would officially add *staycation* to the institutionally recorded American lexicon.[39] Slow-time USA had quickly found a new popular past time. The invention of the staycation implicitly manufactured a particular ideological version of the slow life when alternative forms of the good life and the need for social change were looming on the horizon. The wheels were turning across the nation, people were doing the math, and the critique of American spectacular consumer culture could almost become mainstream. "Do Americans overconsume, overdrive, and overdesire?" talking heads on the nightly news from MSNBC and Fox, would ask. Yes, everyone seemed to agree.

Slowing down seemed progressive. Slowness became part of the popular vernacular of corporate America and the national psyche. The staycation emerged as a palatable form of slowness that was good for the U.S. economy and also for the nuclear family, not to mention "the environment." The staycation was shown to be good for the self-enterprising individual, family values, consumer citizenship, and the overall health of the nation. In a sense, by staycationing, the economic crisis could be averted and the guilt of consumption and overspending could be alleviated. If there were a national debt, the American middle-class nuclear family would help repay it this summer by staying at home for once. In fact, converting the private home into a destination would create an exciting place to wait for the crisis to be over.

The proprietors for the great American staycation were finding all sorts of dark corners in the American psyche to extol the virtues of staying at home. While taking to the road was an American right, this road was not always that easy to navigate—it was often diverse. The staycation capitalized on the latent xenophobic tendencies of the insular family. A CNN .com article that ran after the *Weekend Report* mentioned earlier quoted a life coach who argued that staycations were more fitting for many Americans because the "strangeness of different cultures or languages, figuring out foreign currencies or worrying about lost luggage can take a toll."[40] The staycation sustains a culture of insularity, consumption, escapist distraction, and fear, but in doing so it serves the national economic interests quite well. Stay at home, shop, grill, watch television and movies—these were the economic directives programmed by mass media and retail giants. As such, the staycation trend was a cultural phenomenon similar to the rest of the mundane life of the suburbs. This time, however, the slow banalities of the humdrum became something to get excited over.

The economic slowdown has been a challenge to a deeply national sense of being on the go, the imagined pace and path that justifies American-style middle-class consumption. The emergence of the staycation occurred precisely at a time when Americans could see that their mobility and their locales, including domestic spaces, are structurally bound to larger geopolitical forces and the uneven and inequitable social system they sustain. Constructing the staycation was a pretty good investment for those threatened by this potential change in pace and path. The big three television networks, big-box stores, financial advisors, and George W. Bush's instructions for Americans to shop all had a part to play in instructing Americans how to stay at home.

The underlying goal of this economic directive was to maintain the movement of capital and the illusion of untrammeled mobility at a time when the crisis of capital contained seeds for an alternative version of the good life. Perhaps the cultural transformation could have ruptured the unquenchable desire to live in constant and unlimited motion. The circulation of capital could have stalled. But it didn't. Instead it was effectively slowed and reoriented to a new site. The great cultural transformation was directed toward revamping the home, the stable reference of middle-class dreams, and making it the ultimate destination, again.

The still citizen is a threatening figure for capital. In *Polar Inertia* Paul Virilio argues that at the heart of capitalism is a state of permanent mobility.[41] The staycation fits completely within his frame, as it provides a context of mobile immobility. The flow needs to keep flowing; when people are stationary, still, and calm, the market suffers. It has often been argued that the advertising industries construct dissatisfaction while also marginally eliminating it through the promises of various products, yet ultimately leaving the individual in a constant state of being almost satisfied but never really. The fact that the staycation is a mode of waiting makes it a perfect way to produce this complacent dissatisfaction. The subjective and experiential dimensions of living in a capitalist society are experienced through one's relationship to time and staying on the right path. The economic slowdown and the energy crisis are crises in pace, energy flow, and time. The mobility and tempo, the pace and path that capital relies on, have become unhinged and vulnerable to a resistant reshaping. The staycation recalibrates the tempo of suburbia to meet the new needs of an economic slowdown and financial crisis. Following the directive to staycate is not necessarily a new form of false consciousness; it is an intensified technological and economic mode of subjecthood that depends on already established cultural anxieties about time and mobility. But what makes the staycation unique and worthy of consideration is that capitalists and other disciplinary institutions of power, in this case big media, construct new and innovative ways to control people's time and regulate their movements in space. The staycation is a reterritorialization of the temporal and spatial dimensions of home, work, and leisure. It is a remaking of space to deal with a change in pace.

Conclusion: The Myth of a Slow Public

In *The Politics of the Very Worst*, Virilio argues: "The measure of the world is our vast freedom. Knowing that the world is vast, being aware of this is an element of human freedom and greatness, even if we don't take advantage of it."[42] In *Slow Living*, cultural theorists Wendy Parkins and Geoffrey Craig offer an account of a year living the slow life in Italy. They similarly contend: "An emphasis on contemplation and attention requires a kind of withdrawal—of body and of consciousness—from certain kinds of spaces or places (figured as fast or noisy, the two often conflated so that a slow space is also a quiet one) at least for a period of time, for rest or refreshment."[43] Particular spaces allow for the right practice of time. They continue:

> Slow living involves the conscious negotiation of the *differential temporalities* which make up our everyday lives, deriving from a commitment to occupy time more attentively. Implicit in the practices of slow living is a *particular conception of time* in which "having time" for something means investing it with significance through attention and deliberation. To live *slowly in this sense, then, means engaging in mindful rather than mindless practices* which make us consider the pleasure or at least the purpose of each task to which we give our time.[44]

Within this slow living imaginary, time is treated as something to which we all have equal access. Temporal differences are said to exist because people treat time differently. For example, the multiplicity of time refers to the different ways one can choose to spend one's time on a daily basis. It is the ability to manage one's time that "creates a temporality conducive to ethical relations with others."[45]

There is a dominating sensibility within this discourse on slowness that being a "good" political citizen requires transcendence. Transcendence pervades in both taking the necessary time out and abstracting oneself from the energy and traffic of everyday life. But this traffic conditions the very possibility for some to transcend. Slowness does not and cannot acknowledge its material preconditions or the diversity of demands that sit outside its concrete edifices and sacred spaces. Many of these material relations are fast paced, mindless, and mundane; slowness hides the rhythm of material relations, the very condition of its possibility.

Slowness is a strategy of normalization that naturalizes an appropriate temporal order. Slowness organizes the pace and structure of time as well as the spaces in which it should unfold. Instead of creating a new liberatory relationship to time, slow practices reassert the power of institutional space in people's lives. These spatial solutions to the problem of speed work upon people's sense of time in order to keep them fixed within a confining relationship to capital. Without a temporal imaginary, it does not occur to the proponents of slow food to include the wage laborers, night shifters, farmworkers, or those in the service of the slow lifers in the explicit value system and prescription of right behaviors of the slow-living manifesto. How would a slow lifer do the night shift? Can a slow politics be enacted outside the order of normalized or exceptional time? Who labors quickly to clean the slow-food restaurants? Who washes the dishes so that the next table can be served?

The reassertion of space through slowness is part of a greater political tendency of the Left to focus attention on new space and a new relationship to tempo as a solution to many of the democratic dilemmas of civic life. To temper speed with slowness does not alleviate the fact that slow spaces have their own biopolitical economy of time. Few people are economically or culturally positioned to occupy such space. And fewer still can claim its progressive, political, or sustainable promise. The rising infrastructure of slowness speaks to a spatial bias in all realms of social and political life, from both edges of the political spectrum. An overly spatial cultural imaginary is detrimental to the cultural politics of time. More space is not the path to a more democratic time. In the spatializing of slowness through buildings and theme parks, slow spaces sustain uneven temporalities.

The detours taken through slow space in this chapter do not lead me to the conclusion that the political possibilities inherent in slowness need to be rescued. “Go slow” as a directive—or as a mantra, such as “be where you are” and “I control my time,” both of which we have learned to question—may better be abandoned in exchange for a deeper sense of the temporal. In the next chapter, I conclude this book with some possible ways in which to inhabit the world through the temporal, as a critical perspective with political implications.

Conclusion

TOWARD A TEMPORAL PUBLIC

I began this book with a power-chronographic scan of Shibuya Crossing in Tokyo. Immersed in the rhythm of this iconic setting, I set the stage for my argument that the popular notion that the world is speeding up was less an accurate depiction of the moment than it is a productive ideological discourse symptomatic of global capital's spatial imaginary. I argued that theoretical critiques of the culture of speed had not paid sufficient attention to the institutional, cultural, and economic arrangements that produce specific tempos for different populations. A myopic theoretical focus on speedup had obscured the necessity of tracing how *differential* relationships to time organize and perpetuate inequalities. The concern over speedup is less about time than it is about space. The speedup narrative is based in a critique of a newly unruly tempo that threatens the spatial virtues of democracy.[1] Such a perspective seems determined to envision time and space as competing cultural values rather than intertwined facts of life. The political salience of speed is not just a theoretical matter. When time is approached from below, based on a cultural approach to the everyday, the anxiety over speed looks very different. Individualistic orientations toward time and its management have normalized the exploitation of others' time.

These dual concerns, in theory and everyday culture, are the impetus for *In the Meantime*'s introduction of power-chronography as a way of locating how temporality operates as a key relation of power that manifests in the minutes, days, and lifetimes of different populations. Time is lived at the intersection of a range of social differences that includes class, gender, race, immigrations status, and labor. A temporal perspective offers insight into inequality and recognizes the transecting multidimensionality of social differences. Once acknowledged, the temporal is discernible everywhere.

The Terms of the Temporal

The discourse of speedup is not likely to slow down. Critical thought is replete with spatial metaphors for understanding and naming power: sites, grounds, locations, places, nodes, flows, networks, and formations. The perspective I have offered in this book is an opening to consider more closely how power coalesces temporally, and a switch to focus on time requires new temporal terms. The terms of temporality offer a way of keeping differential, lived time within the critical and cultural discussions of time and space. The terms also offer a way of inhabiting the world in time, to name the political struggles over time that have been invisible for far too long. This book exemplified such a perspective by focusing attention on multiple temporalities. The time of business travelers, taxi drivers, yoga instructors, desk workers, and slow lifers were investigated. *In the Meantime* reveals how *temporal inequities* intensify when the dominant way of apprehending time is guided by the discourses of speedup. I found that what most populations encounter is not the fast pace of life but the structural demand that they must *recalibrate* in order to fit into the temporal expectations demanded by various institutions, social relationships, and labor arrangements. There is a looming expectation that everyone must become an entrepreneur of time control within highly differential relationships to time. It is not technological speed that determines one's temporality; instead it results from where one fits within the biopolitical economy of time.

The biopolitical economy of time is maintained by a diffuse set of interlocutors that range across the political spectrum. Examples include workplaces incorporating wellness, pharmaceutical companies creating productivity pills, and upscale slow-food restaurants serving languorous meals. Capital invests in certain temporalities—that is, capital caters to the clock that meters the life and lifestyle of *some* of its workers and consumers. The others are left to recalibrate themselves to serve a dominant temporality.

One of the core features of neoliberalism is widespread disinvestment: the rolling back of the state's regulation of health, welfare, and other public services. But all bodies do not experience such disinvestment in the same way. One of the central paradoxes of neoliberalism is that while the state has disinvested in most bodies, some are reinvested in by more exclusive means through the market. The bodies that are invested in are the ones most vital to contemporary capitalism, precisely because they don't need to work in order to survive. They have enough wealth to survive, but they work in order to conspicuously consume or meet other ideological needs. Across the landscape of everyday life, interventions into time are presented as invitations to experience a novel temporal experience—a midday yoga class, an aromatherapy and light-enhanced plane ride, or a leisurely meal—within a culture that is largely constructed as technologically driven and speeding out of control.

Desk workers, slow lifers, and frequent business travelers are encouraged to exercise an otherwise unknown amount of control over not just their hours of work but also the meaning of time in their lives. This search for a meaningfulness of time is met by an expansive and exclusive *temporal architecture of time maintenance*. Temporal architectures consist of technologies, commodities, policies, plans, and programs as well as the labor of others. Whether manifest in napping pods, yoga at the desk, or a slow-resort holiday, this temporal architecture continuously confirms and maintains the same structures of power that drain, tire, and exploit other people's time, while elevating one group's sense of temporal importance.

Along with new temporal forms of management, there are new forms of temporal exploitation. A temporal perspective offers new insight into the exacerbation of older, persistent structural inequalities. Cab drivers transport the rushed. Hotel maids receive training to deal especially with the jet-lagged. Sleep concierges labor in hotels across the globe. Queue holders make their wages by standing in line for others. Call-center employees straddle multiple time zones in order to uphold the work and leisure demands of people on the other side of the globe. Slow-food restaurants employ sped-up labor; undocumented dishwashers work long hours with little pay.[2] Throngs of immigrant farmers overheat and dehydrate in the fields while picking organic grapes. Some die.[3] Power-chronography forces us to recognize how the off-hours of social possibility become increasingly marginalized for many so that every moment can be made rich, meaningful, and productive for another.

Subjects lacking in temporal worth, such as the ones who need to work in order to survive, have no system of temporal investment to which they can turn. Instead, their temporality is expected to uphold the time of others while existing outside normative time. Rather than being able to call on a capital-devised architecture of time maintenance to meet their needs, they must devise their own mechanisms, what I referred to as *subarchitectures of time maintenance*. Interestingly, it is the taxi drivers' daily experience of time that would best correspond to a life lived "in the instant," but they are the least likely to consider the world out there sped up. For the taxi driver, there is no overarching tempo. There are only the temporal needs of specific others. The drivers struggle to navigate their own time even as it is to a large degree structured around the time demands of others. They sleep in their cars when they can. They depend on an informal economy—a subarchitecture—of rest stops and places to recalibrate. They hold their bladders until they have a good place to park. They limit their water and caffeine intake because they cannot easily take breaks. They speed up and slow down depending on the time demands of their fares, rhythms of the city, and the time of day they drive. For the taxi drivers, the hours of possibility don't extend too far into the future. Lived time is more immediate. There is no time to think about how to balance time. They have a past that they left behind and uncertain prospects. The dream for the future includes a faint hope that they will no longer drive a taxi.

The Temporal Order of Things

The landscape of uneven time that I have untangled in the chapters of this book is held together by a *normalizing temporal order*. Business travelers claim that they fly above the radar of normal time. They refer to their lives and labor in terms of an exceptional temporality that they believe very few others similarly endure. The places in which their lives unfold and the time practices they engage in only work to confirm this notion for them.

It is also by way of reference to a "normal time out there" against which taxi drivers juxtapose their own time. But this normal time is oppressive. Like the business traveler, taxi drivers too feel always outside time with their night labor and seemingly uncivilized and unpublic hours of work. Even though Abraham disliked the daylight and being around what he called "day people," he did acknowledge a sense of an acceptable and valued order of time that he was not part of. Feeling as if he couldn't fit in, slowly becoming more and more averse to daylight and uncomfortable with how people treated him during the day, he eventually preferred to work late at night and into the early morning. Billie made a business out of structuring his life of taxi driving according to this legitimized ordering of time. He wholeheartedly believed in the legitimacy of nine-to-five business hours as the "right time to be in" and would try his hardest to work accordingly.

The inclusion of yoga at the desk both uses the normalizing day as an ostensible site of resistance while upholding it as the ultimate site of balancing work and life. With the inclusion of yoga and spiritual healing in the workday, the desk worker is instructed to delve into the "power of now" in order to deal with the confining spatial and temporal arrangements of their nine-to-five lives. As for the mobile yoga instructors themselves, they "did their time" and are now released from the temporal and spatial confines of the workaday world. They became entrepreneurs of time control and exist to help others create the appropriate dispositions to live better lives within the temporal order of things.

The slow life is laden with a time orientation devoted to protecting against the encroachment of sped-up life beyond the nine-to-five. Slow lifers alternately attempt to get outside the nine-to-five rat race or look for ways to occupy time "mindfully" within this time frame. Slow-living proponents insist that slow choices result from a rational and thoughtful deliberation process. The goal of slow living isn't so much to achieve a Zen-like state of slowness but to gain the ability and the knowledge to choose "when to be slow and when to be fast." Slow lifers, especially in the slow food movement and at the Caretta Shiodome, consider themselves to be making wise, rational, and sensible choices. The political limits of slowness are most fraught when the perfect slow subject seems to be a Cartesian citizen, able to transcend his or her body, in a properly slow and deliberative public sphere.

I want to make a final argument about the political possibilities of the temporal as it has been advanced in this book. To return to where I first began: Harold Adams Innis argues that cultural notions of time and space not only reflect the technological parameters of possibility but also indicate certain imbalances of power. A balanced space-time approach is culturally necessary for democracy in order keep state power and the market in check. Unless a politics of time challenges and resists the boundaries of normalized time, it fails to be an adequate one. A temporal politics needs to be oriented around something much more complex than merely the maintenance of democratic space and keeping separate the spheres of work, life, and leisure.

My final argument, my very last remark, is that we need a radical politics of time and space that hinges upon temporalizing the spatial categories of democracy. The public is a place in which to start the ongoing project of a radical revising. I now turn to two spaces common to civic life: a public library and a subway car. One is a properly public space and the other a space of public transit. The conception of a temporal public I have in mind depends on two main tenets: (1) that we understand all social space as being in transit; and (2) that politicizing how we inhabit time leads to reimagining time as a collective struggle. This would be a politics for the meantime—keenly aware of the hold that structures of power have upon time. It is a politics unsympathetic to such power and careful to acknowledge how the time of others is always at stake.

A Temporal Public

MORNING AT THE VANCOUVER PUBLIC LIBRARY

The downtown branch of the Vancouver Public Library opens weekdays at 10:00 a.m. The atrium outside the library's front entrance is full of coffee shops and restaurants. It gets steadily busy from 7:00 a.m. onward. Every morning the scene is the same. At 9:30 a.m. a mass of people begins to swell. A very large group gathers outside the library doors. Some sit on the floor and others lean against the walls. By 9:45 there is a crowd of fifty. By 9:58 there are often close to a hundred people. The security guards open the door at 9:59. No one enters. Instead, people wait. The people in the front row roll back and forth on their heels while staring up at the clock and waiting for it to strike 10:00. I witness this scene nearly every weekday morning for a month. It takes little time to figure out who these determined library patrons are. They are a small contingent of Vancouver's homeless. They are also mostly men. Instead of book bags and laptops they carry sleeping bags, thermoses, and coolers.

The security guard nods his head at 10:00. A surge of movement fills the quiet space. The group rushes in. They disperse throughout the library.

Some veer left for the elevators. They are on their way up to the limited number of private carousels on the eighth floor of the stacks. Another large group presses ahead. They run up the escalators in a race to get one of the few public terminals for free unlimited Internet. A few turn right and make their way first to the restrooms. None of them speak to each other. They each have their own routines.

After an hour or so, the library is full of people writing, reading, and surfing but also sleeping. The city's homeless have come to the library to sleep. But they sleep under the guise of other activities because sleeping in the public library is not allowed. On the second floor, where the public terminals are located, one man looks busy surfing, his hand on the mouse as he sits erect at the computer. His impeccable posture makes him hard to miss. Yet he is fast asleep. The top floor of the library has carousels that overlook the city streets. By 11:00 they are full. Here too you will find men fast asleep, but at first glance you would never know. They all look as if they are busy at work.

For almost the entire month of June 2011, I too am seated up on this floor working on this book. I get to know the patterns of my carousel neighbors. A Japanese Canadian man in his sixties arrives every single morning. He carries with him more than twenty newspapers and flyers. He spreads them out to cover the entire surface of his carousel. He takes off his shoes and places them off to the side. He puts on his slippers. His newspapers are spread out like a tatami mat for his resting head. He has a thermos and a cup of tea off to the side against the window. From a certain angle it looks as if he is busily immersed in research, scouring the city's newspapers. This carousel doubles as his *royokan* (a Japanese inn). It is his place to sleep. A few carousels down, there is another man, this one much younger, with his own variation on this theme. He too is fast asleep. He looks to be buried deep in his books cramming for some exam. He has created an even greater screen of privacy, with stacks of books on all sides of his table. The stack is so high that he is able to remain quite hidden. The books block the light coming through the windows, helping to turn day into night.

The security guards walk around the perimeter of the library and through the stacks. The guards know the sleepers, and the guards know what the sleepers are doing. But if these tired souls *appear* to be spending their library time wisely, they will not be asked to leave. Sometimes these patrons hide from the guards as they shuffle the contents of their bags, groom in the bathroom, and take care of other basic needs that don't fall under the rubric of acceptable use of this public space during its working hours—the time in which the normalizing temporality is wide awake and hard at work. The rules of the temporal order are well established. Overall, the Vancouver Public Library is well-known as a progressive space in the city, in part for being open to the homeless. One of its explicit civic-minded mandates is to provide both shelter and activities for the homeless during the day. The very design of the library lends itself well to this. Shaped like the Roman Colosseum, it has pockets of shelter to get out of bad weather and provides hidden spaces outside in which to catch up on sleep.

As the security guards secure the space, they secure a *temporal order*. The library's progressive stance on the city's homeless is ultimately spatial. The city provides space, so long as one stays correctly in time. The unstated order is about a moral use of time oriented around being productive.

A RIDE ON THE E TRAIN

In Brooklyn, day laborers refer to the E train as *hotel ambulante* (the roving hotel). The train has become a place to take shelter in order to catch some hours of sleep, rest one's body, or maybe even eat a meal. Due to the recession and the loss of temporary dwellings for many of the city's undocumented workers, this line in New York City's public-transit system has become a significant node within the undocumented worker's temporal infrastructure, a point in the subtemporal architecture of time maintenance for "meantime" temporalities. As the longest ride in the New York City subway, it is more temporally compatible to the laborers' needs than the city's shelters. Sitting down for the entire ride is an everyday strategy of recalibration for many migrant laborers living and working in New York City. In fact, sleeping on the subway is where many New Yorkers recalibrate.[4] But there is public outcry over the supposed nuisance of these "undesirables" sleeping on trains while others are trying to "get to work."[5] When migrant workers are asleep on the E train, they do not signify a hard day or night of work. They signal a life lived outside acceptable and normalized modes of being productive.

The city's shelters are central to the spatial ordering of the city's denizens. The shelters are there to offer protection, but they are also there to keep people in place and, more important to my argument, to keep them in time. The inhabitants cannot come and go freely at all hours of the day. For the migrant workers, staying in the shelters means they will not be able to get out early enough to look for work. The shelters' hours of operation deem the beginning of the laborer's day as part of the (normalized) night. But by six in the morning, the most lucrative jobs, ones that would last the whole day, are gone. Starting later in the day, when the shelter doors are open for those needing to leave, means that the labor for the day will last into the night. Long hours into the night will exceed the "acceptable" curfew. The shelters' spatial provisions—locked doors during night hours—is absolutely necessary given these laborers' particular predicaments, but they are incongruent to laborers' temporalities. The hours of operation for shelters reflect a normalized conception of what constitutes the parameters of an ordinary "day." The shelters adhere to a temporal order that these laborers actually toil to maintain for others, yet this very temporal order is exclusionary to laborers' specific temporal requirements.

The day laborers' chronopolitical dilemmas are compounded by their geopolitical predicament. Day laborers risk being identified and deported if they stay at certain shelters. In the train they have less chance of sleep but a better chance of anonymity.[6] Hotel ambulante is indicative of the greater geopolitical and chronopolitical tension these laborers continuously balance. Immigration status is itself based on a set of spatial exclusions and restrictions, but they are temporally experienced. And immigrants' temporal experiences go well beyond being out of the rhythm of the temporal order. They include the inability to secure other forms of temporal maintenance, such as health care. Being out of place is experienced as a form of temporal disinvestment. It is an enduring temporal and spatial predicament.

The shelter, the library, and the train are all part of the spatial ordering of daily life in the city. But these examples reveal that the ordering and regulation of populations is also temporal. There is a cultural expectation that people must do their best at all times to fit within the temporal order. One must appear to be properly in time while out in public. For Vancouver's homeless, their ability to adhere to a temporal order ultimately allows them space for relief. Both populations are given space as a solution to their predicament—shelter and public space. But what they need is attention to their temporal plights and predicaments. The laborers in the hotel ambulante and the homeless in the Vancouver Public Library are not trying to convene a public, nor are they trying to keep up with the pace of technological speedup and accelerated capitalism. Instead they are employing strategies of staying in time, but they are also using time as a strategy of survival. These spatial forms of outreach are in some ways out of synch with the very populations for which they exist. They are indicative of a cultural imbalance in how to approach space and time. There is no amount of space or free time that can alleviate the fact that these two populations, Vancouver's homeless and New York City's undocumented underclass, are out of time.

PUBLICS IN TIME

A confining spatial canopy hangs over the political imaginary. Public-sphere theorists, philosophers, occupiers, outreach workers, public-space activists, and airport designers all sustain the same ideal of shared space.[7] Shared space is quite often treated as an intrinsic social good, the condition of possibility for democracy. In her intervention with theories of democracy and publics in the 1990s, Iris Marion Young argued that the imagined unity of deliberative democracy is falsely exaggerated.[8] Instead, she maintained, "the unity that motivates politics is the facticity of people being thrown together, finding themselves in geographical proximity and economic interdependence such that activities and pursuits of some affect the ability of others to conduct their activities. A polity consists of people who live together, who are stuck with one another."[9] But as *In the Meantime* has shown, there is no common experience of time, no universal free time in which the spatialized ideals of democracy and social change can be realized. In short, the radical revising of the public via spatial pluralism requires temporal pluralism.

While publics are currently almost solely understood as spatial constructs, they are also temporal. That publics have power-chronographies necessitates a balanced conception of public space-time. To recognize the power-chronography of it all is to acknowledge that time is a structuring relation of power, exercised over the self and others. Power-chronography challenges a conception of productive political space as that space where differences collide in equal terms by virtue of shared space. While we may share space and time in a certain snapshot of social life or in the crossing of trajectories, on another fundamental level the dream of shared space occurs at the expense of acknowledging the uneven time politics that underlie coming together in space.[10] More often than not, the sharing of space and a moment in time with one another is part of a synchronic relation of power.

To fixate on a space for free time is politically futile, and it is also central to maintaining inequitable temporal politics. This book has made questionable the politics and ethics of imagining an autonomous free time true to any one individual. The *temporal public* is an understanding of the public oriented around a *nonautonomous time*. A sufficiently critical temporal politics does not recognize free time in a public space but rather a relational time, one that is tangled and layered, bound to the time of others.

PUBLICS IN TRANSIT

A temporal public approaches all spaces as transit spaces. It is important to remember that speed theory posits transit space as public space's denigrated Other. Transit spaces are pacified places of hypermobility—the subway car, the airport terminal—*free* from the constraints of local time and geographical world space. But a temporal public is not based on the oppositions between public space and private space. Rather, a temporal public recognizes that all social spaces produce publics. In what we traditionally recognize as transit spaces (airports, hotels, shopping malls, train stations, bus depots) multiple states of temporal being exist: waiting, having time on your hands, transcending time, catching up on time, sleeping, and taking time out.

At the airport many labor to support airplane schedules: ground-traffic control, security personnel, baggage loaders, taxi drivers, hotel maids, and flight attendants, to name a few. These populations undergo related shifts in their own experiences of space and time. Further, they have different horizons of political possibility tied to where they exist within a larger temporal order. Who they are changes depending on where these spaces are and which temporality their own labor works to maintain. Thus, within a temporal public the geopolitical and chronopolitical are not dueling characteristics, with one being virtuous (space) and the other democratic deleterious (time). Instead, there is a complex relationship between the two. And it is an enduring one. The composition of temporal labor and the architecture of time maintenance differ by location. In Raleigh-Durham, where I live, the shoe shiners servicing the frequent business travelers at the airport are African American men. In Toronto, the shoe shiners are older South Asian men. A spatio-temporal politics would explain why each population is placed and calibrated in the shoe-shiner role in two very different cultural situations.[11] Transit spaces are the concrete edifices of mediation and mobility, the material spaces where capital, people, goods, and information circulate. While transit spaces act as the switch points for global capital, they also house very specific local relations. They are key sites for the governing and institutionalizing of the temporal order. They are also replete with the contradictions of that order's contents, the multiple temporalities or itineraries, as they intersect and cross. A conception of the public that recognizes these relations has far more political potential than the tendency to disregard them as merely being symptomatic of apolitical practices that threaten so-called true public space. As this project has shown, politicizing the public means addressing time-space, not just a space.

Power-chronography puts otherwise *imagined* stable places, spaces that are not usually recognized as transit spaces, like the home and the private sphere, in flux because it foregrounds the relationships among the multiple temporalities present while it detangles them. With a temporal imaginary, spaces that we do not normally conceive of in terms of transit become highly politicized spaces of movement—places like the workplace, the home, and the organic grocer. Treating all social spaces as transit spaces allows for recognition of the temporal contingency of political or public life. It also allows for recognition of the layers of temporal interdependencies as a particular form of power that plays out in private life. The temporal gives insight into inequities occurring behind closed doors.[12] The home, for example, can be seen for what it is—a space composed of multiple temporalities that is also a node within the circulation of goods, capital, information, and people. If the home is a space where people work, hire cleaners or other forms of domestic help, do online banking, and get packages delivered by commercial enterprises, then it is a space of transit. Understanding the home as a space of transit politicizes the space in a new way. It means that gendered relations in the home become differently perceptible through the lens of time. It means that labor relations are revealed in new ways. Having one's home and yard attended to during the week so the weekend can be spent in leisurely pursuits needs to be understood within a political economy of time. As I have been arguing, there are gendered, raced, and classed itineraries of temporal worth within a heteronormative patriarchal global capital. The temporal public is a theory of the public that is awake to the politics of differential time.

Inhabiting the World in Time

Several years after power-geometry changed the way space was conceived across the disciplines, Doreen Massey argued, in *For Space*, that we need to recognize coevalness: "Coevalness concerns a stance of recognition and respect in situations of mutual implication. It is an imaginative space of engagement: it speaks of an attitude. And it is informed by a background conceptualization of space and time. It is a political act."[13] She means that no matter how spatially distinct people are, we exist as cotemporaneous subjects—in the same time. A different perspective on time, such as the one advanced in this project, has implications for this coevalness as a political act. To be cotemporaneous must also mean acknowledging the tangles of uneven time. How one is implicated in the bounds of time, in the production of temporal vulnerability for others, must be foregrounded. As a political act, temporally aware coevalness means recognizing one's own place within the landscape of uneven time as a relational temporal position.

In "Building Dwelling Thinking," Heidegger provides an opening for thinking about temporal experience as a form of relational world making. These particular relational sets of temporalities exist in what Heidegger terms "worlds of temporal involvement."[14] In *Being and Time* Heidegger argues that being confirms itself through time, and time becomes the basis of being.[15] The world is not experienced in terms of geographical distance or physical parameters of space. Instead, one's world is measured in terms of "closeness" to what is "ready at hand" and in one's involvement with the "equipment encountered."[16] The experience of the world, what constitutes the world, is temporally contingent. This relation is expressed in terms of a bridge that works as a network to give the opposite landscape meaning. The riverbanks emerge as banks only through the creation of a bridge. A temporal perspective makes visible and significant temporal parameters and temporal worlds of involvement.

Inhabiting the world in time doesn't require an anthropological eye or even a repertoire of theories of time. Nor does it depend on a particular place or pace. It is a way of inhabiting the social world with a temporal awareness—a social world that we can no longer conclude is shared in the same way. Living a politics of time is not a devotion to creating free time but to freeing time from this bind. It means eschewing individualistic notions of my time and your time. It means moving beyond the control and management of time as today's central motivating concern related to time. It considers instead the temporal worlds of involvement that people call forth and gather. In other words, living with a temporal awareness means recognizing how one's management of time has the potential to further diminish the time of others. We must begin to recognize the different demands and invitations to recalibrate as they appear across the social fabric of everyday life. Where are recalibrations negotiated, by whom, and for whom? Rather than relish the new times and new spaces that are promised, or bemoan how little time we have, or think about how to better manage our interpolation into regimes of time management, we must also learn to take a temporal perspective. This is done first by asking what new forms of vulnerability are necessitated by the production of temporal novelties or resistances to speed. Whose time and labor is reorchestrated by changes in pace, whether sped up or slowed down?

A temporal perspective does not try to create more free time; it strives to free time from this fixation. It reimagines time, not as being singularly yours or mine for the taking but as uncompromisingly tethered and collective. The world looks vastly different when it is perceived through the lens of bounded time. In the meantime, I have gotten us only so far. What shall we do now with our entangled time?

Notes

Introduction. Tempo Tantrums

1. Howard Rheingold, *Smart Mobs: The Next Social Revolution: Transforming Cultures and Communities in the Age of Instant Access* (Cambridge: Basic Books, 2003), xiii.

2. The first chapter of Rheingold's *Smart Mobs* is aptly titled "Shibuya Epiphany." It was only after my trip to Shibuya and my own epiphany that I realized that Rheingold had also stood in this intersection to argue for the social possibilities of this accelerated technoculture.

3. Paul Virilio, "The Overexposed City," in Paul Virilio, *Lost Dimension*, trans. Daniel Moshenberg (New York: Semiotext(e)), 9–27.

4. Paul Virilio, *Politics of the Very Worst* (New York: Semiotext(e), 1999), 17.

5. Virilio's *Speed and Politics* (New York: Semiotext(e)), was translated to English in 1986.

6. For Jonathan Crary we are witnessing the end of sleep and the political withdrawal of citizens with the rise of 24/7 capitalism. See his *24/7: Late Capitalism and the Ends of Sleep* (London: Verso, 2013). For Robert Hassan this is a "chronoscopic society" marked by abbreviated thinking and a 24/7 network that governs social life. See his *The Chronoscopic Society: Globalization, Time, and Knowledge in the Network Economy* (New York: Peter Lang, 2003) and his edited volume with Ronald E. Purser, eds. *24/7: Time and Temporality in the Network Society* (Stanford: Stanford University Press, 2007). For Hardt and Negri this 24/7 world reconfigures the political potential of labor. John Tomlinson is concerned with the culture of speed where a balancing between slowness and speed is in order. See his *The Culture of Speed: The Coming of Immediacy* (Thousand Oaks, CA: Sage, 2007). John Armitage and Joanne Roberts find a growing polarization between fast classes and slow classes living between chronotopia and chronodystopia. See their *Living with Cyberspace: Technology and Society in the 21st Century* (New York: Continuum, 2003). Gilles Lipovetksy finds the contemporary "hypermodern." See his *Hypermodern Times*, trans. Andrew Brown (Malden, MA: Polity, 2005). For Zygmunt Bauman these are liquid times full of local corpses and vagabonds stuck in space and

displaced by the new temporal binary that emerges between moving in time, free and weightless, as the kinetic elite and tourists do, and those others weighed down by the heaviness of space. Space is exalted, revered and lamented across the board. See his *Liquid Modernity* (London: Blackwell, 2000). See also James Gleick, *Faster* (New York: Vintage, 1999); the online journal edited by Ben Agger, *Fast Capitalism*, http://www.uta.edu/huma/agger/fastcapitalism/edintro.html. See also Heather Menzies, *No Time: Stress and the Crisis of Modern Life* (Vancouver: Douglas and McIntyre, 2005); Bernard Stiegler, *Technics and Time, 2: Disorientation*. trans. Stephen Barker (Stanford: Stanford University Press, 2009).

7. David Abram, *Spell of the Sensuous: Perception and Language in a More-than-Human World* (New York: Vintage 1997); James W. Carey, *Communication as Culture: Essays on Media and Society* (New York: Routledge, 1989); Peter Galison, *Einstein's Clocks, Poincare's Maps: Empires of Time* (New York: W. W. Norton & Company 2003); Paul Glennie and Nigel Thrift, *Shaping the Day: A History of Timekeeping in England and Wales 1300–1800* (Oxford: Oxford University Press, 2009); Jay Griffiths, *A Sideways Look at Time* (New York: Putnam, 1999); David Harvey, *The Condition of Postmodernity: An Enquiry into the Origins of Cultural Change* (Malden, MA: Blackwell, 1989); Stephen Kern, *The Culture of Time and Space, 1880–1918* (Cambridge: Harvard University Press, 1983); Moishe Postone, *Time, Labor, and Social Domination: A Reinterpretation of Marx's Critical Theory* (New York: Cambridge University Press, 1993); Wolfgang Schivelbusch, *The Railway Journey: The Industrialization and Perception of Time and Space* (Berkeley: University of California Press, 1987); and E. P. Thompson, "Time, Work, Discipline and Industrial Capitalism," *Past and Present* 38 (1967). The relationship between temporality and synchronization is a key current in the histories of changing conceptions of time from the advent of the clock toward the rule of real time and the culture of speed. Underlying these critical histories of temporal synchronization is a notion of time as having once been sacred and continuous but is now fragmented and discontinuous. That time was once something sensuous and free, and could be expressed in a multiple of temporal vernaculars, be it the rising sun or the moon, changing seasons, or the candlelight hours of creative energy between stages of shut-eye documented in histories of sleep in the seventeenth century, is common in romanticizing life before the clock. See Abram, *Spell of the Sensuous*; and A. Rogers Ekirch, *At Day's Close: A History of Nighttime* (New York: Norton and Co., 2005); and Griffiths, *A Sideways Look at Time*. The political-economic history of time considers the governmental power of timekeeping devices to manage, control the conduct survey, and alienate the laboring bodies on shop floors (Thompson, "Time, Work, Discipline and Industrial Capitalism"). This power synchronizes bodies, and also economic systems. The standardization of world time to accommodate the transportation systems of imperial powers, at the expense of local and private times, is often understood as another example of the overriding of sacred time. See also Carey, *Communication as Culture*; Kern, *The Culture of Time and Space*; and Schivelbusch, *The Railway Journey*. Altered perceptions of time, the subsequent maladies of the mind, and the fear that new types of fast traffic would dismember slow-moving passengers were all a part of the imaginary surrounding "high-speed" trains and trams at the beginning of European

industrialization. A more recent history that argues that the industrialization of time was more public than Thompson figured is offered by Glennie and Thrift, *Shaping the Day*.

8. See Enda Duffy, *The Speed Handbook: Velocity, Pleasure, Modernism* (Durham, NC: Duke University Press, 2009).

9. Marshall McLuhan, *Understanding Media: The Extensions of Man* (Cambridge: MIT Press, [1964] 1994), 93.

10. Virilio warns of the tyranny of speed in *Politics of the Very Worst*: "Real-time is not very different from classical tyranny, because it tends to destroy the reflection of the citizen in favor of a reflex action" (87). Telepublics and telepresence are substituted for the slower-paced intersubjectivity of traditional political systems. In *Desert Screen: War at the Speed of Light* (London: Continuum, 2002), he argues "Politics depends upon having time for reflection. Today, we no longer have time to reflect, the things that we see have already happened. And it is necessary to react immediately. Is a real-time democracy possible? An authoritarian politics, yes. But what defines democracy is the sharing of power. When there is not time to share, what will be shared." (43).

11. Zygmunt Bauman in *Globalization: The Human Consequences* (New York: Columbia University Press, 1998) maintains that "the inhabitants of the first world live in a perpetual present, going through a succession of episodes hygienically insulated from their past as well as future. These people are constantly busy and perpetually short of time, since each moment in time is non-extensive" (88). As for the slow class, he goes on to say: "People marooned in the opposite world are crushed under the burden of the abundant, redundant and useless time they have nothing to fill with. In their time nothing ever happens. They do not 'control time'—but neither are they controlled by it, unlike the clocking in, clocking out ancestors subject to the faceless rhythm of factory time" (88).

12. Political economists such as Vincent Mosco and Herbert Schiller provide important correctives to the aphoristic work of theorists like Virilio, Bauman, and McLuhan. Mosco in *The Digital Sublime: Myth, Power, and Cyberspace* (Cambridge: MIT Press, 2005), argues that these "cosmic thinkers," like Virilio and others in the style of McLuhan, continue to provide the digital age and its forms of sociality their "sacred canopy" (82). In general, the work of Mosco and Schiller is an important reminder of the uncritical assertions regarding the "death of geography" and the "end of history" that continues to animate critical analyses of new media and technology.

13. Suggestively, Mosco asks: "History, the rough and tumble analog of bodies, classes, and power gives way to a new digital beginning. Or does it?" *The Digital Sublime* (82). While the work of political economists is key, it too can remain abstracted from lived experience. In a sense, political economy is unable to fully address Mosco's analog world of bodies and power. I suggest that a biopolitical analysis of temporality allows for an embodied political-economic analysis because it places the body at the center of capitalist production. See Donald Lowe, *The Body in Late-Capitalist USA* (Durham, NC: Duke University Press, 1995).

14. Moishe Postone (*Time, Labor, and Social Domination*) has investigated capital and finance in terms of the role of clocks and other timekeeping devices to control

workers. Part of this analysis includes attention to the new social formations that arise because of accelerated capital and technologies, including the changing quantity of labor time versus leisure time. He aligns with Marx's formulation of socially necessary time: "Socially necessary labor time is then the labor time required to produce any use value under the condition of production normal for a given society and with the average degree of skill and intensity prevalent in that society." Karl Marx, *Capital: Volume 1; A Critique of Political Economy 1867* (London: Penguin, 1992), 129. Socially necessary labor time becomes the key site of measuring changes in the speed of human activity.

15. See Thompson, "Time, Work, and Industrial Capitalism." The process of synchronization has been relayed through the example of England and the imposition of world standard time (see Carey, *Communication as Culture*; Kern, *Culture of Time*, 1983; and Schivelbusch, *The Railway Journey*). These critical histories of synchronization provide an opening to examine the micropolitics of synchronization at the level of everyday interactions. The synchronizing of natural time to capital's time is understood as having an asynchronous pattern and effect. In *The Real World of Technology* (Toronto: Anansi, 1999), Ursula Franklin writes: "Now we have the prevalence of asynchronicity—indicated by the loosening if not abandonment, of previously compulsory time and space patterns" (151). She asserts that the pattern of temporal being changes from a synchronous being in sync with one another and the earth's movement to the decoupling of patterns and sequences from their essential functions. In other words, a true and natural relationship to time is increasingly threatened.

16. See Adrian Mackenzie's *Transductions: Bodies and Machines at Speed* (New York: Continuum, 2002), he moves beyond the clock and considers the mediation of time broadly. For Mackenzie, all "technical mediation, insofar as it folds, deforms and shifts relations between living and non-living elements of a sociotechnical ensemble, eventualizes times and spaces." (95).

17. Kern, *Culture of Time and Space*. See also Michelle Bastian, "Fatally Confused: Telling the Time in the Midst of Ecological Crises," *Journal of Environmental Philosophy* 9, no. 1 (2012).

18. I want to acknowledge here the important work being done in queer theory on temporality. Most significantly Judith Halberstam's and Lee Edelman's work on queer temporality acknowledges this sense of temporal difference and bodies who are out of time. See for example, Judith Halberstam, *In a Queer Time and Place: Transgender Bodies, Subcultural Lives* (New York: New York University Press, 2005) and Lee Edelman, *No Future: Queer Theory and the Death Drive* (Durham, NC: Duke University Press, 2004). However, there is still a power-chronography to the forms of temporal normativity and queer temporality that they point to in their work. Power-chronography is a potentially useful political concept for getting at the political economy and labor politics of heteronormative temporality. See also Shannon Bell, *Fast Feminism* (New York: Autonomedia, 2010) for a critical discussion on the feminist liberatory potential of speedup. See also Kath Weston's *Gender in Real Time: Power and Transience in a Visual Age* (New York: Routledge, 2002) where she advocates for a more nuanced conception of gendered space-time.

19. Doreen Massey first mentions power-geometry in 1991 in her article "Global

Sense of Place" in *Marxism Today* (June 24, no. 38), 24–29. Like the chronograph that keeps time and stops time, power-chronography is interested in this mastery at the level of individual micropolitics and the various ways that individuals attempt to start, pause, and stop time. *Chronograph* is derived from the Greek words *chronos* (time) and *graph* (chart). A chronograph is a watch or timepiece that functions as a both a timekeeper and as a stopwatch. To put it simply, a chronograph can measure time in more ways than one. A chronograph dial has several subdials with a scale. A central second hand can be started and stopped without interfering with the continuous time. Power-chronography allows us to see that in a finite human life there are only subdials of time control.

20. Doreen Massey, *Space, Place, and Gender* (Minneapolis: University of Minnesota Press, 1994), 149.

21. Massey, *Space, Place, and Gender*, 151.

22. Massey, *Space, Place, and Gender*, 165.

23. Neil Smith's work on uneven time makes a similar intervention into such theories of time-space compression that Massey is also objecting to. See Neil Smith, *Uneven Development: Nature, Capital, and the Production of Space* (Athens: University of Georgia Press, 2008).

24. Massey makes implicit that a politics of space depends on how one conceives of the object. For her, social space is understood "in terms of the articulation of social relations which necessarily have a spatial form in their interactions with one another." She goes on: "One way of thinking about place is as particular moments in such intersecting social relations" (*Space, Place, and Gender*, 120). Power-geometry makes possible a similar intervention into the temporal. The geographies of intersection that result from Massey's work provide an opening to move beyond speed to consider how the temporal operates as a form of material social struggle. Massey's power-geometry is a powerful corrective to a dominating and difficult spatial imaginary, but it does not necessarily offer a means to deal with the privileging of space across the disciplines. This is not a lack or a limit of Massey's work—instead, it is a necessary next intervention. In her later work, *For Space* (Thousand Oaks, CA: Sage, 2005), Massey promotes a politics based on a sense of co-temporality, of being alive at the same time. If there is a potential politics to recognizing co-temporality, the interdependencies of time need more attention. Power-chronography, as I conceive of it, is a means to finally balance space-time—to realize Massey's invoking of space-time.

25. Edward Soja has summarized the spatial turn as "an attempt to develop a more creative and critically effective balancing of the spatial/geographical and the temporal/historical imaginations." Edward Soja, "Taking Space Personally," in *The Spatial Turn: Interdisciplinary Perspectives*, ed. B. Warf and S. Arias (New York: Routledge, 2009), 12.

26. Even when time is treated as multiple in various social theories, such as in Barbara Adam's *Timewatch: The Social Analysis of Time* (Cambridge, UK: Polity, 1995), or in need of protection as in James Carey's work on the Sabbath (*Communication as Culture*), time is not treated as differential relation of power.

27. Ronald Walter Greene, in an introduction to a special issue on spatial materialism in the journal *Critical Studies in Media Communication*, wonderfully articulates the

limits of the turn, one that we might understand as spinning on its head: "Today, the spatial turn is a well-recognized commonplace. As such, taking a spatial turn seems less like going off the beaten track and more like entering a busy and congested intersection of inquiry." Ronald Walter Greene, "Spatial Materialism: Labor, Location, and Transnational Literacy," *Critical Studies in Media Communication* 27, no. 1 (2010): 105. See also Tim Cresswell's *On the Move: Mobility in the Modern Western World* (New York: Routledge, 2006), which argues that mobility is not just a spatial dynamic; to look at mobility is to study both spatialized time and temporalized space.

28. Nigel Thrift, "Time and Theory in Human Geography: Part I," *Progress in Human Geography* 65 (1977): 65.

29. Torsten Hägerstrand, *Innovation Diffusion as a Spatial Process*, trans. A. Pred (Chicago: University of Chicago Press, 1967). Hägerstrand was ultimately concerned with bringing to geography questions of embodiment and quality of life that only time, or a balanced space-time approach, could articulate. His conceptualizations and mapping of different space-time paths made the ways in which individuals encounter their environments politically significant. See also Alan Pred, ed. *Space and Time in Geography: Essays Dedicated to Torsten Hägerstran* (Lund, Sweden: CWK Gleerup, 1981) and Don Parkes and Nigel Thrift, *Times, Spaces, and Places* (New York: John Wiley, 1980).

30. Nigel Thrift, "Owners Time and Own Time: The Making of Capitalist Time Consciousness, 1300–1880," in *Space and Time in Geography: Essays Dedicated to Torsten Hägerstrand*, ed. Allan Pred (Lund, Sweden: CWK Gleerup, 1981).

31. See Mike Crang, "Rhythms of the City: Temporalized Space and Motion," in *TimeSpace: Geographies of Temporality*, ed. Jon May and Nigel Thrift (London: Routledge, 2001), 187–207; and Mike Crang, T. Crosbie, and S. D. N. Graham, "Technology, Timespace and the Remediation of Neighbourhood Life," *Environment and Planning A* 39 (2007).

32. In *The Bias of Communication* (Toronto: University of Toronto Press, 1951), Harold Innis argues that in order for a civilization to endure, it has to maintain a balance between space and time. The introduction of a new media, by altering the space-time bias, would ultimately transform the culture; therefore it was necessary to maintain a sense of balance through homeostasis—wherein one media checks or offsets the next. For example, Innis maintains that because of the way the printing press was institutionalized in the United States, with a disregard for the necessary balance between space and time, the possibilities for homeostasis in the United States remained forever bleak. Innis reminds us that the time-changing and space-altering capacities of new technologies, as they link to capitalism and the spread of economic and cultural empires, is not the end point of thinking about the relationships between technologies, culture, and power. Rather, it is a place to start thinking from.

33. Innis, *The Bias of Communication*, 6. For a discussion on the centrality of Innis to media and cultural studies see Jody Berland, *North of Empire: Essays on the Cultural Technologies of Space* (Durham, NC: Duke University Press, 2009).

34. To summarize Innis, the rise of a particular complex of media forms arise out of social, economic, and cultural struggles that are tied to physical geography as well as different forms of political organization. See Harold A. Innis, *A History of the Cana-*

dian Pacific Railway (Toronto: University of Toronto Press, 1971). At heart, Innis was a political economist of media technology who recognized the importance of culture as the strategic ground where ideas about time and space are formed. See Harold A. Innis, *Empire and Communication* (Toronto: University of Toronto Press, 1950/1972).

35. Innis, *Empire and Communication*, 7.

36. Innis, *Bias of Communication*, 24.

37. Publics figure almost exclusively within the theoretical imaginary as spatial constructs. Delineations are made between ideal publics and the other space: for the public sphere (agora) and the private sphere (oikos), see Jürgen Habermas, *Structural Transformations of the Public Sphere* (Cambridge: MIT Press, 1999); for public space and oppositional space, see Nancy Fraser, "Rethinking the Public Sphere: A Contribution to the Critique of Actually Existing Democracy," in *Habermas and the Public Sphere*, ed. C. Calhoun (Cambridge: MIT Press, 1992); for anthropological public space and nonplace, see Marc Augé *Non-places: Introduction to an Anthropology of Supermodernity* (London: Verso, 1995), and for public space and speed spaces, see Chris Decron, "Speed-Space," in *Virilio Live: Selected Interviews*, ed. John Armitage (London: Sage, 2001), 69–81. The spatial logic of liberal democracy is also evident in the constant questioning of where publics might be—are they local, global, subaltern, national, or regional? Are they here or are they there? Is the television talk show a new public space (Sonia Livingstone and Peter Lunt *Talk on Television: Audience Participation and Public Debate*, [London: Routledge, 1993]) and what about the Internet today (Mark Poster, *Information Please: Culture and Politics in the Age of Digital Machines*, [Durham, NC: Duke University Press 2006])? The newest technologies looming on the horizon are often met with questions of how they might change social space and the ways that individuals interact with each other in space (Adriana de Souza de Silva and Jordan Frith, *Mobile Interfaces in Public Spaces: Locational Privacy, Control, and Urban Sociability*, [New York: Routledge, 2006]).

38. For example, see the chapters by Seyla Benhabib, Michael Warner, Craig Calhoun, and Nancy Fraser in Craig Calhoun, ed., *Habermas and the Public Sphere* (Cambridge: MIT Press, 1992).

39. See William Scheuerman, *Liberal Democracy and the Social Acceleration of Time* (Baltimore, MD: The Johns Hopkins University Press, 2004).

40. See for example, Sheldon Wolin's essay "What Time Is It?" in *Theory and Event*, Vol. 1. Issue 1, 1997. The essay captures perfectly the normalizing democratic expectation that there must be shared time within a political constituency. Wolin points out the disjuncture between political time and the time of the social and advocates for the necessity of slow time.

41. See Nicholas Garnham, *Emancipation, the Media, and Modernity: Arguments about the Media and Social Theory* (New York: Oxford University Press, 2000). Garnham insists the bourgeois public sphere becomes a new political class precisely because it is able to sustain itself through a network of institutions of civil society, such a coffee houses, libraries, and newspapers. Underlying the ideal of the public sphere is the guarantee of free time that being a private citizen promises.

42. See Arjun Appadurai, *Modernity at Large: Cultural Dimensions of Globalization*

(Minneapolis: University of Minnesota Press, 1996); Manuel Castells, *The Rise of the Network Society* (Malden, MA: Blackwell, 1996); Saskia Sassen, *Globalization and Its Discontents* (New York: New Press, 1998); and Saskia Sassen, "Spatialities and Temporalities of the Global: Elements for a Theorization," *Public Culture* 12, no. 1 (Winter 2000). Sassen's work on globalization has also provided extensive and wonderful accounts of the spatial and temporal politics of the modern in the context of globalization or multiple modernities. She considers the different temporalities inherent in the local, the nation, and the global. But in all of these works, the element of time is about rapidity or speeds or spatialized time, even if the sense is of multiple modernities that flow into each other. The multiplicity of temporalities that power-chronography investigates is not the layers of time of the modern or those brought on because of different spatial boundaries or entities.

43. Lisa Parks's "Kinetic Screens: Epistemologies of Movement at the Interface" in *Media/Space: Place, Scale and Culture in a Media Age*, ed. Nick Couldry and Anna McCarthy (London: Routledge, 2004), is an invaluable book chapter with affinities to my approach to power-chronography. Parks's chapter focuses on computer and television waste as a new way to conceive of "life at the interface," which challenges the media studies work that continues to focus on the privileged itinerary of the surfer, for example.

Appadurai posits five scapes or imagined worlds to account for different dimensions of cultural flows in *Modernity at Large*: ethnoscapes (movement of people from groups as diverse as tourists and refugees), mediascapes (distribution of information), technoscapes (technology's rate of speed across borders), financescapes (disposition of global capital to move rapidly), and ideoscapes (the role of the imagination in the context of these flows, where lines between fictional and real landscapes are blurred). For Appadurai, the individual actor is "the last locus of this perspectival set of landscapes" but these landscapes "are eventually navigated by agents who both experience and constitute larger formations, in part from their own sense of what these landscapes offer" (33). Important for power-chronography is that these are perspectival constructs that have to do with a range of actors, from intimate face-to-face groups to diasporic communities to multinational corporations. Nonetheless, Appadurai's focus on scapes is ultimately spatial.

44. Examining how individuals and social groups experience time differently has been a predominant theme in anthropology, sociology, philosophy, and geography. Barbara Adam, a key sociologist of time, has been a leading theorist of examining the differences time makes. Adam's theory of the timescape ascertains that space, time, and context are mutually and equally important. She works to grasp the multiplicity of timescapes and multiplicity of social times that constitute the world in varying differentiations: biology, gender, environment, digital time, body time, clock time, and social time. See Barbara Adam, *Time and Social Theory* (Cambridge, UK: Polity, 1990); and Barbara Adam, *Timewatch: The Social Analysis of Time* (Cambridge, UK: Polity, 1995). Similarly, the work of Adam has been critical in pointing out how the gendered nature of social times often translates into experiences of temporal Othering, wherein access to public life is negated. See Barbara Adam, *Time* (London: Blackwell,

2004). Adam's work is linked to other important research on different organizations of time, beyond the phenomenological and existential frameworks, where the relationship between temporality and knowledge in the everyday lifeworld is central. See, for example, Carole Greenhouse, *A Moment's Notice: Time Politics across Cultures* (Ithaca, NY: Cornell University Press, 1996). Adam also has some affinities with the time geographers and the chronogeographic school of thought. Their focus is largely on how people differently experience different temporalities and social times that in turn reflect different relationships to knowledge and different positions within the network of intersubjective relations. See also Pierre Bourdieu, "The Attitude of the Algerian Peasant Toward Time," in *Mediterranean Country Men*, ed. J. Pitt-Rivers (Paris: Mouton and Co. 1963). The chronogeographers relay how there are differences yet these differences aren't understood as systemic. Adam, on the other hand, argues that contemporary social theories are too firmly embedded in Newtonian science and classical dualist philosophy to adequately account for the contemporary world of standardized time, nuclear power, computers, and global telecommunication. In Henri Lefebvre's rhythm analysis, time is a rhythm that occupies a given space. For Lefebvre, rhythm is a relation of a time within a space, a localized time, or if one wishes, a temporalized place. See Henri Lefebvre, *Rhythmanalysis: Space, Time and Everyday Life*, trans. S. Elden and G. Moore (Continuum: London, 2004), 230. Rhythms are to be listened to and analyzed. They can be heard, but not seen. His focus was on comparative rhythms.

This notion of a hierarchy of time similar to the speed theorists' was prevalent in sociology in the 1980s with Jeremy Rifkin's *Time Wars: The Primary Conflict in Human History* (New York: Simon and Schuster, 1987). There, he argued, an impending social conflict was on the horizon between the time rich and time poor. In terms of different experiences of time, Edward T. Hall's popular *Dance of Life: The Other Dimension of Time* (New York: Anchor, 1983) presents different cultural attributes to varying international approaches to time. The problem with these intercultural or comparative approaches is that time is spatialized to be discrete rather than interdependently experienced and structurally tied. Time is treated as if it were subject to a spatialized linearity where different peoples, civilizations, populations, and places are imagined to be behind the times. Temporal explanations for difference have too often depended on articulating time to specific groups—colored people's time is slower, women's time is fluid, and entire ethnic groups are relegated to the past. The focus on singular identities leads to the anachronistic tendency that Johannes Fabian refers to in *Time and the Other* (New York: Columbia University Press, 1983), where he outlines the tension within ethnology where the referent is always placed in a time other than the present of the informer. Temporal differences are either reduced to essential biological functions or examined for how they can be brought up to speed. While there are exciting potentials here, the focus in power-chronography is concerned with the interdependence of rhythms. Power-chronography does not provide a comparative analysis of discrete forms of time. Instead the experience of time and discourses about time are understood to be always-already relational.

45. Massey, *Space, Place, and Gender*, 148.

46. Massey points out that "different social groups, and different individuals, are placed in very distinct ways in relation to these flows and interconnections," 149.

47. Joel Garreur, "The Great Awakening: With a Pill Called Modafinil, You Can Go 40 Hours Without Sleep—and See into the Future," *Washington Post*, accessed June 17, 2002. http://wallycourie.com/1Classes%20Fall%2004/Drugs/washPost-Provigil.html.

48. Timothy Ferris, *The 4-Hour Workweek: Escape 9–5, Live Anywhere, and Join the New Rich* (New York: Crown Publishers, 2007).

49. Michel Foucault, *The History of Sexuality*, trans. Robert Hurley (New York: Pantheon, 1978), 141.

50. The biopolitics of temporal difference are constituted by differential investments into life by institutions of modern power. Governing occurs through strategies, regulations, and techniques specifically for the management of problems of living. See Nicholas Rose, ed., *Foucault and Political Reason: Liberalism, Neo-liberalism and Rationalities of Government* (Chicago: University of Chicago Press, 1996). Within a biopolitical perspective, we can recognize that capital must make a stake, an investment, into the living life and also lifestyle of its workers and consumers. This stake is made by a diffuse set of interlocutors. See also Elizabeth Freeman's definition of *chrononormativity* as the "the use of time to organize individual human bodies into maximum productivity" in *Time Binds: Queer Temporalities, Queer Histories* (Durham NC: Duke University Press, 2010), 3.

51. Lauren Berlant in "Slow Death (Sovereignty, Obesity, Lateral Agency)," *Critical Inquiry* 33, no. 4 (2007) builds on Foucault and forefronts the temporal aspects of biopower. Berlant, who was especially concerned with obesity as a chronic and terminal condition under capital, defines biopower in the context of this slow expenditure of bodies. It is the "scene of administration, discipline, and recalibration of what constitutes health" (756). The sacrifice of bodies within the machinery of capital does not occur as a fast catastrophe, a crisis of the labor force of capital. It instead occurs at a slow and arduous pace.

52. Foucault "Chapter 11" of *Society must be Defended: Lectures at the College de France 1975–1976*, ed. Mauro Bertani and Alessandro Fontana (New York: Penguin, 2003), 239–264.

53. For a discussion of the most recent forms of labor that are getting outsourced see Arlie Hochschild's *The Outsourced Self: Intimate Life in Market Times* (New York: Metropolitan Books, 2012).

54. Innis, *Bias of Communication*, 33–34.

Chapter One. Jet-Lag Luxury

1. See John D. Kasanda and Greg Lindsay, *Aerotropolis: The Way We'll Live Next* (New York: FSG, 2011). It is also interesting to note that as early as 1927, U.S. corporations were reconfiguring the sky as a means for reaching "some distant meeting place in advance of business competition." Alastair Gordon, *Naked Airport: A Cultural History of the World's Most Revolutionary Structure* (New York: Metropolitan Books, 2004), 33. By the 1960s the airport was proclaimed a "city for businessmen" and the *Wall Street Jour-*

nal had a new name for this itineratti, the "corporate gypsies" (Gordon, *Naked Airport*, 186). The livability and workability of transit space has been encapsulated by the architectural term *dwelltime*. As Justine Lloyd writes, "Instead of experiencing waiting time as wasted time, which inevitably leads to boredom and alienation from one's environment, the urban traveler is invited to use transit time to accumulate useful experiences of leisure and work." Justine Lloyd, "Dwelltime: Airport Technology, Travel, and Consumption," *Space and Culture* 6, no. 2 (2003), 94. As dwelltime goods and services increase, the space becomes familiar to the ebb and flow of everyday life. It accounts for the fact that you can go to church, shop, eat, get a manicure, work, and even get a prescription filled. In fact, *layover lifestyle*, a term coined by the *New York Times* journalist Joshua Kurlantzick, is meant to capture this new investment into waiting time at the airport. See his "Project Runway," *New York Times*, March 29, 2007, accessed March 29, 2010, http://www.nytimes.com/interactive/2007/03/29/travel/escapes/20070330_AIRPORT_SLIDESHOW.html.

2. See Marc Augé, *Non-places: Introduction to an Anthropology of Supermodernity* (London: Verso, 1995); M. Crawford, "The World in a Shopping Mall," in *Variations on a Theme Park: The New American City and the End of Public Space*, ed. M. Sorkin (New York: Hill and Wang); Mark Gottdeiner, *Life in the Air: Surviving the New Culture of Air Travel* (Lanham, MD: Rowman and Littlefield, 2000); Fredric Jameson, *Postmodernism, or, The Cultural Logic of Late Capitalism* (Durham, NC: Duke University Press, 1991); and Paul Virilio, *Pure War* (New York: Semiotext(e), 1997). A great quote that captures a similar sentiment found in all of this work is by Gottdiener: "Could the airport, as a distinct milieu that is increasingly dwelled in as we adjust to lives spent in air travel, be helping to create or amplify a new social character—the uncaring detached, self-contained individual armed with a laptop, walk-man, credit cards, cellular phone, Palm Pilot and business agenda?" (34).

3. Paul Virilio, *Crepuscular Dawn* (New York: Semiotext(e), 2002), 74.

4. Paul Virilio, *Pure War* (LA: Semiotext(e), 1997), 77–79.

5. Virilio, *Pure War*, 77.

6. Manuel Castells's *The Rise of the Network Society* (Malden, MA: Blackwell, 1996) draws attention toward the increasing socioeconomic power of a rising class of itinerant elite who are linked together by their time-sharing practices. The airport exists within the "connecting lines of the spaces of flows" (417). For Castells, the airport's first-class business lounges and VIP services for international business were part of a larger development of "secluded space across the world along the connecting lines of the spaces of flows" so that "the traveler is never lost; and a system of travel arrangements, secretarial services, and reciprocal hosting that maintains a close circle of the corporate elite together through the worshipping of similar rites in all countries" (417).

7. John Naisbit. *High-Tech/High-Touch: Technology and our Accelerated Search for Meaning*. (Boston: Nicholas Brealey, 2001).

8. Annie Davies, "The Bra that won't get alarm bells ringing" in *The Telegraph* (May 18 2002), http://www.telegraph.co.uk/travel/724269/Bra-that-wont-set-alarm-bells-ringing.html. Accessed June 19, 2013.

9. Stephen Arterburn and Sam Gallucci, *Road Warrior: How to Keep Your Faith, Relationships, and Integrity When Away from Home* (Colorado Springs, CO: WaterBrook Press, 2008).

10. Robert L. Jolles, *The Way of the Road Warrior: Lessons in Business and Life from the Road Most Traveled* (San Francisco: John Wiley, 2005).

11. See the websites http://www.womanroadwarrior.com, http://www.globalroadwarrior.com, and http://www.roadwarriortips.com.

12. Kathleen Ameche, *The Woman Road Warrior: A Woman's Guide to Domestic and International Business Travel*, 2nd ed. (Chicago: Agate, 2007).

13. Tracy Clark-Flory, "The End of Menstruation," Salon, February 4, 2008, accessed June 10, 2008, http://www.salon.com/2008/02/04/menstruation_2/.

14. Pico Iyer, *Global Soul: Jet-Lag, Shopping Malls, and the Search for Home* (New York: Vintage, 2001), 160.

15. Francine Parnes, "Constant Travelers Wear Their All-Nighters as a Badge of Pride," *New York Times*, December 6, 2005, accessed September 10, 2010, http://www.nytimes.com/2005/12/06/business/06sleep.html?_r=1.

16. Parnes, "Constant Travelers Wear Their All-Nighters as a Badge of Pride."

17. Air rage, incidents of violence, yelling, and unruly passenger behavior is an increasingly common topic in the travel section of the *New York Times* and CNN's travel reports. These are all part and parcel of the new pathology of air travel related to the intensification of symptoms of jet lag. The jet-lag reduction expert Diana Fairechild argues that air rage is due to recirculated air in the airplane cabin, which causes ear pain, restricts oxygen, and makes deep breathing difficult. See Diana Fairechild, *Jet Smarter*, Flyana Books, 1995.

18. Graham Lawton, "Get Ready for 24-Hour Living," *New Scientist*, February 18, 2006 (39).

19. Alexandra Gill, "Sleep No More," *Globe and Mail*, April 1, 2006, F9.

20. "Sydney research lab 'hotel' to study sleep disorders, "The Telegraph "(Feb. 7 2009). Accessed March 2010. http://www.news.com.au/breaking-news/welcome-to-sydneys-hotel-isolation/story-e6frfkp9-1111118777958.

21. Diana Fairechild, *Jet Smarter*.

22. Michel Foucault, *Care of the Self* (New York: Vintage, 1988), 101.

23. See Nikolas Rose, "Governing 'Advanced' Liberal Democracies," in *Foucault and Political Reason: Liberalism, Neo-liberalism and Rationalities of Government*, ed. Andrew Barry, Thomas Osborne and Nikolas Rose, 37–64 (Chicago: University of Chicago Press, 1996).

24. "Westin Hotels and Resorts Debuts Hotel-Room Laboratory to Combat Jetlag," Westin Hotels and Resorts, press release, June 25, 2008. Accessed March 27, 2010, http://www.newscenter.philips.com/main/standard/about/news/press/20080903_westin_concept_room.wpd.

25. Arthur Estrada, Amanda M. Kelley, Catherine M. Webb, Jeremy R. Athy, and John S. Crowley, "Modafinil as a Replacement for Dextroamphetamine for Sustaining Alertness in Military Helicopter Pilots," *Aviation, Space, and Environmental Medicine* (Vol. 83, No. 6 June 2012), 556–564.

26. Joel Garreau, "The Great Awakening: With a Pill Called Modafinil, You Can Go 40 Hours Without Sleep—and See into the Future," *Washington Post*, June 17, 2002, C1.

27. As quoted in Garreau, "The Great Awakening," C1.

28. Foucault, *Care of the Self*, 99–100.

29. Graham Lawton, "Get Ready for 24-Hour Living," Issue 2539, February 18, 2006, 34–39. Accessed June 19, 2013. http://www.newscientist.com/article/mg18925391.300-get-ready-for-24hour-living.html.

30. Lawton, "Get Ready for 24-Hour Living," 39.

31. See Tim Cresswell, *On the Move: Mobility in the Modern Western World* (New York: Routledge, 2006).

32. Patricia Ticineto Clough, "Introduction" in Patricia Ticineto Clough and Jean Halley, eds., *The Affective Turn: Theorizing the Social* (Durham, NC: Duke University Press, 2007), 4.

33. Rachel Sherman's *Class Acts: Service and Inequality in Luxury Hotels* (Berkeley: University of California Press, 2007) on class and labor at luxury hotels. She refers to this desire for home away from home as indicative of longing for "a fantasy mother's house" where the aspects of care within luxury services are precisely those that are eliminated in the privatization of health care (46–47). Sherman points out that this type of fantasy mother's care, where nothing can go wrong and the individual is nurtured, is the primary source of profit in luxury services.

34. Kerry McDermott, "Now You Can Catch the Dreamliner," *Daily Mail UK Mail Online*, December 14, 2012, accessed June 19, 2013, http://www.dailymail.co.uk/news/article-2247892/Boeing-787-Dreamliner-Qatar-Airways-unveils-jetlag-busting-aircraft-operate-Heathrow.html.

35. Emirates Airlines, "Welcome to Emirates," accessed March 27, 2010, http://www.emirates.com.

36. See Laurie Ouellette and James Hay, *Better Living through Reality TV: Television and Post-welfare Citizenship* (Malden, MA: Blackwell, 2008).

37. See their website http://www.okura.nl/en/services/jetlag-program.html. Accessed June 19, 2013.

38. http://parktoronto.hyatt.com/hyatt/pure/spas/treatments/massage.jsp, http://www.foxprovidence.com/dpp/rhode_show/rhode_show_got_blue_thumbs_pda_massage_20090602. Accessed June 19, 2013.

39. http://www.cntraveler.com/spas/2009/07/Spa-Plus-The-Businessperson. Accessed June 19, 2013.

40. See the "Nemorelax" page of the company website, http://www.nemorelax.com (accessed March 25, 2010). Resting in public is also a common practice in shopping malls with shiatsu-massage chairs in atriums. IKEA has played with the *sovhotel* (the sleep hotel) in busy shopping malls for those who have literally shopped until they've dropped.

41. Jolles, *The Way of the Road Warrior*, 192.

42. For a discussion of these labor practices and circadian rhythm technologies see Martin Moore-Ede, *The Twenty-Four-Hour Society: Understanding Human Limits in a World That Never Stops* (Reading, MA: Addison Wesley, 1993).

43. Alastair Gordon explains the architect John Walter Wood's argument from 1930: "A successful airport, he concluded, should be operated like a 'smoothly functioning organism, providing a steady and fluent movement of aircraft, passengers, merchandise, mail, and surface vehicles'" (Gordon, *Naked Airport*, 104). The airport architect Joseph Hudnot maintains that "passage from airplane to automobile is so direct and so effortless that one is scarcely conscious of an architecture: an experience that which would appear to be happily consistent with the nature of an organization whose merchandise is time" (quoted in Gordon, *Naked Airport*, 104). The airport was imagined as a circulatory machine, in a sense a switch point, where the multiple flows are kept separate and moving at different speeds.

44. An American market analysis company, Airport Interviewing and Research Inc., stated that in 2005 (in the United States) on average a passenger spent eighty-six minutes in the airport after clearing security. Airport Interviewing and Research Inc., "Traveler Insights." Accessed November 23, 2005. http://www.pri-air.com/air/travel.html.

45. "Airport Waiting Time Costs British Business Half a Billion Pounds," *Times of London*, March 30, 2005. Accessed April 22, 2013. http://www.thetimes.co.uk/tto/travel/businesstravel/article1742850.ece.

46. Ameche, *The Woman Road Warrior*, 20.

47. Jeremy Rifkin, *Time Wars: The Primary Conflict in Human History* (New York: Simon and Schuster, 1987), 190.

48. Pierre Bourdieu, *Pascalian Meditations*, trans. Richard Nice (Stanford: Stanford University Press, 2000), 224.

Chapter Two. Temporal Labor and the Taxicab

1. I have explored this topic in Sarah Sharma, "Taxicab Publics and the Production of *Brown Space* after 9/11," *Cultural Studies* 24, no. 2 (March 2010): 183–199. See also Brett Neilson, "The World Seen from a Taxi: Students-Migrants-Workers in the Global Multiplication of Labour," *Subjectivity* 29 (2009).

2. Giorgio Agamben, *Homo Sacer: Sovereign Power and Bare Life*, trans. Daniel Heller-Roazen (Stanford: Stanford University Press, 1998), 175.

3. I have explored this idea at length in three different articles: "Baring Life and Lifestyle in the Non-place," *Cultural Studies* 23, no. 1 (2009): 129–148; "Taxicab Publics and the Production of *Brown Space* after 9/11"; and "Taxis as Media: A Temporal Materialist Reading of the Taxi Cab," *Social Identities: Journal of Race, Nation, and Culture* 14, no. 4 (July 2008).

4. Toby Miller's concept of the "new international division of cultural labor" provides a way of understanding the new labor requirements of mobile middle-class culture. Temporal labor could be understood as an instantiation of this new international division of labor that Miller refers to Toby Miller et al., *Global Hollywood* (London: British Film Institute; Berkeley: University of California Press, 2001).

5. Michel Foucault, *The History of Sexuality*, trans. Robert Hurley (New York: Pantheon, 1978).

6. Michael Hardt, "Prison Time," *Yale French Review*, no. 91 (1997): 64–79.

7. Hardt, "Prison Time," 67.

8. Hardt, "Prison Time," 66.

9. Pico Iyer, *Global Soul: Jet-Lag, Shopping Malls, and the Search for Home* (New York: Vintage, 2001), 112.

10. See Michael Hardt and Antonio Negri, *Commonwealth* (Cambridge: Harvard University Press, 2009); Michael Hardt and Antonio Negri, *Empire* (Cambridge: Harvard University Press, 2000); Michael Hardt and Antonio Negri, *Multitude* (Cambridge: Harvard University Press, 2004); and Jason Read, *Micropolitics of Capital* (New York: SUNY Press, 2003).

11. Read, *Micropolitics of Capital*, 133.

12. Pierre Bourdieu, *Pascalian Meditations*, trans. Richard Nice (Stanford: Stanford University Press, 2000), 228.

13. Bourdieu, *Pascalian Meditations*, 255.

14. *Designing the Taxi* (New York: Design Trust for Public Space, 2005), accessed April 22, 2013. http://designtrust.org/publications/publication_05destaxi.html.

15. Inextricably bound to Westin's jet-lag concept rooms and the Hilton's Serenity beds for the socially jet-lagged are extraneous conditions of labor. The new mattresses in the Serenity line weigh 113 pounds, with 16 extra pounds for the new luxury linens. A report from the Canadian Center for Occupational Health and Safety says: "A hotel housekeeper changes body position every three seconds while cleaning a room. If we assume that the average cleaning time for each room is twenty-five minutes, we can estimate that a housekeeper assumes 8,000 different body postures every shift." Hotel Workers Rising, *Creating Luxury, Enduring Pain: How Hotel Work Is Hurting Housekeepers*, A Unite Here Publication, April 2006. Accessed April 15, 2007. http://www.google.com/search?client=safari&rls=en&q=Creating+Luxury,+Enduring+Pain:+How+Hotel+Work+Is+Hurting+Housekeepers&ie=UTF-8&oe=UTF-8, explains the new components of care in a jet-lag luxury suite: "A housekeeper who changes one Serenity Bed™ per room and cleans fifteen rooms per day strips over 500 pounds of soiled linen and replaces it with 500 pounds of clean linen. Further, the sheets and blankets are tucked under the mattress requiring the housekeeper to lift the heavy mattress at least eight times in the course of making a single bed." The average workload often far exceeds fifteen rooms a day. The report includes firsthand accounts from workers in the hotels. One housekeeper who has worked at the Hilton Hawaiian Village for eighteen years states, "There is so much to do on the new bed that we have to rush constantly. And when you are rushing and lifting extremely heavy mattresses or punching pillow after pillow into their cases, we hurt. I have pain in my lower back and shoulders and my knees swell up. I have trouble sleeping at night because of the fatigue and pain. I often have to get out of bed and work the stiffness out of my body."

16. The outsourced call center is another obvious place of temporal coordination and standardization. This is a standardization of time that involves differential bodies rather than time zones, clocks, airplanes, trains, or ships. An empire of space gives way to the empire of time—of a new order and new magnitude. The sedentary call-center employee recalibrates, much like the mobile taxi driver, to live within the tempo of business hours elsewhere, subordinated to the time demands of another population.

It is only in this context that these two time zones, temporal paths, cross. That is, if one recalibrates and synchronizes to the time of another. These call-center employees, like other cab-lagged individuals, are a growing form of expendable temporal reserve labor that works within a temporal architecture erected by Expedia, Hewlett-Packard, and Verizon. Diabetes, depression, chronic fatigue, backaches, dizziness, digestive problems, headaches, and repetitive strain injuries are commonly cited by call-center employees in Delhi, whose rhythm of business must synch five hours back for the United Kingdom and twelve hours back for the United States. As reported in the *Australian*, the health of employees matters little when there is a reserve army of labor. For example, in this article a corporate well-being manager claims: "Indian companies are the least concerned for the health of the employee because everything boils down to money." "Call Center Youth Face Burn Out," *The Australian*, October 2, 2007. Accessed March 12, 2011. http://www.theaustralian.com.au/australian-it-old/call-centre-youth-faces-burn-out/story-e6frgano-1111114546442. This echoes Claire's comment in chapter 1 that the floor workers don't require emotional intelligence because they are just there for the money, which reveals that the reserve labor force is always a site of disinvestment, and thus technologies of the self are the last resort. With slim chances of regulation within the industry, the rise of heart attacks for workers in their mid-twenties, and the quick turnover of workers, there are now preventive corporate wellness solutions, such as yoga, salad bars, and distress hotlines that are increasingly incorporated. These forms of temporal rescue do little to increase the material well-being of the employees or lessen time spent on the job. Instead this rescue normalizes their sense of living on the outside of time, but with a few healthful choices. With yoga in the office in the United States or the United Kingdom, the nine to five that workers are recalibrating toward is only their own. Instead this situation in India is temporal labor. While at work employees synchronize to a nine to five overseas, revalidating a temporal order of normalization, writ globally. While the call-center employees are temporal laborers for the United States, they are also imbricated within a structural politics of time in the locations in which they are placed.

Chapter Three. Dharma at the Desk

1. For an interesting discussion of the rhythm of waiting as it relates to television, see Anna McCarthy, *Ambient Television: Visual Culture and Public Space* (Durham, NC: Duke University Press, 2001).

2. Rarely does concern with the sedentary life on these popular sites focus on the structural or cultural variables of sedentary living, which would then have to explain the fact that the largest sedentary population is in fact women. According to the Center for Disease Control, it is specifically African American women living below the poverty line who are at risk. Cynthia L. Ogden, Molly M. Lamb, et al. Obesity and Socioeconomic Status in Adults: United States, 2005–2008. Accessed March 10, 2012. http://www.cdc.gov/nchs/data/databriefs/db50.pdf.

But these women are already sick by the terms and conditions of contemporary capitalism. Sickness is, after all, defined as the inability to work. And by all expectations of capitalism, it is rather sick not to work. These women are not subjects of investment or intervention; they are not subjects of value, but reminders of the end of the spectrum. Instead, the sedentary life drawing the most attention is the office worker, ones who are doing time at the desk.

3. Oliver Ryan, "How To Succeed in Business: Meditate," *Fortune Magazine* online edition, July 23 2007. Accessed March 15, 2012. http://money.cnn.com/magazines/fortune/fortune_archive/2007/07/23/100135590/.

4. Susi Hately Aldous, *Yoga for the Desk Jockey* (sha-press, 2005).

5. Karl Marx, *Capital: Volume 1; A Critique of Political Economy* (London: Penguin, 1867/1992).

6. Slavoj Žižek *On Belief* (New York: Routledge, 2001), 13. For a discussion of the rise of competitive capitalism within new age industry see also Kimberly Lau, *New Age Capitalism: Making Money East of Eden* (Philadelphia: University of Pennsylvania Press, 2000.) I am not concerned here with the real or potential effects of yoga at work—that is, if it actually alleviates stress for the employee and increases productive output for the employer. As Nikolas Rose and Peter Miller argue in relation to the United Kingdom's Quality of Working Life Reforms, "To analyse such a process is not to arbitrate on whether it is essentially humanizing or dehumanizing, liberating or imprisoning. For to do so would be to presuppose that a particular device or argument is 'good' or 'bad' in and of itself." It is exactly this! Peter Miller and Nikolas Rose, *Governing the Present: Administering Economic, Social and Personal Life* (Malden, MA: Polity, 2008), 197.

7. The yoga instructors have become experts in governmentality, fit for rehabilitating the tired out worker. As Nancy Fraser argues: "The result is a new, postfordist mode of subjectification. Neither the Victorian subject of individualizing normalization nor the fordist subject of collective welfare, the new subject of governmentality is the actively responsible agent. A subject of (market) choice and a consumer of services, this individual is obligated to enhance her quality of self through her own decisions." Nancy Fraser, "Rethinking the Public Sphere: A Contribution to the Critique of Actually Existing Democracy," in *Habermas and the Public Sphere*, ed. C. Calhoun (Cambridge: MIT Press, 1992), 127.

8. Nikolas Rose, *Governing the Soul: The Shaping of the Private Self*, 2nd ed. (New York: Free Association Books, 1999), 103–4. For a perspective outside of the governmentality literature, see Peter Fleming, *Authenticity and the Cultural Politics of Work: New Forms of Informal Control* (Oxford: Oxford University Press, 2009); and Andrew Ross, *No-Collar: The Humane Workplace and Its Hidden Costs* (Philadelphia, PA: Temple University Press, 2003).

9. Gilles Deleuze, Postscript on the Societies of Control *October. Vol.* 59, (Winter, 1992), 3–7.

10. Fred Alan Wolf, *The Yoga of Time Travel: How the Mind Can Defeat Time* (Wheaton, IL: Quest Books, 2004), 12.

11. Carol Greenhouse in *A Moment's Notice: Time Politics across Cultures* (Ithaca, NY: Cornell University Press, 1996) contends that a linear conception of time enabled Western cultures to look toward the future and construct some sense of agency within the reality of the temporal structure. This progressive sense of history and time is

argued to have had profound implications on geopolitical and alternative constructions of time. The desire for agency in the temporal structure produced notions of progress that marginalized Others' conceptions of time. There has been an important stream of literature that examines modernity's rejection of alternative temporal horizons found in superstition and magic. Maureen Perkins, in *The Reform of Time: Magic and Modernity* (London: Pluto, 2001), argues that these alternative constructions of time were discursively constructed as deviant and dangerous.

12. Wolf, *The Yoga of Time Travel*, 12.

13. Wolf, *The Yoga of Time Travel*, 18.

14. As quoted on their website. Accessed June 19, 2013. http://www.take5moment.com/mhtml/about.html.

15. See, for example, Mark Coté and Jennifer Pybus, "Learning to Immaterial Labour 2.0: MySpace and Social Networks," *Ephemera* 7, no. 1 (2007); Fleming, *Authenticity and the Cultural Politics of Work*; Melissa Gregg, *Work's Intimacy* (Cambridge: Polity, 2011); Michael Hardt and Antonio Negri, *Empire* (Cambridge: Harvard University Press, 2000); Ross, *No-Collar*; Tiziana Terranova, *Network Culture: Politics for the Information Age* (Ann Arbor, MI: Pluto Press, 2004). Beyond this focus on new labor arrangements for what are arguably mostly professional and creative types, most attention within works on globalization and labor has been with the politics and material struggles of physically unhinged populations who move—either because of others' excessive lifestyle requirements or when regimes of dependence force people to move. For example, critical focus on the underside of globalization is concerned with the multiple mobilities that are the byproduct of the exploitative labor demands of the jet-setters: domestic labor, personal shoppers, and dog walkers, as well as the new flows of migration that result from foreign direct investment. See Zygmunt Bauman, *Globalization: The Human Consequences* (New York: Columbia University Press, 1998); Doreen Massey, *Space, Place, and Gender* (Minneapolis: University of Minnesota Press, 1994); and Saskia Sassen, *Globalization and Its Discontents* (New York: New Press, 1998).

16. Paul Virilio's entire theory of speed is based on an argument about the displacement of one's sense of space. What he calls the "three-T revolution" is changes in transport, transmission, and transplant that alter the measure of the world. When the measure of the world contracts, the individual is left without a point of reference. The transport revolution was dominated by the media of the automobile and its message: the restructuring of cities, creation of communicative routes known as highways, and the loss of space realized in the question "how much longer is it?" as opposed to how much farther is it. The transmission revolution refers to the era of telepresence, tele-reality, and television. It is an audio-visual revolution where the speed of information reigns over the content of the information. The final revolution in this triad, transplant, is a late realization of the social Darwinism of the Second World War. Here Virilio is concerned with eugenics, cloning, and the growing field of biotechnology research and experimentation wherein nanotechnologies can be implanted in the human body. This final revolution signals the end of the animal body and a loss of the world proper. Paul Virilio, *Crepuscular Dawn* (New York: Semiotext(e), 2002), 93.

17. The expanding scope of human resources to book office yoga therapy is indica-

tive of the movement of the production of life and the subject toward the center of capitalist modes of production. This is what Hardt and Negri and Jason Read label "real subsumption." See Hardt and Negri, *Empire*; and Michael Hardt and Antonio Negri, *Multitude* (Cambridge: Harvard University Press, 2004); and Jason Read, *Micro-politics of Capital* (New York: SUNY Press, 2003). This departs from Marx's notion that free time were possible—in fact, it was free time that would create the conditions for worker rebellion. For Marx this free time is taken by the worker: "The time during which the worker works is the time during which the capitalists consumes the labor power he has bought for him. If the worker consumes his disposable time for himself, he robs the capitalist" (*Capital*, 342). But disposable time maintains the fiction of a clear separation of the working day. As David Harvey argues in *Spaces of Hope* (Berkeley: University of California Press, 2000), echoing Marx and the autonomists, bodies embedded in a social process such as the circulation of variable capital are never to be construed as docile or passive: "The transformative and creative capacities of the laborer always carry the potentiality (however unimaginable in the present circumstances) to fashion an alternative mode of production, exchange, and consumption" (117). But yoga in the office represents a rather dire situation in terms of worker resistance. It presents itself as this alternative mode of production, exchange, and consumption. It promises a new quality of time to be gained while at work, but ultimately for work. The workplace is maintained as the absolute center of existence.

18. Marx, *Capital*, Volume 1, 223.

19. Frederick Winslow Taylor, *Principles of Scientific Management* (London: Harpers and Brothers, 1911). Frank B. Gilbreth and Lillian M. Gilbreth, *Fatigue Study: The Elimination of Humanity's Greatest Waste; A First Step in Motion Study*. (Easton, PA: Hive, 1973). For a discussion of Taylor and Gilbreth as it relates to mobility and time-discipline see Tim Cresswell's chapter "Workplace and the Home" in his *On the Move: Mobility in the Modern Western World* (New York: Routledge, 2006).

20. Michel Foucault, *Discipline and Punish* (New York: Vintage, 1977), 152.

21. This is a generic advertisement uploaded to slideshare for anyone interested in starting a corporate yoga business. Its presence on slideshare evidences the pervasiveness of the discourse. Accessed March 10 2012, http://www.slideshare.net/KAN CHANSIRIAH/yoga-in-business.

22. Foucault, *Discipline and Punish*, 161.

23. Henry Braverman, *Labor and Monopoly Capital: The Degradation of Work in the Twentieth Century* (New York: Monthly Review Press, 1974), 310.

24. Braverman, *Labor and Monopoly Capital*, 310.

25. As advertised on their website. Accessed June 19, 2013. http://www.lotus-exchange.com/on-site-massage.shtml.

26. Pierre Bourdieu, *In Other Words: Essays Towards a Reflexive Sociology* (Stanford: Stanford University Press, 1990), 190.

27. Jean-Luc Nancy, *Corpus*, trans. Richard A. Rand (New York: Fordham University Press, 2008), 110.

28. See Nate Holdren's definition: "The basic point of the concept is that value production and resistance to value production do not occur only in determinate and

recognized workplaces and in activity by waged workers. This concept of the social factory has a polemical force against the factoryist political and organizational model that centers on workplaces and waged work" in "Glossary," in *Constituent Imagination: Militant Investigations, Collective Theorization*, ed. Stevphen Shukaitis, David Graeber, and Erika Biddle (Oakland, CA: AK Press, 2007), 318.

29. Lawrence Pintak, "Balancing Business with Buddha," Belief.net (December 2011), http://www.beliefnet.com/Faiths/Buddhism/2001/06/Balancing-Business-With-Buddha.aspx?p=4#. Accessed March 10, 2012.

30. Ken Hillis, *Digital Sensations: Space, Identity, and Embodiment* (Minneapolis: University of Minnesota Press, 1999), 102.

31. As quoted on their website http://www.lotus-exchange.com/funk.shtml. Accessed March 27, 2010.

32. http://www.lotus-exchange.com/corporate-yoga-classes.shtml. Accessed March 27, 2010.

33. Michael Carroll, *Awake at Work: 35 Practical Buddhist Principles for Discovering Clarity and Balance in the Midst of Work's Chaos* (Boston: Shambhala, 2004), 205.

34. Carroll, *Awake at Work*, 205.

35. Marx, *Capital*, 376.

Chapter Four. Slow Space.

1. Pico Iyer, "The Joy of Quiet," *New York Times*, December 29, 2011. Accessed January 1, 2012. http://www.nytimes.com/2012/01/01/opinion/sunday/the-joy-of-quiet.html?pagewanted=all&_r=0.

2. For example, see Penelope Green, "The Slow Life Picks up Speed," *New York Times*, January 31, 2008. Accessed April 25, 2013. http://www.nytimes.com/2008/01/31/garden/31slow.html?pagewanted=all; and Michael Kimmelman, "Pleasures of Life in the Slow Lane," *New York Times*, November 7, 2011. Accessed April 25, 2013. http://www.nytimes.com/2011/11/08/arts/design/a-bike-lane-perch-for-the-urban-show.html?pagewanted=all.

3. Wendy Parkins and Geoffrey Craig, *Slow Living* (Sydney: UNSW Press, 2006), 55.

4. Marshall McLuhan, *Understanding Media* (New York: McGraw Hill, 1964), 150.

5. McLuhan, *Understanding Media*, 150.

6. Stewart Brand, *The Clock of the Long Now: Time and Responsibility and the Idea Behind the World's Slowest Computer* (New York: Basic Books, 1995).

7. See the foundation's website, http://longnow.org/about/. Accessed January 5, 2008.

8. Brand, *The Clock of the Long Now*, 2.

9. Brand, *The Clock of the Long Now*, 27.

10. See the organization's website, http://www.sloth.gr.jp/E-index.htm.

11. See Sharon Otterman, "Haste, Scorned: Blogging at a Snail's Pace," *New York Times*, November 23, 2008, ST10.

12. Carl Honore, *In Praise of Slow: How a Worldwide Movement Is Challenging the Cult of Speed* (New York: Harper, 2004); Carlo Petrini, *Slow Food: The Case for Taste*, trans. W. McCuaig (New York: Columbia University Press, 2001).

13. John Tomlinson in *The Culture of Speed: The Coming of Immediacy* (Thousand Oaks, CA: Sage, 2007) and William E. Connolly in *Neuropolitics: Thinking, Culture, and Speed* (Minneapolis: University of Minnesota Press, 2002) in their own ways advocate the institutionalizing of slow zones or brakes into the regimes of modern life. Connolly recognizes that there are asymmetries in speed while also being attune to the fact that speed can create conditions of pluralism (179). Thus slowness is another speed of which Connolly argues it is critical that citizens in a variety of walks of life be provided with structural opportunities for periodic escape and retreat from a fast-paced life (144). Tomlinson asks, "How, whilst rejecting uniform deceleration, can we preserve deliberative time-space in both personal-existential and institutional forms?" (157). Tomlinson argues for balance as a way of taking control over life: "It is not a regressive or nostalgic slow value. It does not imply self-scrutiny or self-control according to any traditional or fixed precepts. It does not look for life formulas or try to achieve settled state of inner harmony. Balance as control is not about coming to rest. It's more or less the opposite: a process of constant reflexive rebalancing in the face of contingency" (158). He continues, "It is to experience ourselves as capably and sensitively attuned to our fast-moving environment and so as existentially flexible, responsive and resilient" (159). This notion of "rebalancing in the face of contingency" would have to recognize still the uneven rhythm of social relations. More space and more time are not the solution to material inequalities, nor is a better relationship to space and time. What needs to be balanced is not speed with slowness, or more space for time, or more time for time for that matter. Instead what is needed is a deeper awareness of the politics of time.

14. McLuhan was widely critiqued for a theory that fell so easily into the hands of marketers and corporations, and slowness can suffer the same fate. But the commodification of slowness with its flimsy discursive terrain and contradictory manifestations is not what makes it problematic, nor is this surprising. Rather it is this attention to a single *pace* as a politics that distracts and derails recognition of the deeper politics of time as it is actually lived and waged in material struggles.

15. "About Us," *Ruddy Potato*. Accessed March 15, 2012. http://www.ruddypotato.com/about.html (quote no longer available).

16. See Cathy N. Davidson's *36 Views of Mt Fuji: On Finding Myself in Japan* (Durham, NC: Duke University Press, 2006).

17. "Facilities," Caretta Shiodome. Accessed May 5, 2009. http://www.caretta.jp/english/floorguide/index.html.

18. Original article appeared in the daily metro magazine *Metropolis Tokyo*, April 4, 2003. Accessed June 19, 2013. http://jerde.com/news/202.html.

19. "What Is Slow Food," Slow Food USA. Accessed March 15, 2011. http://www.slowfoodusa.org/index.php/slow_food/.

20. Slow Food USA website. *Slow Food International Manifesto*. Accessed March 1, 2008. www.slowfoodusa.org/about/manifesto.html.

21. Slow Food USA website. *Slow Food International Manifesto*. Accessed March 1, 2008. www.slowfoodusa.org/about/manifesto.html.

22. Slow Food USA website. *Slow Food International Manifesto*. Accessed March 1, 2008. www.slowfoodusa.org/about/manifesto.html.

23. See the Restaurant Opportunities Center of New York's website, http://www.rocny.org/. The organization is responsible for organizing workers for better working conditions.

24. Toby Miller, *Cultural Citizenship: Cosmopolitanism, Consumerism, and Television in a Neoliberal Age* (Philadelphia: Temple University Press, 2007), 111.

25. Slow Food USA website. *Slow Food International Manifesto*. Accessed March 1, 2008. www.slowfoodusa.org/about/manifesto.html.

26. Citta Slow website, *Citta Slow Charter*. Accessed March 27, 2008, http://www.cittaslow.org/section/association/philosophy.

27. Paul L. Knox, "Creating Ordinary Places: Slow Cities in a Fast World," *Journal of Urban Design* 10, no. (2005): 7.

28. Slow Food USA website. Accessed April 15, 2008. www.slowfoodusa.org.

29. See Richard Wilk, ed., *Fast Food/Slow Food: The Cultural Economy of the Global Food System* (Lanham, MD: AltaMira Press, 2006).

30. Miller, *Cultural Citizenship*, 114.

31. Miller, *Cultural Citizenship*, 114.

32. Connolly, *Neuropolitics*, 162.

33. CNN highlighted the staycation as a "1st Issue" in its *Weekend Report*. Debra Alan "Staycations: Alternative to pricey, stressful travel," CNN.com, June 12, 2008. Accessed June 30, 2008. http://www.cnn.com/2008/LIVING/worklife/06/12/balance.staycation/index.html?iref=allsearch.

34. "Plan a Backyard Staycation," The Early Show, CBS News, July 3, 2008, 1:30 PM. http://www.cbsnews.com/video/watch/?id=4230174n.

35. Lynn Spigel, *Make Room for TV: Television and the Family Ideal in Postwar America* (Chicago: University of Chicago Press, 1992); and Lynn Spigel, *Welcome to the Dreamhouse: Popular Media and Postwar Suburbs* (Durham, NC: Duke University Press, 2001).

36. Spigel, *Welcome to the Dreamhouse*, 60–61.

37. "Staycation! Many Opting to Stay Home," ABCLOCAL, May 24, 2008. Accessed June 1, 2008. http://abclocal.go.com/wtvd/story?section=resources/lifestyle_community&id=6161484.

38. Rebecca Ray and John Schmidt, *No-Vacation Nation* (Washington, D.C.: Center for Economic and Policy Research, May 2007), 3.

39. "Staycation" *Merriam-Webster's Collegiate Dictionary*, Eleventh Edition, 2009.

40. Debra Alban, "Staycations: Alternative to Pricey, Stressful Travel," CNN.com, June 12, 2008. Accessed June 30, 2008. http://www.cnn.com/2008/LIVING/worklife/06/12/balance.staycation/index.html?iref=allsearch.

41. Paul Virilio, *Polar Inertia*. (Thousand Oaks, CA: Sage, 2000).

42. Paul Virilio, *The Politics of the Very Worst* (New York: Semiotext(e), 1999), 43.

43. Parkins and Craig, *Slow Living*, 4.

44. Wendy Parkins, "Out of Time: Fast Subjects and Slow Living," *Time and Society* 13, no. 2–3 (2004): 64, my emphasis.

45. Parkins and Craig, *Slow Living*, 51.

Conclusion. Toward a Temporal Public

1. To reiterate, one of the reasons the temporal is obscured is that space continues to be the privileged site of thinking about power. In fact, the critique of speed masquerades as a time politics but is really a concern about time's effect on space. This appears within speed theory in at least three ways: (1) concern over the acceleration of linear time of history into a global real time where geopolitics is replaced by a chronopolitics; (2) speed as a tempo of modern life that produces nondeliberative, fast, and hasty subjects who threaten the political possibilities of public space and the sanctity of what are actually quite normalized social spheres of existence, such as work, home, and leisure; and (3) the production of temporal denizens, understood as fast and slow classes, who live in diametric experiences of time and are imagined to have no spatial relationship (i.e., are never in the same place at the same time).

2. Anisha Hingorani, "Cheap Food for Diners, but at What Cost?," Institute for Food and Development Policy/Food First, February 5, 2012. Accessed April 5, 2012. http://www.foodfirst.org/en/labor+in+the+food+system.

3. Julie Guthman, "Fast Food/Organic Food: Reflexive Tastes and the Making of 'Yuppie Chow,'" *Social and Cultural Geography* 4, no. 1 (2003).

4. It is interesting, to the say the least, that the *New York Times* and the *New York Times Magazine* ran two interactive pieces in 2011 related to sleeping on the subway. The first pictures a series of everyday people sleeping in transit: on the subway, in trains, and at stations. The article is titled "How Little Sleep Can You Get Away With?" The article is about sleep deprivation and the countermeasures to sleep that exist in the course of an average day: bright lights, noise, coffee, and work demands. Maggie Jones, "How Little Sleep Can You Get Away With?" *Sunday Magazine, New York Times*, April 15 2011, MM41. Accessed April 22, 2011. http://www.nytimes.com/2011/04/17/magazine/mag-17Sleep-t.html?_r=0. Eight months later "To Sleep on the Subway, Maybe? Poor Chance to Dream" was published. It is an interactive article that pictures a neurologist asleep on the A train. He is sleeping for a research study on how much sleep can be obtained while riding on the subway. His breath, brain function, and heart rate are being monitored while riding. The article invites readers to submit their own stories about sleeping on the subway. Christine Haughney, "To Sleep on the Subway, Maybe? Poor Chance to Dream," *New York Times*, December 7, 2011. Accessed December 15, 2011. http://www.nytimes.com/2011/12/08/nyregion/to-sleep-on-the-subway-maybe-but-to-dream-poor-chance.html.

5. Trevor Kapp, "Homeless Advocates Rally at Penn Station for City to Back off Sleeping in Public Places," *New York Daily News*, July 26, 2011. Accessed July 30, 2011. http://articles.nydailynews.com/2011-07-26/local/29834378_1_penn-station-public-places-homeless-activists.

6. Fernanda Santos, "In the Shadows, Day Laborers Left Homeless as Work Vanishes," *New York Times*, January 1, 2010. Accessed April 26, 2013. http://www.nytimes.com/2010/01/02/nyregion/02laborers.html.

7. Gillian Fuller and Ross Harley, in *Aviopolis: A Book about Airports* (London: Blackdog, 2004), find in the airport one of the most diverse and rich social spaces: "Airports

mix multiple forms of life, matter, and information into a series of new and constantly changing relations between bodies and the sky, between local landscapes and global capital. They do this by creating thresholds that enable disparate systems to meet each other. At the airport, the relatively slow and individuated systems of ground transportation meet with faster mass systems of aviation. It is at this intersection that local urban ecologies begin to entwine with the global. The airport is a structure that is also an infrastructure. It is a structure designed for connection" (104). Marc Augé's argument in *In the Metro*, trans. Tom Conley (Minneapolis: University of Minnesota Press, 2002), succinctly captures this sentiment when he says: "We might consider the existence of an intersection without gods, without passions, and without battles these days represents the most advanced stage of society and prefigures the ideal of all democracies" (66). In fact, airplanes were often referred to as democracy in the air because of the novelty of passengers from different "walks of life," although the socio-economic brackets are more similar than one would find in the metro. In *Neuropolitics: Thinking, Culture, Speed* (Minneapolis: University of Minnesota Press, 2002), William Connolly, considering the temporal aspect of being connected, argues for the necessity of thinking through "how to work with and against a world moving faster than heretofore to promote a positive ethos of pluralism. There are no guarantees in this domain. But variations of speed do sometimes encourage people to become more modest about what they are in relation to what they are not" (143). Connolly emphasizes a sense of the relational as a form of recognition within a polity. That different people were together sharing space, even for a brief moment, is a popular point of departure for work on mobility. As John Urry writes in *Mobilities* (Polity: London, 2007), "air travel and its visible inequalities are a synecdoche of the increasingly global pattern of inequalities deriving from huge variations in network capital" (152).

8. Iris Marion Young, *Justice and the Politics of Difference* (Princeton: Princeton University Press, 1990).

9. Iris Marion Young, "Communication and the Other: Beyond Deliberative Democracy," in *Democracy and Difference*, ed. Seyla Benhabib (Princeton: Princeton University Press, 1996), 126.

10. These pluralist accounts emphasize the importance of routes and paths as an attribute of political space. Like the time geographers, this perspective into publics acknowledges how different labor practices and daily routines mean that some paths will cross more than others and that some routes are shared. The overriding sense is that these intersections lead toward certain types of experience, which then produce certain types of knowledge about the self and others. Important here are the intersections and collisions between types of people who wouldn't be meeting in town halls, town squares, and the other institutions of "traditional" theorizing of the public sphere.

11. Toby Miller's concept of the new international division of cultural labor provides a way of understanding the new labor requirements of mobile middle-class culture. See Toby Miller, Nitin Govil, John McMurria, and R. Maxwell, (*Global Hollywood*. London: British Film Institute; Berkeley: University of California Press, 2001). Both the new international division of cultural labor and temporal labor speak to the relational

forms of labor that persist in a world too often mythically described by the attributes of clean and fast technologies.

12. See Sarah Sharma, "Baring Life and Lifestyle in the Non-place," *Cultural Studies* 23 (2009). I have argued elsewhere that transit spaces are historically contingent sites of knowledge and power production because they are constituted by specific economic, cultural, and political forces at particular conjunctures or times.

13. Doreen Massey, *For Space* (Thousand Oaks, CA: Sage, 2005), 70. Johanes Fabian makes a similar point in *Time and the Other* (New York: Columbia University Press, 1983). There he argues that "coevalness aims at recognizing contemporaneity as the condition for the truly dialectical confrontation" (154).

14. Martin Heidegger, "Building, Dwelling, Thinking," in *Poetry, Language, and Thought*, trans. Albert Hofstadter (New York: Harper, 1971).

15. Martin Heidegger, *Being and Time* (New York: Harper, 1962).

16. Heidegger, "Building, Dwelling, Thinking," 143.

Bibliography

Abram, David. *Spell of the Sensuous: Perception and Language in a More-than-Human World*. New York: Vintage 1997.

Adam, Barbara. *Time*. London: Blackwell, 2004.

———. *Time and Social Theory*. Cambridge, U.K.: Polity, 1990.

———. *Timewatch: The Social Analysis of Time*. Cambridge, UK: Polity, 1995.

Agamben, Giorgio. *Homo Sacer: Sovereign Power and Bare Life*. Trans. Daniel Heller-Roazen. Stanford: Stanford University Press, 1998.

Aldous, Susi Hately. *Yoga for the Desk Jockey*. sha-press, www.sha-press.com, 2005.

Ameche, Kathleen. *The Woman Road Warrior: A Woman's Guide to Domestic and International Business Travel*. 2nd ed. Chicago: Agate, 2007.

Appadurai, Arjun. *Modernity at Large: Cultural Dimensions of Globalization*. Minneapolis: University of Minnesota Press, 1996.

Armitage, John, and Joanne Roberts. *Living with Cyberspace: Technology and Society in the 21st Century*. New York: Continuum, 2003.

Arterburn, Stephen and Sam Gallucci. *Road Warrior: How to Keep Your Faith, Relationships, and Integrity When Away from Home*. Colorado Springs: WaterBrook Press, 2008.

Augé, Marc. *In the Metro*. Trans. Tom Conley. Minneapolis: University of Minnesota Press, 2002.

———. *Non-places: Introduction to an Anthropology of Supermodernity*. London: Verso, 1995.

Bastian, Michelle. "Fatally Confused: Telling the Time in the Midst of Ecological Crises." *Journal of Environmental Philosophy* 9, no. 1 (2012): 23–48.

Bauman, Zygmunt. *Globalization: The Human Consequences*. New York: Columbia University Press, 1998.

———. *Liquid Modernity*. London: Blackwell, 2000.

Bell, Shannon. *Fast Feminism*. New York: Autonomedia, 2010.

Benhabib, Seyla. "Models of Public Space: Hannah Arendt, The Liberal Tradition and

Jürgen Habermas." In *Habermas and the Public Sphere*, ed. C. Calhoun, 421–61. Cambridge: MIT Press, 1992.

Berland, Jody. *North of Empire: Essays on the Cultural Technologies of Space*. Durham, NC: Duke University Press, 2009.

Berlant, Lauren. "Slow Death (Sovereignty, Obesity, Lateral Agency)." *Critical Inquiry* 33, no. 4 (2007): 754–80.

Bourdieu, Pierre. "The Attitude of the Algerian Peasant Toward Time." In *Mediterranean Country Men*, ed. J. Pitt-Rivers, Paris: Mouton and Co. 1963, 55–72.

———. *In Other Words: Essays Towards a Reflexive Sociology*. Stanford: Stanford University Press, 1990.

———. *Pascalian Meditations*. Trans. Richard Nice. Stanford: Stanford University Press, 2000.

Brand, Stewart. *The Clock of the Long Now: Time and Responsibility and the Idea behind the World's Lowest Computer*. New York: Basic Books, 1995.

Braverman, Henry. *Labor and Monopoly Capital: The Degradation of Work in the Twentieth Century*. New York: Monthly Review Press, 1974.

Calhoun, Craig, ed. *Habermas and the Public Sphere*. Cambridge: MIT Press, 1992.

Canning, Megan, Savannah Gorton and Deborah Marton. *Designing the Taxi*. New York: Design Trust for Public Space, 2005.

Carey, James W. *Communication as Culture: Essays on Media and Society*. New York: Routledge, 1989.

Carroll, Michael. *Awake at Work: 35 Practical Buddhist Principles for Discovering Clarity and Balance in the Midst of Work's Chaos*. Boston: Shambhala, 2004.

Castells, Manuel. *The Rise of the Network Society*. Malden, MA: Blackwell, 1996.

Clark-Flory, Tracy. "The End of Menstruation." Salon.com, February 4, 2008. Accessed June 10 2008 http://www.salon.com/2008/02/04/menstruation_2/.

Clough, Patricia Ticineto, and Jean Halley, eds. *The Affective Turn: Theorizing the Social*. Durham, NC: Duke University Press, 2007.

Connolly, William E. *Neuropolitics: Thinking, Culture, Speed*. Minneapolis: University of Minnesota Press, 2002.

Coté, Mark, and Jennifer Pybus. "Learning to Immaterial Labour 2.0: MySpace and Social Networks." *Ephemera* 7, no. 1 (2007): 88–106.

Crang, Mike. "Rhythms of the City: Temporalized Space and Motion." In *TimeSpace: Geographies of Temporality*, ed. Jon May and Nigel Thrift. London: Routledge, 2001: 187–207.

Crang, Mike, T. Crosbie, and S. D. N. Graham. "Technology, Timespace and the Remediation of Neighbourhood Life." *Environment and Planning A* 39 (10) (2007): 2405–22.

Crary, Jonathan. *24/7: Late Capitalism and the Ends of Sleep*. London: Verso, 2013.

Cresswell, Tim. *On the Move: Mobility in the Modern Western World*. New York: Routledge, 2006.

Davidson, Cathy N. *36 Views of Mt Fuji: On Finding Myself in Japan*. Durham, NC: Duke University Press, 2006.

Decron, Chris. "Speed-Space." In *Virilio Live: Selected Interviews*, ed. John Armitage. London: Sage, 2001. 69–81.
Delueze, Gilles "Postscript on the Societies of Control" *October. Vol. 59. (Winter, 1992)*, 3–7.
Duffy, Enda. *The Speed Handbook: Velocity, Pleasure, Modernism*. Durham, NC: Duke University Press, 2009.
Edelman, Lee. *No Future: Queer Theory and the Death Drive*. Durham. NC: Duke University Press, 2004.
Ekirch, A. Rogers. *At Day's Close: A History of Nighttime* New York: Norton and Co. 2005.
Estrada, Arthur, Amanda M. Kelley, Catherine M. Webb, Jeremy R. Athy, and John S. Crowley. "Modafinil as a Replacement for Dextroamphetamine for Sustaining Alertness in Military Helicopter Pilots." *Aviation, Space, and Environmental Medicine* (Vol. 83, No. 6 June 2012) 556–564.
Fabian, Johannes. *Time and the Other*. New York: Columbia University Press, 1983.
Ferris, Timothy. *The 4-Hour Workweek: Escape 9–5, Live Anywhere, and Join the New Rich*. New York: Crown Publishers, 2007.
Fleming, Peter. *Authenticity and the Cultural Politics of Work: New Forms of Informal Control*. Oxford: Oxford University Press, 2009.
Foucault, Michel. *Care of the Self*. New York: Vintage, 1988.
———. *Discipline and Punish*. New York: Vintage, 1977.
———. *The History of Sexuality*. Trans. Robert Hurley. New York: Pantheon, 1978.
———. "Chapter 11" of *Society must be defended: lectures at the Collège de France, 1975–76*, ed Mauro Bertani and Alessandro Fontana; translated by David Macey. London: Penguin, 2004, 239–264.
Franklin, Ursula. *The Real World of Technology*. Toronto: Anansi, 1999.
Fraser, Nancy. "Rethinking the Public Sphere: A Contribution to the Critique of Actually Existing Democracy." In *Habermas and the Public Sphere*, ed. C. Calhoun, 108–42. Cambridge: MIT Press, 1992.
Freeman, Elizabeth. *Time Binds: Queer Temporalities, Queer Histories*. Durham NC: Duke University Press, 2010.
Fuller, Gillian, and Ross Harley. *Aviopolis: A Book about Airports*. London: Blackdog, 2004.
Galison, Peter. *Einstein's Clocks, Poincare's Maps: Empires of Time*. New York: W. W. Norton & Company, 2003.
Garnham, Nicholas. *Emancipation, the Media, and Modernity: Arguments about the Media and Social Theory*. New York: Oxford University Press, 2000.
Garreau, Joel. "The Great Awakening: With a Pill Called Modafinil, You Can Go 40 Hours Without Sleep—and See into the Future." *Washington Post*, June 17, 2002, C1.
Gilbreth, Frank B, and Lillian M. Gilbreth. *Fatigue Study: The Elimination of Humanity's Greatest Waste; A First Step in Motion Study*. Easton, PA: Hive, 1973.
Gill, Alexandra. "Sleep No More." *Globe and Mail*, April 1, 2006, F9.
Gleick, James. *Faster*. New York: Vintage, 1999.

Glennie, P., and Nigel Thrift. *Shaping the Day: A History of Timekeeping in England and Wales 1300–1800*. Oxford: Oxford University Press, 2009.

Gordon, Alastair. *Naked Airport: A Cultural History of the World's Most Revolutionary Structure*. New York: Metropolitan Books, 2004.

Gottdiener, Mark. *Life in the Air: Surviving the New Culture of Air Travel*. Lanham, MD: Rowman and Littlefield, 2000.

Gregg, Melissa. *Work's Intimacy*. Cambridge: Polity, 2011.

Greene, Ronald Walter. "Spatial Materialism: Labor, Location, and Transnational Literacy." *Critical Studies in Media Communication* 27, no. 1 (2010): 105–10.

Greenhouse, Carol. *A Moment's Notice: Time Politics across Cultures*. Ithaca, NY: Cornell University Press, 1996.

Griffiths, Jay. *A Sideways Look at Time*. New York: Putnam, 1999.

Guthman, Julie. "Fast Food/Organic Food: Reflexive Tastes and the Making of 'Yuppie Chow.'" *Social and Cultural Geography* 4, no. 1 (2003). 45–58.

Habermas, Jürgen. *Structural Transformations of the Public Sphere*. Cambridge: MIT Press, 1999.

Hägerstrand, Torsten. *Innovation Diffusion as a Spatial Process*. Trans. A. Pred. Chicago: University of Chicago Press, 1967.

Halberstam, Judith. *In a Queer Time and Place: Transgender Bodies, Subcultural Lives*. New York: New York University Press, 2005.

Hall, Edward T. *The Dance of Life: The Other Dimension of Time*. New York: Anchor, 1983.

Hardt, Michael. "Prison Time." *Yale French Studies*, no. 91 (1997): 64–79.

Hardt, Michael, and Antonio Negri. *Commonwealth*. Cambridge: Harvard University Press, 2009.

———. *Empire*. Cambridge: Harvard University Press, 2000.

———. *Multitude*. Cambridge: Harvard University Press, 2004.

Harvey, David. *The Condition of Postmodernity: An Enquiry into the Origins of Cultural Change*. Malden, MA: Blackwell, 1989.

———. *Spaces of Hope*. Berkeley: University of California Press, 2000.

Hassan, Robert. *The Chronoscopic Society: Globalization, Time, and Knowledge in the Network Economy*. New York: Peter Lang, 2003.

Hassan, Robert, and Ronald E. Purser, eds. *24/7: Time and Temporality in the Network Society*. Stanford: Stanford University Press, 2007.

Haughney, Christine. "To Sleep on the Subway, Maybe? Poor Chance to Dream," *New York Times*, December 7, 2011. Accessed December 15 2011. http://www.nytimes.com/2011/12/08/nyregion/to-sleep-on-the-subway-maybe-but-to-dream-poor-chance.html.

Heidegger, Martin. *Being and Time*. New York: Harper, 1962.

———. *Poetry, Language, and Thought*. Trans. Albert Hofstadter. New York: Harper, 1971.

Hillis, Ken. *Digital Sensations: Space, Identity, and Embodiment*. Minneapolis: University of Minnesota Press, 1999.

Hochschild, Arlie. *The Outsourced Self: Intimate Life in Market Times.* New York: Metropolitan Books, 2012.

Holdren, Nate. "Glossary" in *Constituent Imagination: Militant Investigations, Collective Theorization*, ed. Stevphen Shukaitis, David Graeber, and Erika Biddle (Oakland, CA: AK Press, 2007), 38.

Honore, Carl. *In Praise of Slow: How a Worldwide Movement Is Challenging the Cult of Speed.* New York: Harper, 2004.

Hotel Workers Rising. *Creating Luxury, Enduring Pain: How Hotel Work Is Hurting Housekeepers.* A Unite Here Publication, April 2006. Accessed April 15, 2007 http://www.google.com/search?client=safari&rls=en&q=Creating+Luxury,+Enduring+Pain:+How+Hotel+Work+Is+Hurting+Housekeepers&ie=UTF-8&oe=UTF-8.

Innis, Harold A. *The Bias of Communication.* Toronto: University of Toronto Press, 1951.

———. *Empire and Communication.* Toronto: University of Toronto Press, 1972.

———. *A History of the Canadian Pacific Railway.* Toronto: University of Toronto Press, 1971.

Iyer, Pico. "The Joy of Quiet." *New York Times*, December 29, 2011. Accessed January 1, 2012. http://www.nytimes.com/2012/01/01/opinion/sunday/the-joy-of-quiet.html?pagewanted=all&_r=0.

———. *Global Soul: Jet-Lag, Shopping Malls, and the Search for Home.* New York: Vintage, 2001.

Jameson, Fredric. *Postmodernism, or, The Cultural Logic of Late Capitalism.* Durham, NC: Duke University Press, 1991.

Jolles, Robert. *The Way of the Road Warrior: Lessons in Business and Life from the Road Most Traveled.* San Francisco: John Wiley, 2005.

Jones, Maggie. "How Little Sleep Can You Get Away With?" *Sunday Magazine, New York Times*, April 15, 2011, MM4, accessed April 22, 2011. http://www.nytimes.com/2011/04/17/magazine/mag-17Sleep-t.html?_r=0.

Kapp, Trevor. "Homeless Advocates Rally at Penn Station for City to Back off Sleeping in Public Places," *New York Daily News*, July 26, 2011. Accessed July 30 2011. http://articles.nydailynews.com/2011-07-26/local/29834378_1_penn-station-public-places-homeless-activists.

Kasanda, John D., and Greg Lindsay. *Aerotropolis: The Way We'll Live Next.* New York: FSG, 2011.

Kern, Stephen. *The Culture of Time and Space, 1880–1918.* Cambridge: Harvard University Press, 1983.

Knox, P. L. "Creating Ordinary Places: Slow Cities in a Fast World." *Journal of Urban Design* 10, no. 1 (2005): 1–11.

Kurlantzick, Joshua. "Project Runway." *New York Times*, March 29, 2007. Accessed March 29, 2010. http://www.nytimes.com/interactive/2007/03/29/travel/escapes/20070330_AIRPORT_SLIDESHOW.html.

Lau, Kimberly. *New Age Capitalism: Making Money East of Eden.* Philadelphia: University of Pennsylvania Press, 2000.

Lawton, Graham. "Get Ready for 24-Hour Living." *New Scientist*, February 18, 2006.

Lefebvre, Henri. *Rhythmanalysis: Space, Time and Everyday Life*. Trans. S. Elden and G. Moore. London: Continuum, 2004.

Leidner, R. *Fast Food, Fast Talk: Service Work and the Routinization of Everyday Life*. Berkeley: University of California Press, 1993.

Lipovetsky, Gilles. *Hypermodern Times*. Trans. Andrew Brown. Malden, MA: Polity, 2005.

Livingstone, Sonia and Peter Lunt. *Talk on Television: Audience Participation and Public Debate*. London: Routledge, 1993.

Lloyd, Justine. "Dwelltime: Airport Technology, Travel, and Consumption." *Space and Culture* 6, no. 2 (2003): 93–109.

Lowe, Donald. *The Body in Late-Capitalist USA*. Durham, NC: Duke University Press, 1995.

Mackenzie, Adrian. *Transductions: Bodies and Machines at Speed*. New York: Continuum, 2002.

Marx, Karl. *Capital: Volume 1; A Critique of Political Economy (1867)*. London: Penguin, 1992.

Massey, Doreen. *For Space*. Thousand Oaks, CA: Sage, 2005.

———. *Space, Place, and Gender*. Minneapolis: University of Minnesota Press, 1994.

McCarthy, Anna. *Ambient Television: Visual Culture and Public Space*. Durham, NC: Duke University Press, 2001.

McLuhan, Marshall. *Understanding Media: The Extensions of Man*. Cambridge: MIT press: 1964/1994.

Menzies, Heather. *No Time: Stress and the Crisis of Modern Life*. Vancouver: Douglas and McIntyre, 2005.

Miller, Peter, and Nikolas Rose. *Governing the Present: Administering Economic, Social and Personal Life*. Malden, MA: Polity, 2008.

Miller, Toby. *Cultural Citizenship: Cosmopolitanism, Consumerism, and Television in a Neoliberal Age*. Philadelphia: Temple University Press, 2007.

Miller, Toby, J. McLurria, N. Govil and R. Maxwell. *Global Hollywood*. London: British Film Institute; Berkeley: University of California Press, 2001.

Mosco, Vincent. *The Digital Sublime: Myth, Power, and Cyberspace*. Cambridge: MIT Press, 2005.

Moore-Ede, Martin. *The Twenty-Four-Hour Society: Understanding Human Limits in a World That Never Stops*. Reading, Mass.: Addison Wesley, 1993.

Naisbit, John. *High-Tech/High-Touch: Technology and our Accelerated Search for Meaning*. Boston: Nicholas Brealey, 2001.

Nancy, Jean-Luc. *Corpus*. Trans. Richard A. Rand. New York: Fordham University Press, 2008.

Neilson, Brett. "The World Seen from a Taxi: Students-Migrants-Workers in the Global Multiplication of Labour." *Subjectivity* 29 (2009): 425–44.

Otterman, Sharon. "Haste, Scorned: Blogging at a Snail's Pace." *New York Times*, November 23, 2008, S10.

Ouellette, Laurie, and James Hay. *Better Living through Reality TV: Television and Post-welfare Citizenship*. Malden, MA: Blackwell, 2008.

Parkes, Don, and Nigel Thrift. *Times, Spaces, and Places*. New York: John Wiley, 1980.
Parkins, Wendy. "Out of Time: Fast Subjects and Slow Living." *Time and Society* 13, no. 2–3 (2004): 363–82.
Parkins, Wendy, and Geoffrey Craig. *Slow Living*. Sydney: UNSW Press, 2006.
Parks, Lisa. "Kinetic Screens: Epistemologies of Movement at the Interface." In *Media/Space: Place, Scale and Culture in a Media Age* ed. Nick Couldry and Anna McCarthy, London: Routledge, 2004. 37–57.
Parnes, Francine. "Constant Travelers Wear Their All-Nighters as a Badge of Pride," *New York Times*, December 6, 2005. Accessed September 10, 2010. http://www.nytimes.com/2005/12/06/business/06sleep.html?_r=1.
Perkins, Maureen. *The Reform of Time: Magic and Modernity*. London: Pluto, 2001.
Petrini, Carlo. *Slow Food: The Case for Taste*. Trans. W. McCuaig. New York: Columbia University Press, 2001.
Poster, Mark. *Information Please: Culture and Politics in the Age of Digital Machines*. Durham, NC: Duke University Press, 2006.
Postone, Moishe. *Time, Labor, and Social Domination: A Reinterpretation of Marx's Critical Theory*. New York: Cambridge University Press, 1993.
Pred, Alan., ed. *Space and Time in Geography: Essays Dedicated to Torsten Hägerstrand*. Lund, Sweden: CWK Gleerup, 1981.
Ray, Rebecca, and John Schmitt. *No-Vacation Nation*. Washington, DC: Center for Economic and Policy Research, May 2007.
Read, Jason. *Micropolitics of Capital*. New York: SUNY Press, 2003.
Rheingold, Howard. *Smart Mobs: The Next Social Revolution: Transforming Cultures and Communities in the Age of Instant Access*. Cambridge: Basic Books, 2002.
Richmond, Lewis. *Work as Spiritual Practice" A Practical Buddhist Approach to Inner Growth and Satisfaction on the Job*. New York: Three Rivers Press, 2000.
Rifkin, Jeremy. *Time Wars: The Primary Conflict in Human History*. New York: Simon and Schuster, 1987.
Rose, Nikolas, ed. *Foucault and Political Reason: Liberalism, Neo-liberalism and Rationalities of Government*. Chicago: University of Chicago Press, 1996.
———. "Governing 'Advanced' Liberal Democracies." In *Foucault and Political Reason: Liberalism, Neo-liberalism and Rationalities of Government*, ed. Andrew Barry, Thomas Osborne, and Nikolas Rose, Chicago: University of Chicago Press, 1996. 27–64.
———. *Governing the Soul: The Shaping of the Private Self*. 2nd ed. New York: Free Association Books, 1999.
Ross, Andrew. *No-Collar: The Human Workplace and Its Hidden Costs*. Philadelphia: Temple University Press, 2003.
Sassen, Saskia. *Globalization and Its Discontents*. New York: New Press, 1998.
———. "Spatialities and Temporalities of the Global: Elements for a Theorization." *Public Culture* 12, no. 1 (Winter 2000): 215–32.
Scheuerman, William. *Liberal Democracy and the Social Acceleration of Time*. Baltimore: The Johns Hopkins University Press, 2004.
Schiller, Dan. *How to Think about Information*. Urbana: University of Illinois Press, 2010.

Schivelbusch, Wolfgang. *The Railway Journey: The Industrialization and Perception of Time and Space*. Berkeley: University of California Press, 1987.

Sharma, Sarah. "Baring Life and Lifestyle in the Non-place." *Cultural Studies* 23, no. 1 (2009): 129–48.

———. "Taxicab Publics and the Production of *Brown Space* after 9/11." *Cultural Studies* 24, no. 2 (March 2010) 183–199.

———. "Taxis as Media: A Temporal Materialist Reading of the Taxi-Cab." *Social Identities: Journal of Race, Nation, and Culture* 14, no. 4 (July 2008): 457–464.

Sherman, Rachel. *Class Acts: Service and Inequality in Luxury Hotels*. Berkeley: University of California Press, 2007.

Smith, Neal. *Uneven Development: Nature, Capital, and the Production of Space*. Athens: University of Georgia Press, 2008.

Soja, Edward. "Taking Space Personally." In *The Spatial Turn: Interdisciplinary Perspectives*, ed. B. Warf and S. Arias, 11–35. New York: Routledge, 2009.

Sorkin, S., ed. *Variations on a Theme Park: The New American City and the End of Public Space*. New York: Hill and Wang, 1992.

Spigel, Lynn. *Make Room for TV: Television and the Family Ideal in Postwar America*. Chicago: University of Chicago Press, 1992.

———. *Welcome to the Dreamhouse: Popular Media and Postwar Suburbs*. Durham, NC: Duke University Press, 2001.

Stiegler, Bernard. *Technics and Time, 2: Disorientation*. Trans. Stephen Barker. Stanford: Stanford University Press, 2009.

Taylor, Frederick Winslow. *The Principles of Scientific Management*, London: Harper & Brothers, 1911.

Terranova, Tiziana. *Network Culture: Politics for the Information Age*. Ann Arbor, MI: Pluto Press, 2004.

Thomas, Geoffrey. "New Jets to Combat Jet Lag." *Australian*, May 30, 2008, accessed March 25, 2010, http://www.news.com.au/new-jets-to-combat-jet-lag/story-e6frfrg9-1111116487356.

Thompson, E. P. "Time, Work, Discipline and Industrial Capitalism." *Past and Present* 38 no 1 1 (1967): 56–97.

Thrift, Nigel. "Owners' Time and Own Time: The Making of Capitalist Time Consciousness, 1300–1880." In *Space and Time in Geography: Essays Dedicated to Torsten Hägerstrand*, ed. Allan Pred, Lund, Sweden: CWK Gleerup, 1981. 56–84.

———. "Time and Theory in Human Geography: Part I." Vol 1 no 1 *Progress in Human Geography* (1977). 65–101.

Tomlinson, John. *The Culture of Speed: The Coming of Immediacy*. Thousand Oaks, Calif.: Sage, 2007.

Urry, John. *Mobilities*. Polity: London, 2007.

Virilio, Paul. *Crepuscular Dawn*. New York: Semiotext(e), 2002.

———. *Desert Screen: War at the Speed of Light*. London: Continuum, 2002.

———. "The overexposed city," in *Lost Dimension*, trans. Daniel Moshenberg, New York: Semiotext(e) 9–27.

———. *Polar Inertia*. Thousand Oaks, CA: Sage, 2000.

———. *Politics of the Very Worst*. New York: Semiotext(e), 1999.
———. *Pure War*. New York: Semiotext(e), 1997.
———. *Speed and Politics*. Trans. Mark Polizzotti. New York: Semiotext(e), 1986.
Warner, Michael. "Publics and Counterpublics." In *Habermas and the Public Sphere*, ed. C. Calhoun, 22–63. Cambridge: MIT Press, 1992.
Weston, Kath. *Gender in Real Time: Power and Transience in a Visual Age*. New York: Routledge, 2002.
Wilk, Richard, ed. *Fast Food/Slow Food: The Cultural Economy of the Global Food System*. Lanham, MD: AltaMira Press, 2006.
Wolf, Fred Alan. *The Yoga of Time Travel: How the Mind Can Defeat Time*. Wheaton, IL: Quest Books, 2004.
Wolin, Sheldon. "What Time It It?" in *Theory and Event* Vol. 1. Issue 1, 1997.
Young, Iris Marion. "Communication and the Other: Beyond Deliberative Democracy." In *Democracy and Difference*, ed. Seyla Benhabib, 120–135. Princeton: Princeton University Press, 1996.
———. *Justice and the Politics of Difference*. Princeton: Princeton University Press, 1990.
Žižek, Slavoj. *On Belief*. New York: Routledge, 2001.

Index

Page numbers in *italics* denote illustrations.